SUGAR AND POWER IN THE DOMINICAN REPUBLIC

Eisenhower, Kennedy, and the Trujillos

MICHAEL R. HALL

Contributions in Latin American Studies, Number 13

GREENWOOD PRESS
Westport, Connecticut • London

Library of Congress Cataloging-in-Publication Data

Hall, Michael R., 1960–
    Sugar and power in the Dominican Republic : Eisenhower, Kennedy,
and the Trujillos / Michael R. Hall.
        p.   cm—(Contributions in Latin American studies, ISSN
    1054–6790 ; no. 13)
    Includes bibliographical references (p.   ) and index.
    ISBN 0–313–31127–7 (alk. paper)
    1. United States—Foreign relations—Dominican Republic.
    2. Dominican Republic—Foreign relations—United States.   3. United
    States—Foreign relations—1953–1961.   4. United States—Foreign
    relations—1961–1963.   5. Economic sanctions—Dominican Republic.
    6. Economic sanctions—Latin America Case studies.   7. Sugar trade—
    Dominican Republic—History—20th century.   8. Tariff on sugar—
    United States.   9. Democratization—Dominican Republic.   I. Title.
    II. Series.
    E183.8.D6H35   2000
    327.7307293′09′045—dc21   99–16101

British Library Cataloguing in Publication Data is available.

Library of Congress Catalog Card Number: 99–16101
ISBN: 0–313–31127–7
ISSN: 1054–6790

First published in 2000

Greenwood Press, 88 Post Road West, Westport, CT 06881
An imprint of Greenwood Publishing Group, Inc.
www.greenwood.com

Printed in the United States of America

The paper used in this book complies with the
Permanent Paper Standard issued by the National
Information Standards Organization (Z39.48–1984).

10 9 8 7 6 5 4 3 2 1

SUGAR AND POWER IN THE DOMINICAN REPUBLIC

Eisenhower, Kennedy, and the Trujillos

MICHAEL R. HALL

Contributions in Latin American Studies, Number 13

GREENWOOD PRESS
Westport, Connecticut • London

Library of Congress Cataloging-in-Publication Data

Hall, Michael R., 1960–
    Sugar and power in the Dominican Republic : Eisenhower, Kennedy,
and the Trujillos / Michael R. Hall.
       p. cm—(Contributions in Latin American studies, ISSN
  1054–6790 ; no. 13)
    Includes bibliographical references (p.) and index.
    ISBN 0–313–31127–7 (alk. paper)
    1. United States—Foreign relations—Dominican Republic.
2. Dominican Republic—Foreign relations—United States. 3. United
States—Foreign relations—1953–1961. 4. United States—Foreign
relations—1961–1963. 5. Economic sanctions—Dominican Republic.
6. Economic sanctions—Latin America Case studies. 7. Sugar trade—
Dominican Republic—History—20th century. 8. Tariff on sugar—
United States. 9. Democratization—Dominican Republic. I. Title.
II. Series.
E183.8.D6H35 2000
327.7307293′09′045—dc21   99–16101

British Library Cataloguing in Publication Data is available.

Library of Congress Catalog Card Number: 99–16101
ISBN: 0–313–31127–7
ISSN: 1054–6790

First published in 2000

Greenwood Press, 88 Post Road West, Westport, CT 06881
An imprint of Greenwood Publishing Group, Inc.
www.greenwood.com

Printed in the United States of America

The paper used in this book complies with the
Permanent Paper Standard issued by the National
Information Standards Organization (Z39.48–1984).

10 9 8 7 6 5 4 3 2 1

This book is dedicated to my grandparents.

Contents

List of Tables

Preface

This book is an examination of the powerful impact that sugar had on US-Dominican relations between 1958 and 1962. It seeks to understand why Presidents Dwight D. Eisenhower and John F. Kennedy used sugar quota legislation to maintain US hegemony in the Dominican Republic and push Rafael Leonidis Trujillo Molina and his successors along the path toward democracy, and how the Dominican government used the communist threat to US hegemony in the Western Hemisphere to justify its desire for an increased share of the preferential US sugar market.

The first three chapters provide the background necessary to put the 1958–1962 period into historical perspective. Emphasis is placed on the role of sugar in the Dominican political economy since the colonization of Hispaniola and the political and economic aspects of US-Dominican relations from 1900 to 1957.

Drawing heavily upon US and Dominican government documents, the final chapters of this study argue that the Eisenhower administration initiated economic sanctions against Trujillo's authoritarian regime in an effort to gain hemispheric support against Fidel Castro's regime in Cuba. Kennedy expanded those economic sanctions, especially as they pertained to Dominican participation in the preferential US sugar market, in an attempt to liberalize the Dominican political system and stave off the possibility of a Castro-like communist takeover of the Dominican Republic. After Trujillo's assassination on 30 May 1961, the Kennedy administration used threats and promises revolving around the sugar quota to push the dictator's successors along a path toward democracy. Juan Bosch's election on 20 December 1962 and the subsequent allotment of a generous sugar quota indicated the apparent (albeit temporary) success of US policy toward the Dominican Republic.

My interest in US-Dominican relations sprouted in early 1984 when I joined the US Peace Corps and was sent to the Dominican Republic. Since that time, an untold number of people have provided invaluable intellectual guidance and moral support. A few people, however, merit special mention. In the United States, I wish to thank Gifford Doxsee, Michael Grow, Alonzo Hamby, Judson Kratzer, Harold Molineu, Jeffery Morris, Eric Roorda, and Thomas Walker. In the Dominican Republic, I wish to thank Gineida Castillo, Martica Féliz Matos, Sucre Muñoz, Luis Sánchez Noble, Carmen Iris Olivo, Bernardo Vega, and Violeta Wú.

Introduction

Sugar was the primary vehicle of reciprocal manipulation between the United States and the Dominican Republic from 1958 to 1962. A focus on sugar policy, therefore, elucidates the contrasting definitions of national interest that US and Dominican leaders have applied in their dealings with each other. Unlike traditional studies of US-Latin American relations, which approach their topic from a unilateral perspective—focusing on US interests, US actions, US policies, and the overshadowing weight of US influence in Latin America—this book provides a bilateral perspective that gives due attention to the US perspective but attaches equal significance to Dominican interests and ambitions as influential, and occasionally predominant, factors in determining hemispheric relations. In addition, this study is a potential source of insight into US relations with other Latin American nations.[1]

The Monroe Doctrine, which sought to isolate Latin America from European influence and expand US political and economic hegemony, conditioned the way that US policy makers thought about the Dominican Republic.[2] US policy makers, striving to maintain political and economic hegemony, consistently used economic threats and rewards to manipulate Dominican domestic and foreign policy. By exploring the steps leading to the application of economic coercion against the Dominican Republic between 1958 and 1962, and the objectives and concrete impact of that coercion, it is possible to develop some useful generalizations about the role of economic diplomacy as a tool of US foreign policy.

US economic diplomacy invariably fell into two categories. Positive economic diplomacy involved the granting of specific rights or privileges, such as preferential quotas, in order to achieve political or military goals. Negative economic diplomacy involved the withholding or ending of specific privileges, such as participation in preferential quotas, or the imposition of particular constraints, such as punitive taxation.[3] During the Cold War, the United States frequently used both positive and negative economic diplomacy. In 1960, the removal of the Cuban sugar quota and its redistribution to other foreign nations—the so-called Cuban windfall—provided the United States with an enticing economic opportunity to manipulate Dominican policy.

Between 1958 and 1962, the United States played an instrumental role in the transition from authoritarian dictatorship to democracy in the Dominican Republic.[4] Since sugar was the basis of the Dominican political economy, the principal vehicle of persuasion used by the United States to push the Dominican Republic along the path toward democracy was the promise of a generous preferential sugar quota. The Dominican government, however, also manipulated the United States. Dominican policy makers used the threat of international communism, especially after Fidel Castro's success in Cuba, to increase the US sugar quota, ostensibly to provide the economic resources that would help forestall communist infiltration. In reality, the funds were used by Dominican elites for their own self-serving purposes.

Four events, all of which revolved around the Dominican sugar industry, made 1961 a pivotal year in US-Dominican foreign relations: (1) President Kennedy canceled General Trujillo's participation in the Cuban windfall quota; (2) Trujillo was assassinated and his twelve sugar mills became state property; (3) Dominican President Joaquín Balaguer, in return for the promise of a generous preferential sugar quota, began moving his nation along the road to democracy; and (4) plans were made to lift US economic and political sanctions against the Dominican Republic and enlarge the Dominican sugar quota. In 1961, John D. Barfield, the US Consul in Ciudad Trujillo, stated: "The most significant period in the history of the Dominican Republic vis-à-vis the United States may well be the period 1958 to the present and there is every reason to believe the near future will be even more pregnant with significance for US policy objectives."[5]

The extremely fluid Dominican political situation from Trujillo's assassination on 30 May 1961 to the establishment of a *Consejo de Estado* (Council of State) in January 1962 allowed the sugar quota to be a very effective political tool. The US offer to expand the sugar quota became an increasingly useful incentive to Dominican political change, and likewise the withholding of the sugar quota became a conceivable US deterrent to political digression in the Dominican Republic.[6] On the other hand, however, Dominican threats that the failure to obtain a generous preferential sugar quota inhibited the Dominican government's efforts to thwart possible communist menaces that might arise at home invariably conditioned US initiatives and responses.

NOTES

1. Howard J. Wiarda and Michael J. Kryzanek, *The Dominican Republic: A Caribbean Crucible* (Boulder, CO: Westview, 1982), p. xiii. According to Wiarda and Kryzanek, the Dominican Republic is "a microcosm of the immense changes sweeping all of Latin America and the Third World, a test case, a crucible of the issues and wrenching conflicts of the development process."

2. Kenneth Coleman, "The Political Mythology of the Monroe Doctrine: Reflections on the Social Psychology of Hegemony," in *Latin America, the United States, and the Inter-American System* ed. John Martz and Lars Schoultz (Boulder, CO: Westview, 1980), p. 95. According to Coleman, "Hegemony—the establishment by a dominant power of limits for the behavior of other actors beyond which direct control by force will be invoked—implies an implied homeostasis; ie, so long as the behavior of the subordinate parties remains within the prescribed limits, rule by force is not invoked."

3. Diane B. Kunz, "When Money Counts and Doesn't: Economic Power and Diplomatic Objectives," *Diplomatic History* 18 no. 4 (fall 1994): 451–62. According to Kunz, the idea of economic sanctions as a substitute for military action is firmly rooted in the US consciousness.

4. Wiarda and Kryzanek, *The Dominican Republic: A Caribbean Crucible*, p. 135. After World War II, the foreign policy issues of US-Dominican relations revolved around anticommunism and, to a lesser extent, the desire to create a model of liberalism and democracy in the Caribbean. After 1958, the United States sought to preserve stability and prevent communism not by aiding authoritarian dictators but by supporting liberal democrats.

5. John D. Barfield to the State Department, 17 April 1961; Decimal File 739.00/4-1761, Box 1637; Dominican Republic, 1960–1963; General Records of the Department of State, Record Group 59 (hereafter RG 59), US National Archives, Washington, DC (hereafter NA).

6. According to Jonathan Hartlyn, "Although it did not last, democracy advanced further in the country at this time due to the role of international factors than one would have expected based on the country's past history and the legacies of the Trujillo era." See Jonathan Hartlyn, *The Struggle for Democratic Politics in the Dominican Republic* (Chapel Hill: University of North Carolina Press, 1998), pp. 68–69.

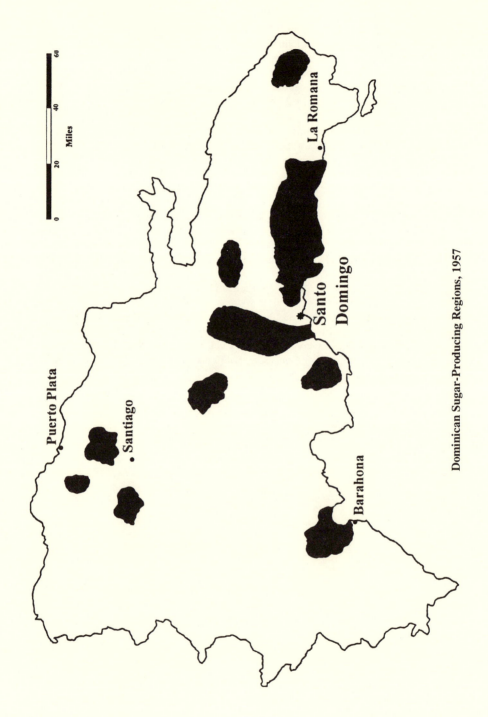

Dominican Sugar-Producing Regions, 1957

Chapter 1

The Role of Sugar in the Dominican Political Economy to 1957

Three factors determined the evolution of the sugar industry in the Dominican political economy: (1) monetary importance in the national economy, (2) ownership of the means of production, and (3) the political role of sugar. This evolution occurred within five distinct time periods. Until 1869 the sugar industry was dominated by Dominican *criollos* (Europeans born in America) and occupied a minor role in the Dominican political economy.[1] Between 1870 and 1899 the Dominican sugar industry was controlled by Cuban, Spanish, and Italian entrepreneurs. Taxes on sugar exports were an important source of revenue for the Dominican government. By 1900 sugar was not only the chief Dominican export product, it was also the center of Dominican society, the nucleus around which all Dominican political and economic activity rotated.[2] US capital dominated the Dominican sugar industry from 1900 to 1929. Taxes on sugar exports were the principal source of revenue for the Dominican government.[3] Not only did the country count heavily on sugar exports to provide foreign exchange, but internal trade and employment were influenced widely by the international market, which determined how much—and at what price—Dominican sugar could be sold abroad. Although US capital continued to dominate the Dominican sugar industry from 1930 until 1947, authoritarian dictator General Rafael Trujillo, who represented a social shift in the Dominican Republic's social hierarchy, used sugar export taxes to implement an economic program of import substitution industrialization. Finally, between 1948 and 1957, Trujillo, in an attempt to consolidate his control over the Dominican political economy, worked to monopolize the Dominican sugar industry. By 1957, Trujillo was the undisputed owner of almost three-quarters of that industry.[4]

To understand the history of Dominican sugar, however, one must understand the less-than-illustrious history of the Dominican Republic.[5] To comprehend what appears to be chaos in modern Dominican history, former US ambassador to the Dominican Republic John Bartlow Martin suggests, "one should know the lunacy that went before."[6]

THE SUBORDINATE POSITION OF THE SUGAR INDUSTRY
IN THE DOMINICAN POLITICAL ECONOMY, 1492–1869

From the initial period of conquest until 1869 the sugar industry occupied a minor position in the Dominican political economy. Although Christopher Columbus introduced sugar cane cultivation to Hispaniola in 1493, during the colonial era of Dominican history (1492–1795) and well into the nineteenth century, the few criollos and *peninsulares* (Europeans living in America) involved in this second-rate economic activity made an insignificant contribution to the economy. Although mining was the main economic activity of the island during the first decades of colonization, in the early sixteenth century a few landowners in the southern parts of the island began to experiment with sugar cane cultivation.[7] Gonzalo de Velosa, a wealthy landowner, built the first *trapiche* (a rudimentary sugar mill operated by human and animal labor) near Santo Domingo in 1515.[8] Although de Velosa initiated limited sugar exports to Spain, the Spanish Hapsburgs never encouraged the exploitation of sugar in Santo Domingo to the extent that it was promoted by the French Bourbons in neighboring Saint Domingue. Whereas the French colony in Saint Domingue became a profitable sugar-producing colony during the seventeenth and eighteenth century, the minimal amounts of sugar produced in Santo Domingo were primarily for internal consumption.[9]

The initial expansion of the Dominican sugar industry was also inhibited by insufficient labor. Forced labor and European disease had wiped out Hispaniola's indigenous population by 1530.[10] Unlike the wealthy criollo elite in French-speaking Saint Domingue, the modest resources of the Spanish-speaking criollo elite in Santo Domingo prohibited the importation of vast numbers of slaves to tend the sugar cane fields.[11] Although the Dominicans never imported enough slaves to significantly expand the sugar industry, the incipient colonial sugar industry experienced modest growth and became thoroughly tied to the institution of slavery.[12]

The Dominican struggle for independence, a series of wars and violent conflicts between 1795 and 1844 that debilitated the economy, precipitated a further decline in the Dominican sugar industry. From the moment of the 1795 Treaty of Basil, when the Spanish Crown granted the eastern two-thirds of Hispaniola to France, until 1821 when José Nuñez de Cáceres simultaneously proclaimed the Dominican Republic an independent nation and a protectorate of Gran Colombia, over two-thirds of the Dominican criollos emigrated to other parts of Latin America.[13] During this period, the old Dominican oligarchy, whose wealth had been based primarily on the possession of large cattle ranches, virtually disappeared. Wars and invasions during the first two decades of the nineteenth century decimated the cattle herds and destroyed the economic base of many of those Dominican families who chose to remain in the country.[14]

Following a brief period of nominal independence and nebulous efforts at national economic construction, including the return of several criollo families that had abandoned the island, the Haitian military invaded the Dominican Republic in 1822 and remained until 1844. In addition to seriously wounding Dominican pride, Haitian President Jean-Pierre Boyer drastically altered the small Dominican sugar industry when he abolished slavery in the conquered nation. This reduction in the labor force had a catastrophic impact on the already debilitated Dominican sugar industry.[15] The elimination of slave labor caused levels of production in the first half of the nineteenth century to fall below seventeenth- and eighteenth-century production levels.[16]

Between 1844 and 1861, during the second period of Dominican independence, various *caudillos* (strongmen) attempted to exert political control over the nation, while simultaneously striving to revive the national economy. None of the emerging national elites, however, used sugar as their economic power base.[17] The dominant interests in the south and east wanted to expand the mahogany industry, and the dominant interests from the central Cibao region encouraged tobacco production. As a result, the Dominican economy was supported primarily by tobacco and mahogany exports to Europe.[18]

In 1861, after seventeen years of political strife and economic frustration during the second period of Dominican independence, President Pedro Santana annexed the nation to Spain. Although the economic stability generated by the reunion with Spain provoked a proliferation of small sugar plantations in the southern region of the country, the sugar industry remained insignificant.[19] More important, although annexation by Spain provided a degree of economic stability, the loss of Dominican political sovereignty aroused a nationalistic fervor in many elites that culminated in the 1865 War of the Restoration and the third declaration of Dominican independence within half a century.[20]

In the years immediately following the War of Restoration, exports of fine woods and tobacco to Europe continued to dominate the Dominican export economy. Whereas Cuba and Jamaica had already developed economies based on sugar exports by the 1860s, annually producing 450,000 tons and 148,000 tons, respectively, in 1870 the Dominican Republic exported less than 4,000 tons of sugar.[21] During the last quarter of the nineteenth century, however, a series of internal and external events allowed the Dominican political elites to greatly expand the small sugar industry and use it as a power base to support their political regimes.

MODERNIZATION AND GROWTH OF THE SUGAR INDUSTRY, 1870–1899

Between 1870 and 1899 Spanish, Cuban, and Italian investors vigorously developed and controlled a dynamic Dominican sugar industry that came to occupy an increasingly important position in the Dominican economy. Dominican political elites who saw a self-serving economic advantage in pursuing the liberal, export-led model of economic development energetically supported the modernization of the sugar industry, an increase in sugar exports, and the integration of the Dominican economy into the world economy during the last quarter of the nineteenth century. As a result of increased sugar production, taxes on sugar exports became one of the principal sources of revenue for the Dominican government. Table 1.1 shows the rapid growth of the Dominican sugar industry during the last quarter of the nineteenth century. A crop of minor importance in 1870, sugar by 1900 had become the nation's primary export.

Table 1.1
Dominican Sugar Exports, 1870–1900

Year	Tons
1870	3,899
1888	18,181
1898	36,363
1900	53,000

Source: Oficina Nacional de Estadística de la República Dominicana, *La Industria Azucarera en Marcha* (Ciudad Trujillo: Oficina Nacional de Estadística de la República Dominicana, 1955), pp. 3–27.

In 1865, however, few Dominicans had the intuition that their nation was capable of developing an export-based economy driven by a revitalized, modernized, and greatly expanded sugar industry. The Dominican Republic's small and thinly spread population (estimated at 150,000 in 1870) and the proximity of a more populous and more aggressive Haiti, as well as the demographic, agricultural, and monetary devastation of the country resulting from the political turbulence that preceded and accompanied the annexation and restoration period of Dominican history, were good reasons to doubt the nation's capacity to develop into a viable and economically prosperous nation.[22] After the War of the Restoration, the criollo elite lacked the financial resources to expand and modernize the sugar industry. For this reason, the capital to develop the sugar industry had to come from abroad. This foreign investment initially came from entrepreneurial Spanish, Italian, and Cuban immigrants who ingratiated themselves into the Dominican oligarchy through *compadrazgo* (godfathership), marriage, and other social ties.

Two events brought these investors to the Dominican Republic. First, the 1861–1865 Spanish reannexation of the country brought Spanish and Italian investors interested in the development of commerce and agriculture. Second, and more important, was the Ten Years War of 1868–1878 in Cuba. During the 1870s, 5,000 Cuban entrepreneurs previously engaged in Cuban sugar production fled to the Dominican Republic when revolution and slave revolts at home threatened their survival. According to historian Frank Moya Pons,

The most important effect of the arrival of the Cubans was the decision taken by some of the Cubans to invest the capital they had brought with them in the purchase of land for sugar plantations and in the construction of industrial mills for the manufacture of sugar by modern methods, that is, by using steam-powered machinery and railways for transporting the cane. The opening of those mills began in the south and east, where land was cheaper and where a tradition of sugar production was still alive.[23]

Historian Frank Báez contends that the Cuban immigration was the "primary cause of the transformation of the Dominican sugar industry."[24] This transformation caused a rupture with the pre-capitalist form of sugar production, the trapiche. Between 1870 and 1882, the Cubans built more than thirty steam-powered *ingenios* (modern sugar mills), each with an annual production capacity of over two million pounds of sugar.[25] The first ingenios established were Esperanza and Angelina in 1874 and 1876, respectively. They were followed by Porvenir (1879), Consuelo (1881), Cristóbal Colón (1883), and Santa Fe (1885). The Cuban sugar producers invested over $6 million, had total annual sales of over $3 million, and paid the Dominican government $200,000 per year in export duties.[26]

Also influencing the rapid growth of the Dominican sugar industry were conflicts elsewhere in the world. The Franco-Prussian War of 1870 severely affected European sugar beet production, and the US Civil War had a similar effect on the Louisiana sugar cane industry. The Dominican government took advantage of these situations by encouraging the expansion and modernization of the Dominican sugar industry. Basing his ideas on a positivist philosophy of order and progress, from 1882 to 1899 President Ulíses Heureaux provided the political stability necessary for the expansion of the Dominican sugar industry.[27] Heureaux limited bureaucratic corruption, pushed for economic modernization, imposed political stability, and was responsible for establishing the base of a liberal, export-led economy in the Dominican Republic. In so doing, he used the sugar industry as the economic base of his political control. The establishment and expansion of modern sugar plantations in the southern coastal areas broadened the economic base of the country and widened the sources of credit for the government. Between 1888 and 1898, sugar production doubled from 20,000 to 40,000 tons.[28]

The expansion of the Dominican sugar industry, however, depended on its modernization. During the 1880s, the modernization of the sugar industry—accompanied by increased sugar cane acreage and the construction of new sugar mills—caused the Dominican economy to grow.[29] The Dominican political elites deliberately and energetically supported the modernization of the sugar industry through tariff exemptions for machinery and tools, limited exemption from export tariffs, and extensive government land concessions. Often unwilling or unable to use their own financial resources, Dominican elites encouraged foreign capital investment, which amounted to over $11 million during the 1880s, and energetically sought extensive foreign loans from Europeans. Due to the low cost of land, most of the capital invested was concentrated in the purchase and installation of sugar mill machinery and the development and operation of rail lines to bring cane to the ingenios.[30]

Italian-Dominican sugar magnate Juan Bautista Vicini and other members of the Dominican oligarchy supported Heureaux's efforts to create a stable economic and political environment for foreign capital in the Dominican Republic.[31] Heureaux's dictatorship, therefore, was the political expression of the entrance of the Dominican Republic into the global economy. The last decades of the nineteenth century saw a considerable increase in global sugar consumption. Sugar consumption in the United States increased from one million tons in 1880 to 2,660,000 tons in 1900.[32] Dominican elites took advantage of fortuitous world market opportunities.

Although the short-term monetary advantages of pursuing liberal economic models had been obvious to the Dominican political elites since 1870, the disadvantages of basing the national economy on sugar would not be fully revealed until the Great Depression. Nevertheless, the political elites realized in the 1890s that continued economic prosperity depended on a stable world market price for sugar. They also realized, albeit too late, that they had virtually no control over the price paid for sugar on the world market. Until 1892, the Dominicans benefited from high world prices for their sugar. Between 1892 and 1898, however, the international price of sugar dropped from 6.2 cents per pound to 4.1 cents per pound because of the overproduction of a heavily subsidized sugar beet industry in Europe. Lower sugar prices led to increased foreign debt in the Dominican Republic, as well as to the elimination of ten ingenios and the remaining trapiches in the country.[33]

Although the drop in sugar prices wreaked havoc on the national economy by greatly increasing the national debt and seriously undermining the ability of the Heureaux government to meet its financial obligations, the concentration of the Dominican sugar industry that resulted from the economic downturn was beneficial to two families: the Vicini family of Italian immigrants, owners of five sugar mills in 1893, and the Bass family, US investors who owned two sugar mills.[34] Many of the Cuban and Spanish sugar mill owners, however, were less fortunate. After going bankrupt, many of them sold their interests to US families and corporations. Between 1892 and 1912 Cuban and Spanish interests in more than thirty Dominican ingenios were gradually bought out by US and Canadian investors.

The Heureaux government was even less fortunate than the bankrupt Cuban and Spanish entrepreneurs. Although Heureaux facilitated the modernization of the Dominican sugar industry, his government incurred an extensive foreign debt that undermined the economic foundation of his regime. As such, the arrival of the twentieth century brought with it a new Dominican economic reality. The Dominican Republic had been transformed from a European-oriented producer of tobacco and fine woods into a vulnerable country in which sugar reigned and the United States economic presence predominated.

US CONTROL OF THE SUGAR INDUSTRY BEFORE
TRUJILLO'S RISE TO POWER, 1900–1929

By 1900 sugar cane cultivation was the most important economic activity in the Dominican Republic, and the taxes and duties imposed on sugar exports were indisputably the principal source of revenue for the Dominican government. Sugar accounted for more than 50 percent of Dominican exports.[35] At the same time, US foreign investors began to invest in the Dominican sugar industry. The increased penetration of US interests was the result of Dominican economic and political turmoil as much as a more aggressive US diplomatic and foreign investment policy. The financial chaos and political turmoil that engulfed the Dominican Republic following the 26 July 1899 assassination of President Heureaux coincided with the period in which the United States began extending its hegemonic influence outward over the Caribbean region.[36]

Heureaux's assassination ushered in a new era of instability, characterized by political violence and growing foreign debt. When he was gunned down in Moca by political rival Ramón Cáceres, the Dominican Republic's foreign debt exceeded $30 million. Historian Franklin Knight explains:

The Dominican Republic entered the twentieth century nominally independent, but in political chaos and economic bankruptcy. Heureaux's assassination left the country without the political apparatus or the fiscal solvency to attack its mounting domestic and foreign problems. The most pressing of these problems was an enormous foreign debt.[37]

The revolutionary turmoil that aggravated the country's financial situation after Heureaux's assassination was heightened by a power struggle between two contending factions of Liberal political elites: the Jimenistas who supported Juan Isidro Jiménez from their stronghold in Monte Cristi; and the Santiago-based Horacistas, who supported Horacio Vásquez.[38] Although Jiménez and Vásquez were both opposed to Heureaux's financial policies and relations with foreign capitalists, open hostility between the two factions resulted from their repeated attempts to secure access to the revenues of the Dominican customs houses. According to US Chargé d'Affaires W. F. Powell: "The damage sustained will be another heavy expense added to those that the country will have to pay. The financial condition of the government is worse than bad, if such can be accepted to express the present monetary condition of the Republic."[39]

Within three months of Heureaux's assassination, France threatened to intervene militarily and confiscate all customs revenues unless the Dominican government paid a $280,000 debt. In an attempt to restore stability to the nation, President Juan Isidro Jiménez sent Foreign Minister Francisco Henríquez y Carvajal to the United States and Europe to reassure creditors that they would eventually be paid. However, the failure of the Dominican mission to restore confidence within the international financial community increased the vulnerability of the Dominican sugar industry to US penetration. Unable to obtain new loans and debilitated by the effort to pay off old loans, many of the Spanish, Cuban,

Italian, and Dominican sugar owners who survived the economic crisis of the 1890s went bankrupt during the first decade of the twentieth century and sold their interests to US and Canadian investors eager to find new investment opportunities. By 1912, the Cuban entrepreneurs who had arrived in the Dominican Republic during the 1870s had sold their sugar interests to North Americans.[40]

In October 1903, Carlos Morales Languasco, an ex-priest and disciple of Juan Isidro Jiménez, declared himself chief executive and in so doing alienated Jiménez, who launched yet another revolution. As the Dominican Republic plunged into revolutionary turmoil that further aggravated the country's financial situation, the United States, fearing that Dominican financial irresponsibility might lead to European intervention, began to pressure the Dominican government to allow US agents to take over the collection of customs and thus control Dominican financial affairs. Similarly, Morales Languasco's government, faced with an empty treasury, a $32,280,000 foreign debt (two-thirds of which was held by European creditors), and the inability to secure future loans, began to warm to the idea of greater US participation in the Dominican economy. Since customs house revenues from the island nation's eleven ports represented 90 percent of government revenues, Morales Languasco was interested in restoring stability.[41] The idea of appointing the United States to collect Dominican customs, therefore, was as much a Dominican as a US proposal.

Encouraged by the possibility of securing new foreign loans, Dominican Foreign Minister Juan Sánchez signed an agreement with the United States on 31 January 1904 that committed the Dominican government to pay the United States $4.5 million over an extended period of time in settlement of a claim made against the Dominican government by the San Domingo Improvement Company, a US company that had bought up a large portion of the Dominican foreign debt held by European creditors. The agreement stipulated:

The United States shall appoint a Financial Agent, who shall establish an office in the Dominican Republic. In case of failure to receive during any month the sum then due, the said Financial Agent shall have full power and authority to forthwith enter into possession of the Custom House at Puerto Plata in the first instance, and to assume charge of the collection of the customs duties and Port Dues at that port.[42]

On 27 September 1904, Morales Languasco announced that the Dominican government was unable to meet the terms of the 31 January protocol. Expressing his conviction that European warships were likely to appear in Dominican ports to forcibly collect outstanding debts, Morales Languasco suggested that the best solution to the problem would be "for the United States to take charge of the collection of customs revenues, guaranteeing to the Dominican government enough to live on" while arranging payments to the foreign creditors.[43] Playing on US fears of European involvement in hemispheric affairs, Morales Languasco avoided a potentially catastrophic financial and political situation in the Dominican Republic by encouraging the US government to intervene in his protection.

In response to this situation, on 6 December 1904, President Theodore Roosevelt committed the United States to the role of international policeman in the Caribbean region and warned the Caribbean nations that he would intervene in their internal affairs if they displayed financial irresponsibility.[44] Most Dominican elites, who viewed the European threat to Dominican sovereignty as potentially more enduring and less financially rewarding than the proposed tenets of the Roosevelt Corollary to the Monroe Doctrine, found US hegemony much more attractive than European domination.[45] Therefore, much to the delight of Morales Languasco, on 1 April 1905 the US government established the so-called modus vivendi receivership over Dominican customs before any of the Dominican Republic's European creditors could do likewise.[46] The Dominican Customs Receivership, which was headed by an appointee of the US president, stipulated that 45 percent of the country's future customs revenues would be turned over to the Dominican government for expenses; the remaining 55 percent would be used to pay the Dominican Republic's creditors.[47]

Morales Languasco and his successor, Ramón Cáceres, hoped that the revenues generated by the sugar industry and funneled through the general receivership would be sufficient to pay the foreign debt as well as restore economic and political stability to the Dominican Republic. Cáceres, a member of a wealthy Cibao landowning family (and Vásquez's cousin) who did not use his position exclusively for personal enrichment, ignored Jimenista accusations that he was a *vendepatria* (country seller) and energetically championed the modus vivendi. Cáceres realized that the proportion of customs duties received by the Dominican government gave it a larger and more regularly paid cash income than any previous administration ever had at its disposal. In 1906, the US Customs Receivership paid the Dominican government $1,329,107.[48] According to Finance Minister Federico Velázquez, "Thanks to the modus vivendi, we have lived two years with relative ease and accumulated a respectable amount of money destined to the payment of said debts."[49]

Table 1.2
Dominican Sugar Production, 1902–1915

Year	Tons	Year	Tons
1902	45,723	1909	70,599
1903	50,803	1910	94,496
1904	47,755	1911	91,423
1905	48,069	1912	97,589
1906	55,975	1913	86,020
1907	60,963	1914	107,476
1908	63,234	1915	110,005

Source: James J. Murphy to the State Department, 15 April 1926; Sugar Folder, Box 154; Dominican Republic, Narrative Reports, 1904–39; RG 166; NA.

In an attempt to invigorate the economy and generate government revenue, Cáceres further encouraged the investment of US capital in the Dominican sugar industry. As Table 1.2 shows, sugar production in the Dominican Republic increased dramatically during his administration. In 1906 he enacted a law exempting the sugar companies from all production taxes. In 1907, Cáceres signed a new agreement with the United States that strengthened the 1905 receivership agreement, made the Dominican Republic a virtual protectorate of the United States, and legalized any future US intervention in Dominican affairs. In an attempt to secure sufficient investment dollars for the Dominican sugar industry, Cáceres agreed that his government would neither contract further foreign debt nor modify its current tariff barriers without US permission.[50]

On 19 November 1911, however, Luis Tejera, an irritated Jimenista, fatally shot President Cáceres. Although the Horacistas immediately named Eladio Victoria president, Cáceres's assassination threw the nation back into the all-too-familiar condition of violence and instability. After an extended period of presidential musical chairs and economic chaos in Santo Domingo, the United States militarily intervened in the Dominican Republic.

During the US military occupation (1916–1924), US dominance of the Dominican sugar industry accelerated. Legislation enacted by the US military governor increased the amount of land devoted to sugar cane production, fostered US influence over the sugar industry, and lowered sugar export duties.[51] The amount of land devoted to sugar cane production increased from 34,880 acres in 1893 to 438,132 acres in 1925. Of this total, 355,854 acres belonged to US-owned companies.[52] By 1924, eleven of the twenty-one ingenios belonged to two US conglomerates—the Cuban Dominican Sugar Company and the South Porto Rico Sugar Company—and five others were owned by US citizens. Whereas the profits earned by the Cuban, Italian, and Spanish sugar mill owners during the last two decades of the nineteenth century were reinvested in the Dominican economy, the US development of Dominican sugar mills created an enclave economy that expatriated the profits, which exceeded $35 million during the military occupation. Nevertheless, the Dominican government continued to receive hefty revenues from sugar exports.[53] By 1924, the two US sugar giants, which began their operations in the Dominican Republic during the US military occupation, controlled 80 percent of Dominican sugar production.[54]

The Dominican Republic's political economy underwent drastic changes during the US occupation. One consequence of the military occupation was a modernization of the sugar industry that caused Dominican production to double in six years. As Table 1.3 shows, in 1916 the Dominican sugar industry produced 128,082 tons of sugar; in 1925 it produced 316,268 tons. Sugar production escalated to supply the increased world demand caused by the destruction of the European sugar beet industry during World War I. Increased sugar production was facilitated by extensive transportation systems built by the US Marines. In addition to the nation's first national highway system, the US Marines improved rail, harbor, and port facilities. These improvements to the nation's infrastructure, which enabled the sugar cane to reach the sugar mills quicker, greatly increased sugar production since sugar cane not ground within twenty-four hours of being cut loses over 50 percent of its juices.[55]

The expansion of the sugar industry, however, made the Dominican political economy more dependent than ever before on world sugar prices. The owners of the growing sugar industry understood that if their industry was to continue to prosper, it would require more than economic and political stability. Because of extensive international competition and production gluts it would also require a guaranteed market overseas. According to William Bass, the successful owner of Ingenio Consuelo, "If the Dominican sugar mills are going to prosper they need a preferential market with assured prices."[56] In the early 1920s, however, the Dominican government and the US sugar mill owners were not able to convince the United States that it was to both countries' mutual benefit to guarantee the Dominican Republic a reduced tariff in the US market.[57]

Table 1.3
Dominican Sugar Production, 1916–1929

Year	Tons	Year	Tons
1916	128,082	1923	187,129
1917	132,262	1924	233,056
1918	129,367	1925	316,268
1919	160,850	1926	360,415
1920	178,550	1927	368,196
1921	188,526	1928	354,085
1922	159,666	1929	360,259

Source: Charles B. Curtis to the State Department, 2 June 1931; Sugar Folder, Box 154; Dominican Republic, Narrative Reports, 1904–39; RG 166; NA.

As long as international sugar prices remained stable, however, the increasingly monocultural nature of the Dominican economy did not pose a threat to the nation's economic prosperity. Unfortunately, international economic instability during the 1920s, which was beyond the control of the Dominican government, exposed the serious flaws inherent in the liberal, export model of economic development. Dominican sugar remained dependent on the vagaries of international commodity prices. Although there was a significant increase in world sugar prices between 1914 and 1920, the global depression of 1921 lowered the price to three cents a pound, down from 22.5 cents per pound a year earlier. Having earned $105 million in 1920, Dominican sugar exports fell to a value of $45 million in 1921 and $9 million in 1922.[58]

The global depression of 1921 was not the only event that disrupted the Dominican sugar industry. The Fordney-McCumber Tariff of 1921 placed a tariff of $0.022 per pound on all sugar imported to the United States, with the exception of sugar imports from Cuba, Puerto Rico, the Philippines, and Hawaii.[59] Plagued by the double affliction of low prices and a high tariff, Dominican sugar exports to the United States declined spectacularly during the 1920s. Although the United States bought 76 percent of all Dominican sugar produced between 1911 and 1920, from 1921 to 1930 the United States only bought 11 percent of all Dominican sugar produced. By 1930, the United Kingdom was importing over 70 percent of Dominican sugar exports, whereas the United States only imported 2 percent of Dominican sugar exports.[60] Although the Dominicans were able to redirect their sugar exports to Canadian and Western European markets, they suffered under the constant fear that these markets would also be closed to them as more countries worked out special arrangements for purchasing sugar.[61]

Throughout its entire history—except for periods when the nation was militarily occupied by foreigners—the Dominican Republic had been dominated by a colorful array of Liberal and Conservative elites vying for the spoils of office. Their relentless commitment to export-led growth since 1870 had resulted in unreliable dependence on international commodity prices, an excessive degree of control of the nation's resources by foreign interests, little economic diversification, virtually no industrialization, and no genuine national development. Customs revenues, major banks, and most important businesses were controlled by US capital. The entire Dominican sugar industry, with the exception of those mills owned by the Dominicanized Vicini family, was in foreign hands.[62]

Although the global economy briefly recovered during the mid-1920s and the international price of sugar rose to $0.10 per pound in 1926, world sugar prices promptly began another dreadful price decline. By the end of 1929 the price of sugar fell below the cost of production. The stock market crash of 1929 and the coming of the Great Depression exposed the political and economic bankruptcy of the oligarchical system. Sugar exports to the United Kingdom were virtually cut in half overnight, wages deteriorated rapidly, and the income generated from the sugar industry was lower than at any time since the 1899 assassination of Heureaux. Whereas Dominican sugar exports showed a 117 percent increase from 1920 to 1930, the value of those exports decreased by 78 percent during the same time period. In 1920, the Dominicans exported 158,805 tons of sugar for $45,3-05,620. In 1930, the Dominican Republic exported 345,930 tons of sugar for $9,910,289.[63] The negative consequences of the liberal, export-led economy—laid bare by the Great Depression—caused extreme economic and political instability.

US CONTROL OF THE SUGAR INDUSTRY AFTER TRUJILLO'S RISE TO POWER, 1930–1947

By 1930, the dramatic fall in international sugar prices created a revolutionary atmosphere on the island. It was painfully obvious to many influential Dominicans that liberal export models were incapable of protecting the nation against the economic shock of massive global depression. It was equally obvious that the corrupt and inept Horacio Vásquez government, which had been in power since the US Marines left the island nation in 1924, was unable to effectively guide the nation through the economic crisis. Wealthy landowner Rafael Estrella Ureña, "an impulsive but idealistic demagogue" from Santiago, called the Horacista and Jimenista elites vendepatrias. He was outraged by Vásquez's unconstitutional decision to run for reelection in 1930.[64] Significantly, Estrella Ureña's opposition movement was supported by Rafael Leonidis Trujillo Molina, the leader of the National Guard.[65] In the words of US Minister Curtis: "The measure of popular support which the Revolution received was due to the economic depression, but at bottom the revolution was caused by the unprincipled ambitions of General Trujillo and Estrella Ureña."[66] On 3 March, therefore, Estrella Ureña and Trujillo were sworn in as interim president and vice president, respectively, and elections were scheduled for 24 May. It soon became obvious that Trujillo wanted the commanding position, and Estrella Ureña yielded to Trujillo's ambition.

Trujillo's victory was unlike other military uprisings led by traditional caudillos. This coup marked a definitive rupture with the old political order.[67] Trujillo represented a shift in the sociopolitical power structure.[68] The son of a middle-class family, Trujillo was admitted to the constabulary in 1919 as a second lieutenant and rose rapidly to the upper ranks.[69] The elites, whose local militias had been disarmed during the US occupation, were unable to resist Trujillo's well-armed troops. In addition to blaming the old oligarchy for the Dominican Republic's economic woes, Trujillo held a deep hatred of the aristocratic elite and viciously subordinated them to his personalistic rule.[70] In the words of a US diplomat stationed in the Dominican Republic, Trujillo spent his life "trying to compensate for what he unconsciously considered his inferior origin and background."[71] He created a new oligarchy made up of Dominicans who depended on the largesse of the dictator for their social, economic, and political power. These people are frequently referred to as the *gente de la segunda*, to distinguish them from the traditional elites, the *gente de la primera*.

At the beginning of his presidency, not only did Trujillo have to deal with a confused and ugly internal political situation, but also the worldwide economic depression that was seriously affecting the Dominican economy and causing a decline in governmental revenues. Dominican government revenues had diminished from $14 million in 1929 to less than $7 million in 1931.[72] To this, fate added the calamity of Hurricane Zenón on 3 September 1930, which destroyed most of Santo Domingo. Trujillo, who ironically began his nefarious career as a guard on a US-owned sugar mill, realized that his political hold would remain tenuous unless he was able to control and improve the failing economy.

Trujillo was a nationalist for whom economic growth, as a source of political power, was second in importance only to his own absolute control of that power. Trujillo's driving force was his constant desire for total power. He therefore used the sugar industry as a tool of economic domination to reinforce his political power. He quickly established friendly relations with the directors of the US sugar mills in Santo Domingo, who rushed to support Trujillo as a bastion of stability. At a 1933 banquet at the La Romana Country Club, Edwin Kilbourne, administrator of the West Indies Sugar Corporation, stated that the well-being of the sugar enclaves and the Dominican Republic depended on the continued leadership of the dictator. According to Kilbourne, "We are content to place in his hands our financial interests with the conviction that they could not be placed in better hands."[73]

Trujillo adroitly brought the Dominican economy under his control. Although foreign interests played an important part in the Dominican political economy, especially in the sugar industry, the real power brokers were the Trujillo family assisted by a nouveau riche that had been created by the dictator. Although the traditional elites, including the Vicini, Brugal, Bermúdez, Cabral, Tavares, and Grullón families, did not have their properties expropriated, Trujillo placed his relatives and friends in key positions and created a new elite. Trujillo controlled the salt, insurance, milk, tobacco, meat, cement, cooking oil, and beer industries, to name a few. Frequently, his partners were his relatives or friends.[74] With this unique friends and family network, Trujillo and his cronies came to own half of the nation's assets. By 1938, Trujillo, whose annual salary as president in 1931 was $8,400, had mysteriously amassed a personal fortune worth over $30 million.[75] His supporters, however, attempted to cloak the dictator's graft and corruption in an ideology based on the idea of national reconstruction.[76]

Table 1.4
Sugar Exports as Percentage of Dominican Exports, 1928–1937

Year	Percentage	Year	Percentage
1928	59%	1933	46%
1929	52%	1934	52%
1930	53%	1935	61%
1931	58%	1936	56%
1932	61%	1937	59%

Source: Don V. Catlett to the Secretary of State, 29 January 1943; Sugar Folder, Box 118; Dominican Republic, General Records; RG 84; NA.

Although Trujillo never seriously considered nationalizing the US sugar interests during the 1930s, he realized that without generous revenues from the Dominican sugar industry he would not be able to support his authoritarian regime and consolidate himself in power.[77] As Table 1.4 shows, during the 1930s, sugar exports represented more than half of the Dominican Republic's export earnings. Trujillo, therefore, moved to invest himself with wide powers over sugar production, including the right of fixing production quotas for each company, the supervision of exports, and examination of the companies' books and records.[78] Income generated from sugar sales allowed the dictator to tighten his grip on the Dominican political economy and engage in public works programs that fueled his megalomania. His investment in huge public works projects with high visibility also gained him the support of the masses.

The US sugar mill administrators and Trujillo maintained a very amiable relationship.   Their support enabled Trujillo to consolidate his control in the Dominican Republic.   To reward the sugar mill administrators for their support, Trujillo lifted all taxes on machinery imports.[79]   As Table 1.5 shows, the mill owners expanded production, which rewarded Trujillo with increased revenues.

Table 1.5
Dominican Sugar Production, 1930–1939

Year	Tons	Year	Tons
1930	362,711	1935	449,817
1931	427,621	1936	450,000
1932	359,647	1937	493,302
1933	382,374	1938	348,000
1934	424,157	1939	418,385

Source: Federico García Godoy to Max Henríquez Ureña, 27 June 1938; Sugar Folder, Box 33; Dominican Republic, General Records; RG 84; NA.

Trujillo used the sugar industry, which was of "vital" importance to the economic structure of the Dominican Republic, as the economic base for his political control.[80]   According to US diplomat Robert Mills McClintock,

After evincing early military ability, particularly in matters of discipline and organization, he has since displayed a similar capacity in business and is a shrewd, unscrupulous, avaricious man of affairs. He has the master politician's flair for distributing plums among his underlings, with the genius of knowing when to dangle the fruit higher out of reach of their grasping hands.[81]

Sugar export revenues provided the dictator with operating expenses and the capital needed for his innovative import substitution industrialization programs, the expansion of the export-oriented agrarian sector, and continued improvements in the nation's infrastructure.   Nevertheless, although the steps that Trujillo took gave the appearance of diversifying the national economy, they were simply methods to enhance his control over the political economy.   He provided the gente de la segunda with lucrative economic opportunities in return for complete loyalty. Trujillo's economic policies, which depended on the continued expansion of the sugar industry, actually intensified the monocultural economy based on sugar.[82]

The havoc revisited on Europe's sugar beet crops by World War II, which greatly increased world markets for Dominican sugar, served to further strengthen the Dominican economy.   As shown by Table 1.6, commodity shortages during the war caused the prices for Dominican agricultural exports to rise spectacularly.   In 1941, the United Kingdom agreed to purchase 400,000 tons of Dominican sugar for $0.092 per pound.[83]   In 1942, the British agreed to purchase 400,000 tons of Dominican sugar for an astonishing $0.265 per pound.

Because of wartime disruptions in trans-Atlantic shipping, however, in 1942 the Dominican Republic was only able to export 189,919 tons of sugar. According to a US diplomat in Ciudad Trujillo: "High hopes were held by producers for the future of the industry when they contracted for the price of $2.65 per hundred pounds, but in the course of 1942 it was found that shipping presented a much more serious problem than the sale of sugar."[84] Regardless, because of the higher price, sugar exporters earned more than $7 million in profits and the Dominican government more than $2.6 million from sugar taxes. Trujillo, who had been increasing sugar taxes since 1937, imposed a $0.25 tax per hundred pound bag in 1939 and a tax of 20 percent on sugar sales in excess of $1.50 per hundred pound bag in 1942.[85]

Table 1.6
Dominican Sugar Production and Exports, 1940–1947

Year	Production (in tons)	Exports (in tons)	Value (in dollars)
1940	430,000	414,000	8,470,440
1941	431,705	386,385	7,829,729
1942	484,328	189,919	10,361,792
1943	480,216	406,101	22,156,467
1944	512,089	692,649	37,790,241
1945	370,063	437,869	29,862,665
1946	458,919	388,950	32,944,065
1947	465,428	474,509	44,366,591

Source: US Embassy in the Dominican Republic to Department of State, 12 September 1945; Sugar Folder, Box 157; Dominican Republic, General Records; RG 84; NA.

The British continued to purchase over 400,000 tons of Dominican sugar a year for the duration of the war. In return for a guaranteed price of $2.65 per hundred pounds, Trujillo promised the US ambassador (in secret) not to impose any new taxes on sugar for the duration of the war. Regardless, in 1943 Trujillo's government earned $4.5 million from sugar taxes, while the sugar exporters made profits over $7 million.[86] In 1945, Trujillo's government earned over $6 million from sugar taxes.[87] Since Trujillo had unrestricted access to the national treasury, most of this money found its way into the dictator's personal accounts.[88] For his own financial needs, Trujillo made the economy even more dependent on sugar. For the rest of his life, Trujillo would use political and military power to line his own pockets and enrich his closest supporters. Estimates of his wealth ranged from $300 million to $1 billion.[89]

The price of this progress, however, was the centralization of political and economic power in the hands of Trujillo. The corporatist power structure devised by Trujillo was like a honeycomb:

The military power, the political power, the Church, were all represented in the multiple-cell walls of the comb, but so was every important business interest, every financial power, every permit and license and trade regulation, every tax, every exemption, every law; all joined together in their thousands and harmonized, each unit supporting every other, until the separate strengths of the components were as nothing in comparison with the strength and tenacity of the whole.[90]

To consolidate his control, Trujillo relied increasingly on coercion, repression, and intimidation to maintain his authoritarian state. His regime was bolstered by seven intelligence agencies that infiltrated all levels of Dominican society. A vigilant and unremitting surveillance system was maintained over every aspect of Dominican life. All citizens were obligated to carry a *cédula* (national identification card) as well as surrender their passports upon return from trips abroad. Imprisonment, torture, and murder wiped out thousands of political opponents. At La Cuarenta, the Military Intelligence Service's torture chamber, an electric cattle prod was used for shocking particularly sensitive areas. Those who survived Trujillo's torture chambers were so ruined, mentally and physically, that they no longer posed a threat to the regime.[91]

TRUJILLO TAKES CONTROL OF THE SUGAR INDUSTRY, 1948–1957

In 1948, Trujillo began to build new sugar mills and purchase foreign-owned mills in order to consolidate his control over the Dominican political economy. He wanted to expand the process of import substitution industrialization by moving towards the replacement of the foreign-owned sugar enclaves with domestic control over the chief export sector. Rising world sugar prices also provided the dictator with the essential funds to support paternalistic social welfare programs and make the Trujillo family extraordinarily wealthy. The enormous wealth generated from sugar revenues also enabled him to pay off the entire Dominican foreign debt.[92] Although geopolitical realities demanded subservience to US hegemonic interests, Trujillo's anticommunist rhetoric and support in the United Nations convinced US policy makers to look the other way when the dictator moved to control US sugar interests in the Dominican Republic. Trujillo convinced US sugar mill owners and government officials that the most advantageous path to follow was one that coincided with his attempts to dominate the sugar industry.[93] From 1948 to 1957, then, Trujillo enjoyed US government support, while simultaneously exploiting nationalist sentiments against foreign control of the economy. As Table 1.7 shows, by 1957 he controlled almost three-quarters of the Dominican sugar industry.

In 1947, the Dominican government earned $16,169,063 from taxes on sugar exports. The profits reaped by the foreign owners of the sugar industry, however, attracted the dictator's attention. Between 1945 and 1952, the West Indies Sugar Corporation and the South Puerto Rico Sugar Company earned over $85 million from the sale of Dominican sugar.[94] Trujillo, therefore, moved aggressively into the sugar industry, establishing new ingenios of his own or acquiring others of previously small importance. In 1948, he purchased a second-hand sugar mill in

Puerto Rico. He transported the mill, which he renamed Ingenio Catarey, to a parcel of land he owned on the outskirts of Villa Altagracia.[95] Within a year he started construction of the Central Río Haina.[96] Trujillo boasted (erroneously) that his new sugar mill was the world's largest.

Although initially motivated by high sugar prices in the international market, Trujillo's expansion plans during the 1950s were not wholly in response to a period of booming conditions that could have created false expectations of continuous profits. On the contrary, they were the result of a desire to dominate the sources of foreign exchange no matter what export prices were at the time. Because of the close interrelationship between the government and the Trujillo family, the dictator could operate the sugar industry at a profit under almost any conceivable condition. Trujillo was able to obtain state land free of rent, free transportation provided by the military and convicts, and generous tax reductions that increased the profit-making potential of his sugar industry.[97]

Table 1.7
Percent of Dominican Sugar Industry Controlled by Trujillo

Year	Percent
1951	5.4%
1952	9.5%
1953	16.9%
1954	21.0%
1955	26.3%
1956	33.4%
1957	71.3%

Source: Oficina Nacional de Estadística de la República Dominicana, *Estadística Industrial de la República Dominicana* (Ciudad Trujillo: Oficina Nacional de Estadística de la República Dominicana, 1958), pp. 4–9.

Thus, the Dominican sugar industry continued to expand throughout the 1950s and generate huge revenues for Trujillo and the Dominican government, which were virtually indistinguishable. By 1952, Trujillo's government was earning over $22 million annually from export taxes placed on sugar.[98] The industrial growth of the postwar years and Trujillo's desire to become the foremost sugar producer in the Dominican Republic moved him in 1950 to promulgate Law No. 2236. This Ley de Franquicias Industriales y Agrícolas favored the establishment of new industries dedicated to the production and conversion of domestic raw materials.[99] This law was enacted to protect the investments that Trujillo had been making in the sugar industry. The first companies to receive incentives from the new law were the Central Río Haina and the Ingenio Catarey. Under the new legislation, both mills were exempt from paying import duties on equipment and machinery for twenty years.[100]

During the 1950s, Trujillo continued to absorb the Dominican sugar industry, using both state and personal funds to buy many of the foreign mills operating in his country. To cultivate domestic support for this undertaking, Trujillo launched a campaign filled with nationalistic rhetoric against foreign domination of the sugar industry and increased pressure on foreign sugar companies through export taxes to convince the owners to sell. In 1953, the dictator bought the Ingenio Monte Llano in Puerto Plata from the West Indies Sugar Company, the Central Ozama from a group of Canadians, Ingenio Amistad from a group of Puerto Ricans, and Ingenio Porvenir from the Kelly family.[101] By the end of the year, the only sugar mills not owned by the dictator belonged to the two large US sugar corporations—the West Indies Sugar Corporation and the South Porto Rico Sugar Company—and the Vicini family. Trujillo, therefore, increased the pressure on the remaining foreign sugar companies to sell their interests to him. They were subjected to additional taxation as well as numerous fines for sanitation and labor infringements. This campaign culminated on 13 January 1954, when a law was passed subjecting all foreign sugar company profits over $50,000 annually to a 20 percent income tax.[102]

Trujillo, however, denied allegations that the Dominican government was using excessive pressure on the foreign sugar companies to sell their interests. In a conference held at the National Palace with the representatives of the two large US sugar companies, Trujillo announced: "The Dominican Government has always protected and aided businessmen, regardless of nationality, who dedicate themselves to normal activities."[103] Regardless, the US Embassy in Ciudad Trujillo held that "foreign sugar interests have suffered from serious discrimination."[104]

The fruition of Trujillo's campaign came in 1957 when he purchased the Barahona, Consuelo, Quisqueya, and Boca Chica sugar mills from the West Indies Sugar Corporation for $35.8 million, as well as the Santa Fe sugar mill from the South Porto Rico Company for $2.5 million. Although the acquisition of the West Indies Sugar Corporation was interpreted by many people as a move toward the gradual elimination of all sizable concentrations of foreign capital in the Dominican Republic, the US Embassy in Ciudad Trujillo explained that the West Indies Sugar Corporation purchase was merely "a desire for monopoly control of the sugar industry rather than a manifestation of hostility toward foreign capital."[105] Regardless, the officials of the West Indies Sugar Corporation considered the price that Trujillo paid for their mills to be fair and equitable. According to a spokesman for the West Indies Sugar Corporation, "It is believed that the sale was a constructive move. The price was fair and the Corporation was finally relieved of the difficult and embarrassing problem that it has always faced of reconciling the conflict of interests between the two countries in the US sugar market."[106]

In 1957, Trujillo's three sugar corporations—Azucarera Haina, Azucarera Nacional, and Azucarera Yaque—controlled twelve of the sixteen sugar mills in the country. Dominican newspapers reported that "a new impulse was being given to the sugar policy of the Dominican Republic under the direction of Generalissimo Trujillo."[107] Nevertheless, the South Porto Rico Sugar Company continued to expand its colossal operations at the Central Romana, the largest sugar mill in the country. In return for generous tax concessions, the South Porto Rico Sugar Company, which produced 277,238 tons of sugar that year, agreed to invest over $10 million.[108]

During the 1950s, therefore, despite growing world supplies of sugar, the Dominican sugar industry began to increase sugar production and expand total investment in the industry. Most of this increase was attributable to Trujillo's interest in sugar. As Table 1.8 shows, sugar exports averaged about 500,000 tons annually between 1950 and 1954, but rose sharply thereafter, reaching over one million tons in 1960. In order to obtain an assured market for this expanded production, Trujillo increasingly sought to secure a larger share of the US preferential sugar market.[109]

Table 1.8
Dominican Sugar Production and Exports, 1948–1957

Year	Production (in tons)	Exports (in tons)	Value (in dollars)
1948	421,633	381,200	41,300,000
1949	476,484	436,800	38,300,000
1950	453,000	424,632	37,465,864
1951	481,584	474,474	49,865,775
1952	547,523	530,881	50,509,000
1953	553,479	536,199	33,145,000
1954	532,372	604,032	37,727,000
1955	629,850	579,442	39,800,000
1956	755,114	693,146	56,234,938
1957	794,843	723,400	83,800,000

Source: Alvin Gilbert to Department of Agriculture, 19 June 1959; Sugar Folder, Box 246; Dominican Republic, Narrative Reports, 1955–61; RG 166; NA.

Significantly, Trujillo did not energetically lobby in the United States for a preferential sugar quota until he was personally involved in the Dominican sugar industry. In a speech before the Dominican Congress on 27 February 1951, Trujillo expressed his interest in expanding the export of Dominican sugar to the United States.[110] Although the professed objective of Trujillo's clamoring for increased sugar quotas from the United States was to acquire badly needed foreign exchange, after 1959 much of the profits from sugar—instead of being dumped back into the economy—either made their way into Trujillo's Swiss bank accounts or were used to purchase arms and munitions.

In gaining control of the sugar industry, Trujillo intensified his country's economic dependence on sugar exports.[111] Perhaps Trujillo's sugar expansion policy would not have been an obstacle to overall development if the income generated from sugar exports had been reinvested in the country. To make matters worse, at the end of the 1950s the inevitable cyclical fall in the price of sugar provoked economic tumult. Because sugar played such an important part in the economy, changes in either the volume or price of sugar exports impacted upon all phases of the country's life.[112] Although sugar revenues in 1957 amounted to $84 million, they fell to $55 million in 1958.[113] Heavy expatriation of capital during the 1950s, declining sugar prices, and the failure to achieve a large preferential sugar quota from the United States contributed to the critical economic and social problems that were beginning to undermine Trujillo's monopoly of power.[114]

NOTES

1. Oficina Nacional de Estadística de la República Dominicana, *La Industria Azucarera en Marcha* (Ciudad Trujillo: Oficina Nacional de Estadística de la Oficina Nacional de Estadística de la República Dominicana, 1955), pp. 3–27. In 1870, the Dominican Republic exported a meager 3,889 tons of sugar.

2. Andrés Corten, *Azúcar y Política en la República Dominicana* (Santo Domingo: Taller, 1976), p. 3.

3. Loomis to Thomas C. Dawson, 6 January 1905; *Foreign Relations of the United States* (FRUS, hereafter) *1905*, p. 302. In 1905, over 90 percent of Dominican government revenues were generated from export taxes on agricultural products, especially sugar.

4. Oficina Nacional de Estadística de la República Dominicana, *Estadística Industrial de la República Dominicana* (Ciudad Trujillo: Oficina Nacional de Estadística de la República Dominicana 1958).

5. Dominican historiography is even less illustrious. The study of Dominican history has been impeded in the past by the absence of readable history books. In 1878, José Gabriel García published the poorly written, but still widely used, *Compendio de la Historia de Santo Domingo*. Apart from Juan Bosch and Joaquín Balaguer, whose histories are often colored by political exigencies, the two most laudable Dominican historians of the current century are Bernardo Vega, who has written extensively on the Trujillo years, and Frank Moya Pons, author of *Manual de la Historia Dominicana*.

6. John Bartlow Martin, *Overtaken by Events: The Dominican Crisis from the Fall of Trujillo to the Civil War* (Garden City, NY: Doubleday, 1966), p. 18. Because of the lack of scholarly historical works by Dominicans, studies of Dominican history by Anglo-Americans and Europeans predominate. Although Moya Pons and Vega avoid using the term "lunacy," they would certainly point out inconsistencies similar to those elaborated by Martin.

7. See Roger Plant, *Sugar and Modern Slavery: A Tale of Two Countries* (London: Zed Books, 1987). Sugar is a carbohydrate, and like all carbohydrates its function is to supply energy to the body. The commercial sources of sugar are sugar cane (a perennial grass), grown in tropical climates, and the sugar beet, which flourishes in the temperate zone. When fully refined, beet sugar and cane sugar are identical, and they may be used interchangeably for all purposes.

8. Federico Echenique, "La Industria Azucarera Dominicana en Perspectiva," *Azúcar y Diversificación*, Año 4, no. 31 (May 1975): 27–31.

9. Sidney Wilfred Mintz, *Sweetness and Power: The Place of Sugar in Modern History* (Brattleboro, VT: Elisabeth Sifton Books, 1985), pp. 15–23.

10. Frank Moya Pons, *El Pasado Dominicano* (Santo Domingo: Fundación J.A. Caro Alvarez, 1986), p. 72. Although there were 400,000 Taíno Indians living on the island in 1494, there were only 60,000 in 1508; 33,000 in 1511; 25,000 in 1514; 11,000 in 1517; and fewer than 1,000 in 1521.

11. Ibid., p. 16. During the 1520s, many Dominican criollos emigrated to other parts of Spanish America in search of more lucrative economic opportunities after the supply of precious metals decreased. Cattle breeding became the primary economic activity of the island's remaining criollo elites. The cattle the Spanish colonizers had introduced multiplied rapidly and roamed freely all over the colony.

12. G. B. Hagelberg, "Sugar in the Caribbean: Turning Sunshine into Money," working paper, Woodrow Wilson International Center for Scholars, 1985, p. 4. African slaves cut the sugar cane by hand with a broad, heavy machete, severed the leafy tops, and removed the dry trash from the stalks, which were then loaded manually onto ox-drawn carts headed for the sugar mill.

13. Harry Hoetink, *The Dominican People: Notes for a Historical Sociology* (Baltimore: The Johns Hopkins University Press, 1982), p. 43. Santo Domingo's population declined from 125,000 in 1789 to fewer than 63,000 in 1819.

14. Moya Pons, *El Pasado Dominicano*, p. 199. Although cattle ranching was the economic base of most elite families, most cattle ranching families, especially in the eastern part of the island, operated small trapiches.

15. Corten, *Azúcar y Política*, pp. 37–38. A secure supply of cheap labor was required to make the sugar industry profitable. Dominican criollos and mulattos refused to cut sugar cane.

16. Roberto Cassá, *Historia Social y Economía de la República Dominicana* (Santo Domingo: Alfa y Omega, 1977), p. 226. Haitian President Jean-Pierre Boyer distributed land to former slaves and Haitian officers on the condition that they devote part of it to the production of export crops. In addition, Boyer tried to limit the extensive cattle breeding that damaged potential agricultural lands. During the Haitian occupation, therefore, tobacco production increased from 589,000 to 2,622,000 pounds per year and precious wood exports doubled.

17. Patrick Bryan, "The Transition to Plantation Agriculture in the Dominican Republic, 1870–1884," *Journal of Caribbean History* 10 (1978): 82–105. There was not a single monolithic elite. Rather, there were landowners, businessmen, professionals, prominent families, and religious officials who operated in concert with the military.

18. See Michiel Baud, *Peasants and Tobacco in the Dominican Republic, 1870–1930* (Nashville: University of Tennessee Press, 1995).

19. Franc Báez Evertz, *Azúcar y Dependencia en la República Dominicana* (Santo Domingo: Universidad Autónoma de Santo Domingo, 1978), pp. 7–9. During the period of Spanish reoccupation (1861–1865) many Spanish entrepreneurs began small-scale sugar cane cultivation in the rural southwest.

20. See Luis Martínez Fernández, "Caudillos, Annexationism, and the Rivalry between Empires in the Dominican Republic, 1844–1874," *Diplomatic History* 17 (fall 1993): 571–97.

21. Hugh Thomas, "Cuba, c. 1750–1860," in *Cuba: A Short History*, ed. Leslie Bethell (Cambridge, MA: Cambridge University Press, 1993), p. 15.

22. Harry Hoetink, "The Dominican Republic, c. 1870–1930," in *The Cambridge History of Latin America*, vol. 5, ed. Leslie Bethell (London: Cambridge University Press, 1984), pp. 289–291. Dominican politics were to a great extent governed by the perceived need to secure outside economic, political, and military protection as a countervailing force

against the Haitian menace.

23. Frank Moya Pons, *Manual de la Historia Dominicana* (Santiago: Academia Dominicana de la Historia, 1977), p. 408.

24. Báez, *Azúcar y Dependencia*, pp. 9–10.

25. Echenique, "La Industria Azucarera Dominicana," pp. 27–31. An ingenio is a large sugar mill, originally powered by steam and currently by petroleum. A *central* originally denoted an ingenio without large affiliated plantations that mainly processed the cane of independent growers. Today, the distinction between ingenio and central is blurred.

26. Ibid.

27. Valentina Peguero, *Vision General de la Historia Dominicana* (Santo Domingo: Corripio, 1978), pp. 240–44. Ulíses Heureaux (or Lilís, as he was popularly known) was president from 1882 to 1884, and then again from 1887 to 1899. Between 1884 and 1886, two presidents (Gregorio Billini and Alejandro Woss y Gil) were appointed by Heureaux.

28. Hoetink, "The Dominican Republic, c. 1870–1930," pp. 292–93.

29. Ibid., p. 296. Modernization and the expansion of the sugar industry transformed a barter economy into a money economy. The value of land increased, money began to penetrate all social levels, and agrarian wage labor became more common. The regional notables intermingled frequently with the Cuban, Spanish, and Italian immigrants. This led to the formation of a national bourgeoisie at the end of the nineteenth century.

30. José del Castillo, "La Formación de la Industria Azucarera Moderna en la República Dominicana," in *Tobacco, Azúcar, y Minera*, ed. Antonio Lluberes (Santo Domingo: Banco de Desarrollo Interamericano, 1984), pp. 30–31.

31. Esteban Rosario, *Los Dueños de la República Dominicana* (Santo Domingo: Iodized Editores, 1992), pp. 3–5. Vicini married into a prominent Dominican family and joined the ruling elite.

32. del Castillo, "La Formación de la Industria Azucarera Moderna en la República Dominicana," pp. 45–50.

33. Ibid. By 1900, fourteen ingenios had gone bankrupt: La Fe, Caridad, Esperanza, Dolores, Jainamosa, Duquesa, Encarnación, San Luis, Constanza, Bella Vista, Stella, and Francia in Santo Domingo; San Marcos in Puerto Plata; and Cabeza de Toro in Samaná.

34. Rosario, *Los Dueños*, pp. 4–5. Regardless, the ingenios that survived continued the modernization process by constructing railroads to transport the raw sugar cane and by purchasing new machinery.

35. James J. Murphy Jr. to the State Department, 15 April 1926; Sugar and Molasses Folder, Box 154; Dominican Republic, Narrative Reports, 1904–39; Records of the Foreign Agricultural Service, Record Group 166 (RG 166, hereafter); NA. In 1900, to protect the sugar industry, cattle breeding outside fenced areas was prohibited.

36. See Sumner Welles, *Naboth's Vineyard: The Dominican Republic, 1844–1924* (New York: Payson & Clarke, 1928).

37. Franklin Knight, *The Caribbean: The Genesis of Fragmented Nationalism* (New York: Oxford University Press, 1978), p. 184.

38. Emelio Betances, *State and Society in the Dominican Republic* (Boulder, CO: Westview, 1995), p. 57. Following the 1865 War of Restoration, which proclaimed Dominican independence for the third time in the nineteenth century, the oligarchy split into two factions: Liberals (Reds) and Conservatives (Blues). These groupings, however, were little more than loosely organized entourages of rival caudillos competing for power. Nevertheless, President Heureaux and the Blues dominated the Dominican political economy from 1882 to 1899.

39. W. F. Powell to John Hay, 12 May 1903; *FRUS 1903*, pp. 392–93.

40. Báez, *Azúcar y Dependencia*, pp. 19–21.

41. Loomis to Thomas C. Dawson, 6 January 1905; *FRUS 1905*, p. 302.

42. Award of the Commission of Arbitration under the Provisions of the Protocol between the United States of America and the Dominican Republic for the Settlement of the Claims of the San Domingo Improvement Company of New York and Its Allied Companies, 31 January 1904; *FRUS 1904*, pp. 274–79.

43. Thomas C. Dawson to the Secretary of State, 2 January 1905; *FRUS 1905*, pp. 298–99.

44. *Congressional Record*, 85th Congress, 3rd Session, p. 19. Fearing European intervention in the Western Hemisphere to recover massive Latin American debt, the United States sought to reduce European finance in the Americas. It was not long before the so-called Roosevelt Corollary to the Monroe Doctrine was applied to the Dominican Republic.

45. Peguero, *Vision General,* pp. 291–93.

46. Welles, *Naboth's Vineyard*, p. 624–25. The modus vivendi was in effect until the US and the Dominican Republic ratified the treaty.

47. Thomas C. Dawson to the President, 1 July 1905; *FRUS 1905*, pp. 378–89.

48. Review of the Transactions of the Customs Receivership of Santo Domingo, 31 March 1907; *FRUS 1907*, pp. 331–43.

49. Ibid.

50. Peguero, *Vision General*, pp. 291–94.

51. Ibid., p. 310. The US Marines disarmed the various warring caudillos in order to quell internal instability and promote foreign investment. In the southern sugar areas, the US occupational forces had to contend with armed bandits, known as *gavilleros*, who plundered the sugar plantations. To clear the area of gavillero activities, the Marines forcefully concentrated the rural population into a few towns. The *campesinos* (rural folk) sold their land to speculators, who resold the land at a huge profit to US sugar corporations.

52. Piero Gleijeses, *The Dominican Crisis: The 1965 Constitutionalist Revolt and American Intervention* (Baltimore, MD: The Johns Hopkins University Press, 1978), p. 18. Nearly a quarter of the agricultural land in the Dominican Republic was devoted to sugar cane cultivation.

53. José Manuel Madruga, *Azúcar y Haitianos en la República Dominicana* (Santo Domingo: Amigo del Hogar, 1986), p. 84.

54. Báez, *Azú*car y Dependencia, p. 31. The construction of the Central Barahona and the Central Romana during the US occupation caused an dramatic increase in sugar cane acreage.

55. Charles Evans Hughes to the Secretary of the Navy, 17 December 1921, *FRUS 1921*, pp. 866–67.

56. William Bass, *Reciprocidad* (Santo Domingo: La Cuna de América, 1902), pp. 39–40.

57. James J. Murphy Jr. to the State Department, 20 January 1926; Sugar and Molasses Folder, Box 154; Dominican Republic, Narrative Reports, 1904–39; RG 166; NA. US policy makers believed that their nation could be sufficiently supplied with sugar from newly acquired sources in Cuba, Puerto Rico, the Philippines, and Hawaii.

58. del Castillo, "La Formación de la Industria Azucarera Moderna en la República Dominicana," p. 55. Like the sugar crisis of the 1890s, the crisis of the 1920s caused a concentration of the ingenios. By 1925, the Cuban Dominican Sugar Company owned the Barahona, Consuelo, San Isidro, Quisqueya, and Las Pajas ingenios, which controlled 30 percent of all Dominican sugar production. The West Indies Sugar Corporation bought the

Cuban Dominican Sugar Company properties in 1928.

59. Báez, *Azúcar y Dependencia*, p. 63. Although the Fordney-McCumber Tariff was an economic disaster for the Dominicans, it did not devastate the two large US sugar companies operating in the Dominican Republic. Both corporations owned extensive sugar properties in Cuba and Puerto Rico and were able to sustain their Dominican losses.

60. Ibid., pp. 62–67.

61. E. R. Curry, *Hoover's Dominican Diplomacy and the Origins of the Good Neighbor Policy* (New York: Garland Publishing, 1979), p. 57.

62. Arthur Schoenfeld to Cordell Hull, 10 August 1934; Secret Reports Folder, Box 1; Dominican Republic, Miscellaneous Records; Foreign Service Posts of the Department of State, Record Group 84 (RG 84, hereafter); NA. Angelina, Cristóbal Colon, and the Compañía Anónima de Explotaciones Industriales (CAEI) were the three ingenios owned by the Vicini family. In 1930, they accounted for 10 percent of total Dominican sugar production.

63. Charles B. Curtis to the Secretary of State, 2 June 1931; Sugar Folder, Box 154; Dominican Republic, Narrative Reports, 1904–39; RG 166; NA.

64. Charles B. Curtis to the State Department, 1 June 1930; Secret Reports Folder, Box 1; Dominican Republic, Miscellaneous Records; RG 84; NA. In 1928, Vásquez had removed the article in the Dominican Constitution that prohibited reelection to the presidency.

65. Charles B. Curtis to the Department of State, 1 March 1930; *FRUS 1930*, p. 170. Although Estrella Ureña led the revolution that overthrew Vásquez, Trujillo—who controlled the Guardia Nacional since 1925—supplied the majority of the weapons. In December, Trujillo placed a large cache of arms in the virtually unguarded San Luis Fortress in Santiago, the second largest post of the Dominican Army. On 22 February, these weapons were seized by Estrella Ureña and a small group of supporters. Vásquez resigned six days later.

66. Charles B. Curtis to State Department, 1 June 1930; Secret Reports Folder, Box 1; Dominican Republic, Miscellaneous Records; RG 84; NA. Trujillo led Vásquez to believe that he was trustworthy, when in fact he was plotting against him.

67. See Frank Moya Pons, "The Dominican Republic since 1930," in *The Cambridge History of Latin America, 1930 to Present*, vol. 7, ed. Leslie Bethell (New York: Cambridge University Press, 1990), pp. 510–13.

68. Howard J. Wiarda, *Dictatorship and Development: The Methods of Control in Trujillo's Dominican Republic* (Gainesville: University of Florida Press, 1968), p. 30. According to Wiarda, the upper strata of Dominican society had refused to serve as officers in the US-created constabulary with the result that the military leadership was soon dominated by new elements. The old elite lost its monopoly on military training and leadership. This shift from upper-class to middle-class leadership took place initially in the officer corps. After Trujillo came to power, the change was noticeable in the civilian leadership as well.

69. Ibid., pp. 25–28. Trujillo was born in San Cristóbal, a poverty-ridden community on the southern coast, on 24 October 1891. His humble ancestry can accurately be traced back to José Trujillo Monagas, a Spanish police officer who arrived in Santo Domingo during the 1860s, and Diyetta Chevalier, a Haitian who settled in San Cristóbal during the 1822–1844 Haitian occupation.

70. Ibid., pp. 29–31. During the late 1920s, Trujillo sought admission to some of the nation's exclusive social clubs. Membership implied acceptance and social standing on a level with the Dominican elites. Trujillo's rejection by the principal social club in El Seibo

exacerbated his hatred of the gente de la primera.

71. John D. Barfield to the State Department, 17 April 1961; Decimal File 739.00/4-161, Box 1637; Dominican Republic, 1960–63; RG 59; NA. This is evident from the histories of his era sponsored by himself. They always glorify his ancestors, even tracing some them to the French nobility. Mention of the negro race in his background was systematically suppressed.

72. Rafael Trujillo to Herbert Hoover, 25 August 1931; *FRUS 1931*, vol. 2, pp. 110–11.

73. *Listín Diario*, 23 May 1933.

74. Báez, *Azúcar y Dependencia*, pp. 91–92. Ramón Saviñón Lluberes, Trujillo's brother-in-law, managed the real estate business, the industrial slaughterhouse, and the national lottery; his uncle Teófilo Pina Chevalier was president of the national insurance company; Francisco Martínez Alba, his brother-in-law, managed Read Hardware and exercised control over import permits; former US Marine Colonel McLaughlin, whose daughter eventually married Héctor Trujillo, Trujillo's brother, managed the merchant marine; and María Martínez, Trujillo's wife, operated the army's laundry concession.

75. Herbert L. Mathews, "Dominicans Thrive at Cost of Liberty," *New York Times*, 28 March 1953, p. 7. According to Mathews, it was "a parlor pastime in Ciudad Trujillo to guess how much the Generalissimo has secreted abroad; everyone agrees the total must be fabulous."

76. Wiarda, *Dictatorship and Development*, pp. 102–23. Although some of Trujillo's companies benefitted the national economy by establishing enterprises that represent an improvement over earlier foreign monopolies, he always viewed government as a means for personal aggrandizement.

77. Arthur Schoenfeld to Cordell Hull, 10 August 1934; Secret Reports Folder, Box 1; Dominican Republic, Miscellaneous Records; RG 84; NA.

78. Law No. 1365, 23 August 1937; Archivo Particular del Generalísimo [APG, hereafter]; Archivo del Palacio Nacional Dominicano (PND, hereafter), Santo Domingo (SD, hereafter).

79. Law No. 1719, 12 September 1930; APG; PND; SD.

80. Eugene M. Hinkle to the State Department, 11 April 1940; Sugar Folder, Box 51; Dominican Republic, General Records; RG 84, NA.

81. Robert Mills McClintock to the State Department, 1 November 1938; Secret Reports Folder, Box 1; Dominican Republic, Miscellaneous Records; RG 84; NA.

82. Arthur Schoenfeld to the State Department, 26 February 1937; Sugar Folder, Box 24; Dominican Republic, General Records; RG 84; NA.

83. Robert McGregor Scotten to the State Department, 11 March 1941; Sugar Folder, Box 62; Dominican Republic, General Records; RG 84; NA.

84. David I. Ferber to A. M. Warren, 25 February 1943; Sugar Folder, Box 216; Dominican Republic, Narrative Reports, 1942–45; RG 166; NA. To fuel his megalomania, Santo Domingo was renamed Ciudad Trujillo (Trujillo City) in 1936.

85. Robert McGregor Scotten to the State Department, 12 February 1942; Sugar Folder, Box 91; Dominican Republic, General Records; RG 84; NA.

86. Avra Warren to Cordell Hull, 15 July 1943; Sugar Folder, Box 118; Dominican Republic, General Records; RG 84; NA.

87. George F. Scherer to the State Department, 4 September 1945; Sugar Folder, Box 216; Dominican Republic, Narrative Reports, 1942–45; RG 166; NA.

88. Báez, *Azúcar y Dependencia*, pp. 91–95.

89. Howard J. Wiarda and Michael J. Kryzanek, *The Dominican Republic: A Caribbean Crucible* (Boulder, CO: Westview, 1982), p. 36. Wiarda argues that the monetary figure of Trujillo's wealth is less important than the extent of his control over the entire national economy.

90. Robert Crassweller, *Trujillo: The Life and Times of a Caribbean Dictator* (New York: Macmillan, 1966), p. 124.

91. For an literary example of Trujillo's brutality and corruption, see Julia Alvarez, *In the Time of the Butterflies* (New York: Penguin, 1994). It should be pointed out, however, that Trujillo's terror apparatus was not confined to the Dominican Republic nor was the list of victims limited to Dominican citizens. Critics of the Trujillo regime often became *desaparecidos* (disappeared ones).

92. Ellis M. Goodwin to the Secretary of State, 9 February 1949; Sugar Folder, Box 197; Dominican Republic, General Records; RG 84; NA.

93. H. S. Steele to the State Department, 19 April 1948; Communism Folder, Box 21; Dominican Republic, Confidential General Records; RG 84; NA.

94. Dale E. Farringer to the State Department, 14 January 1948; Sugar Folder, Box 196; Dominican Republic, General Records; RG 84; NA.

95. Richard F. Lankenau to the State Department, 5 June 1950; Sugar Folder, Box 129; Dominican Republic, Narrative Reports, 1950–54; RG 166; NA. Ingenio Catarey began operations on 5 June 1950, the birthday of Trujillo's oldest son, Ramfis.

96. Harry R. Zerbel to the State Department, 3 January 1950; Sugar Folder, Box 129; Dominican Republic, Narrative Reports, 1950–54; RG 166; NA. Although Trujillo spent more than $55 million on the Río Haina enterprise, it was never a good economic proposition: it was too large and rarely produced to capacity. Furthermore, the distance between mill and plantation lowered the amount of sugar obtainable from the cane. The sugar content of the cane deteriorates rapidly after cutting.

97. Gustavo Segundo Volmar, *The Impact of the Foreign Sector on the Domestic Economic Activity of the Dominican Republic from 1950 to 1967* (Ph.D. diss. Columbia University, 1971), pp. 78–80.

98. William Belton to the State Department, 30 April 1952; Sugar Folder, Box 129; Dominican Republic, Narrative Reports, 1950–54; RG 166; NA.

99. Frank Moya Pons, "Import Substitution Industrialization Policies in the Dominican Republic," *Hispanic American Historical Review* 70 (November 1990): 562. Numerous factories were built in the Dominican Republic during the 1940s and 1950s to manufacture products for domestic consumption. In addition to the vast sugar industry, Trujillo and his cronies came to monopolize the production of soft drinks, cigarettes, textiles, furniture, shoes, paper, glass, cement, and electric appliances.

100. William Belton to the State Department, 30 April 1952; Sugar Folder, Box 129; Dominican Republic, Narrative Reports, 1950–54; RG 166; NA.

101. For a fascinating study of the Ozama sugar plantation, and its relationship with the Trujillo regime, see Catherine C. LeGrand, "Informal Resistance on a Dominican Sugar Plantation during the Trujillo Dictatorship," *Hispanic American Historical Review* 75, no. 4 (1995): 555–696.

102. Richard A. Johnson to the State Department, 5 May 1954; Decimal File 739.00/5-554, Box 3384; Dominican Republic, 1950–54; RG 59; NA. Dominican Law No. 3732, promulgated 11 January 1954, set fines up to $2,000 daily of any sugar mill in violation of sanitary rules, as well as prison terms of up to six months for executive personnel.

103. Allen H. Lester to the State Department, 3 February 1954; Sugar Folder, Box 128; Dominican Republic, Narrative Reports, 1950–54; RR 166; NA. In addition, Trujillo always paid the foreign mill owners adequate monetary compensation for their properties and investments.

104. Richard C. Desmond to the State Department, 21 March 1955; Economic Conditions Folder, Box 244; Dominican Republic, Narrative Reports, 1955–61; RG 166; NA. Nevertheless, the US Embassy in Ciudad Trujillo never lodged an official complaint with the Dominican government over Trujillo's sugar industry acquisitions.

105. Francis L. Spalding to the State Department, 25 April 1957; Decimal File 839.2351/4-2557, Box 4384; Dominican Republic, 1955–59; RG 59; NA. In 1956, the West Indies Sugar Corporation produced 191,626 tons of sugar.

106. Henry S. Hammond to the State Department, 20 December 1957; Sugar Folder, Box 246; Dominican Republic, Narrative Reports, 1955–61; RG 166; NA.

107. *El Caribe*, 28 January 1957. Amistad, Esperanza, and Monte Llano are located in the north; Barahona is located in the southwest; Río Haina, CAEI, Catarey, Ozama, and Boca Chica are located in the south central region; and Porvenir, Santa Fe, Quisqueya, Consuelo, Angelina, Cristóbal Colon, and La Romana are located in the east. Because of agricultural diversification efforts and low world sugar prices, CAEI, Angelina, Catarey, and Esperanza were closed in 1987. Amistad, Monte Llano, and Porvenir were closed during the 1990s.

108. Francis L. Spalding to the State Department, 20 May 1957; Economic Conditions Folder, Box 244; Dominican Republic, Narrative Reports, 1955–61; RG 166; NA. The South Porto Rico Sugar Corporation sold the Central Romana to the Gulf & Western Company in 1967. A consortium, headed by the Miami-based Cuban-American Fanjul Brothers, bought the Gulf & Western interests in 1986 with the countenance of the Balaguer government. The Fanjul Brothers were close friends of Ronald Reagan and Dominican Vice President Carlos Morales Troncoso.

109. William Belton to the State Department, 30 April 1952; Sugar Folder, Box 129; Dominican Republic, Narrative Reports, 1950–54; RG 166; NA.

110. Rafael Trujillo, "Message before the Dominican National Congress, 27 February 1951," *Discursos, Mensajes y Proclamas*, vol. 10.

111. *Listín Diario*, 15 December 1995. By the time Trujillo was assassinated in 1961, the sugar industry produced more foreign exchange than all other economic activities combined. By 1995, however, sugar accounted for less than 10 percent of the foreign currency earnings. The three primary sources of foreign currency revenue in 1995 were nickel exports, tourism, and remittances from Dominicans living abroad. Although sugar no longer occupies center stage in US-Dominican relations, its legacy continues: Dominican elites continue to dominate the political economy and the US still maintains economic and political hegemony over the small nation.

112. US Agency for International Development, *From Debt to Development* (Washington, DC: US Agency for International Development, 1985), p. 34. The problem of basing the nation's economy on the monocultural export of sugar is laid bare by the fact that, for the sugar exporter, the 6.3 tons of oil that a ton of sugar could buy in 1960 were reduced to .7 tons of oil by 1983.

113. US Department of Agriculture, *The Dominican Republic: Agriculture and Trade* (Washington, DC: US Department of Agriculture, 1963). Although sugar revenues rose to $85 million in 1960, the damage had been done. In 1958, for the first time since 1921, there was a trade deficit.

114. Francis L. Spalding, Counselor of US Embassy in Dominican Republic, to Department of State, 20 May 1957; economic conditions folder, box 244; Dominican Republic, Narrative Reports, 1955–61; RG 166; NA. The Dominican Republic had experienced a significant outflow of capital after 1955, when Trujillo spent $32 million on an international fair to commemorate his twenty-five years in power.

Chapter 2

US Policy Toward the Dominican Republic, 1900–1957

The Dominican Republic has long been of critical interest to US foreign policy. A US diplomat astutely pointed out:

Because of its proximity to the United States, it has been in the interest of our government and American business to promote the development of the resources of the Republic, to develop strong economic ties, and to particularly discourage European nations from attempting to subjugate it into their colonial framework.[1]

An examination of US foreign policy toward the Dominican Republic from 1900 to 1957 reveals that a fundamental undercurrent of that policy has been the extension of US hegemony. According to political scientist Kenneth Coleman, "The persistent goals of US foreign policy toward independent Latin America have included maximum US geographic expansion and the establishment of political and economic hegemony."[2] US policy toward the Dominican Republic was designed to promote and safeguard strategic, economic, and ideological interests. The United States, therefore, incorporated the Dominican Republic within a US sphere of influence, in which the United States exerted informal hegemonic control over the Dominican political economy.

Since the turn of the century, US policy toward the Dominican Republic has reflected a concern over the strategic importance of the Caribbean. In 1914, the completion of the Panama Canal enhanced that importance of the region. The waterway became a vital national security interest.[3] The State Department's Sumner Welles wrote:

It may be confidently asserted that since the acquisition of the Panama Canal Zone by the United States every American Secretary of State has regarded the preservation of peace and the maintenance of orderly procedures of Government in the region of the Caribbean as a matter of deep concern to the United States.[4]

The United States was dedicated to keeping foreign powers away from an area considered part of its security zone.

Economic factors, especially US investment in the Dominican sugar industry, also played an important part in the formation of US policy. By 1900, the search for raw materials and new markets for the rapidly expanding US economy propelled US business interests toward the Dominican Republic. By 1916, US capital controlled over 60 percent of the Dominican sugar industry, the most important industry on the island.[5] Although Dominican elites continued to generate huge revenues from taxes on sugar exports, they lost control of their national economy and made their nation further dependent on the Colossus of the North. US economic ties to the Dominican Republic were further strengthened by World War I, which severed the Dominican Republic's traditional economic and cultural ties with Europe.[6]

In promoting its ideological goals in the Caribbean, the United States occasionally intervened in the Dominican Republic to nurture democracy on the island nation.[7] According to historian Fredrick Pike, "Periodically, the United States passes through alternating cycles of trying to make the world safe for its type of democracy and of endeavoring to make its type of democracy safe from the world."[8] These periodic democratic outbursts, however, have been characterized by numerous contradictions. US policy makers encouraged democracy only when geopolitical security interests were not imperiled. The promotion of democracy was ultimately a tactical means to defend strategic and economic interests. There has been a disinclination of US policy makers to prize democratic values over security interests. Political scientist John D. Martz explains:

Despite frequent rhetorical obeisance paid to the ideals of democracy as a fundamental diplomatic objective, US policy makers have customarily given highest priority to elements other than the implementation of democratic values. They have exaggerated or misunderstood the differences between meaningful participatory democracy and controlled or nonrepresentative elections, especially when this is convenient to the exigencies of geopolitical and security demands.[9]

US policy makers, therefore, approached this effort to transform Dominican political culture with a mixture of paternalism and arrogance.[10] Dominican policy makers, on the other hand, were inclined to adhere to the nation's indigenous authoritarian political traditions. The result was often a democratic facade covering an authoritarian substructure. Indeed, twentieth-century Dominican political culture developed into a struggle between a personalistic, authoritarian, and caudilloistic tradition brought to the island by the Spanish colonizers and an institutional, legalistic, democratic tradition encouraged by US diplomats and foreign policy makers.[11]

By 1916, after nearly two decades of expansion into the Caribbean region, the United States had created the methods and instruments necessary to establish its hegemony in the Dominican Republic. It had done so for a number of reasons: To achieve economic expansion beyond its borders, promote its ideological goals, indulge its prejudices, and improve its self-image.[12] Most important, from that point forward, the fundamental objective of US policy in the Western Hemisphere was to prevent the coming to power of any government in the Caribbean that could threaten the security of the United States or its predominant economic and ideological position in the region.[13]

Whereas US policy makers sought to protect US national interests by promoting stability and, at times, democracy in the Caribbean and keeping foreign powers out, the Dominican Republic's political elites tended to define their national interests in terms of their ability to obtain stable prices for agricultural exports.   The Dominican elites, regardless of their ideological affiliation, consistently viewed political office as the key to securing access to the country's lucrative customs revenues. In the words of Dominican politician Donald Reid Cabral: "The misery of being exploited by capitalists is nothing compared to the misery of not being exploited at all."[14] Since sugar generated the majority of customs revenues during the twentieth century, the Dominican elites repeatedly made sugar policy the center of their foreign policy. The resulting US-Dominican relationship, accordingly, was one of reciprocal manipulation, in which US and Dominican policy makers attempted to safeguard their respective national interests. A survey of US-Dominican relations between 1900 and 1957 reveals the centrality of reciprocal manipulation as the foundation of the two countries' bilateral relationship. That relationship can perhaps be measured most persuasively by focusing on two criteria: (1) the extent of US control over policy decisions in the Dominican political economy; and (2) the level of self-interested Dominican complicity in facilitating the extension of US hegemony.

THE RISE OF US HEGEMONY, 1900–1915

From 1898, when the United States won the Spanish-American War and became the predominant military force in the Caribbean region, until 1915, the eve of the US military occupation of the Dominican Republic, US policy toward the Dominican Republic was a continuous effort to expand US influence. According to historian Bruce Calder, "The Dominican occupation of 1916 to 1924 was clearly part of a general pattern of expanding US influence in the Caribbean after 1898."[15]

During this period of expanding hegemony, the United States employed political and financial manipulation, frequent threats, and the occasional use of force to steadily increase its influence over the Dominican political economy. The US government advocated the expansion of private US capital in the Dominican Republic, especially in the sugar industry. In addition, US officials encouraged Dominican elites to introduce political and fiscal stability to safeguard those interests. Facilitating this policy were the deliberate and energetic efforts of the Dominican oligarchy to invite greater US involvement in their country.

The financial chaos and political turmoil that engulfed the Dominican Republic following the 1899 assassination of President Heureaux coincided with a period in which the United States began to exert greater influence over the Caribbean region. As the Dominican Republic plunged into revolutionary turmoil that further aggravated the country's financial situation, the United States began to pressure the Dominican government to allow US agents to take over the collection of customs and thus control Dominican financial affairs. In response to this situation, on 5 January 1905, Secretary of State John Hay implemented the newly announced Roosevelt Corollary to the Monroe Doctrine by announcing:

The government of the United States, in view of the continued state of unrest which seems to prevail in Santo Domingo, and in view of the imminent and pressing danger of intervention on the part of certain European creditors to the end of obtaining a settlement of claims overdue, that this government is now disposed to assist the government of Santo Domingo in the work of regulating the finances of the Republic by undertaking the administration of all its customs houses.[16]

The Customs Receivership stipulated that 45 percent of the nation's customs revenues would be turned over to the Dominican government for expenses; the remaining 55 percent would be used to pay the country's creditors. According to Minister Thomas Dawson,

The financial modus vivendi put into effect 1 April by a decree of the Dominican Government was the only means apparent by which the Dominican Government could get money enough to exist and to maintain order and at the same time all the creditors receive a reasonably satisfactory guaranty. Further, the desire to get possession of customs-houses is the principle motive for and incentive to revolutions. Foreign collection and receivership were, therefore, necessary if the creditors were to be paid and civil war to cease.[17]

After the modus vivendi was ratified by the US Congress on 22 June 1907, the United States officially proclaimed the US-Dominican Convention of 1907.[18]

With the approval of Morales Languasco's successor, Ramón Cáceres, the United States reduced and consolidated the Dominican foreign debt with the collaboration of the Guarantee Trust Company of New York. The plan included a $20 million loan by the bank to pay legitimate claims against the Dominican government, thus making the United States the Dominican Republic's only foreign creditor. By 1908, the Dominican foreign debt had been cut in half. Foreign creditors agreed to accept $12,407,000 for debts and claims amounting to about $21,184,000 of face value. The financial arrangements negotiated between 1905 and 1907 established a strong US control over Dominican finance, greatly reduced the Dominican foreign debt, and increased the amount of revenue available to the incumbent Horacista political elites. Although beneficial to the Horacista government, the Customs Receivership's success at restoring fiscal stability and eliminating corruption greatly angered the Jimenistas. Excluded from political office and denied the spoils of graft, Jimenista elites saw their opportunities for enrichment curtailed by the removal of the customs revenues from their reach.[19]

After a disgruntled Jimenista assassinated Cáceres in 1911, US policy makers unsuccessfully tried to reestablish stable government in the Dominican Republic. The United States used incentives and threats to persuade various Dominican governments to carry out fiscal and political reforms. Often, US administrators suspended Customs Receivership payments to the Dominican government or sent naval vessels to Dominican waters to secure compliance with their wishes. Blaming Eladio Victoria's Horacista government for the revolutionary atmosphere, in 1912 US Minister William Russell told the Dominican president that failure to resign would result in the withholding of Custom's Receivership revenues to the government.[20] Indicative of US influence, thirteen days later power was turned over to Monseñor Adolfo Nouel, the apolitical Roman Catholic Archbishop. Following an extended period of pandemonium and revolutionary activity, in 1914 power was turned over to Juan Isidro Jiménez.

The United States immediately pressured Jiménez to accept a broad new set of financial reforms. According to US diplomat James Sullivan, "Without our assistance neither this nor any succeeding government can hope to survive long."[21] Pressured by the United States on the one hand, and meeting tremendous resistance in the Dominican Congress from Horacistas on the other, President Jiménez held a tenuous grip on governmental control. On 17 December 1915, Russell handed Jiménez a series of demands that, if accepted, would have turned the Dominican Republic into a virtual US protectorate. The most onerous of these demands was a plan to make a US government official the financial advisor to the Dominican president. The financial advisor, who could not be dismissed, would draft the national budget and administer it by requiring his signature for all government expenditures. Other reforms included the creation of a constabulary staffed by US Marines, the institution of a national taxation system, and placing the collection of all internal revenues in the hands of the Customs Receivership. President Jiménez argued that approval of these demands would be an "abdication of national sovereignty."[22] Unable to meet US demands and unwilling to accept a US offer to send in US Marines, on 7 May 1916 Jiménez resigned in protest.

US-Dominican relations during this period, however, should not be characterized as a simple process of penetration of victimized Dominicans by imperialists.[23] Dominican elites wantonly facilitated the extension of US hegemony for their own self-interest.[24] Although US investment in the Dominican sugar industry and subsequent imports of Dominican sugar expanded US economic control over the island, many Dominican elites benefited from the increased revenues obtained from taxes of sugar exports. Dominican sugar magnate Juan Bautista Vicini Burgos was eager for continued foreign investment in the Dominican sugar industry. Vicini had numerous agents in the United States searching for investors. According to Vicini, the Dominican sugar industry "would not have witnessed such dramatic growth" without US capital investment.[25] Dominican elites, therefore, consistently sought to strengthen their fragile export-led, raw-material-based economy with increased US investment, regardless of the consequences. The price that they paid for the rewards of US investment in the sugar industry—financial solvency, protection from European encroachment, and a sizable market for Dominican sugar exports—was a burgeoning US hegemony over the island nation.

THE APEX OF US HEGEMONY, 1916–1932

The excessive political and economic turmoil that engulfed the Dominican Republic for five years after Cáceres's assassination, as well as US fears of potential German intervention into the chaotic Dominican political economy during World War I, convinced US policy makers that the most efficient way to expand trade and increase national security was through direct control of the Dominican Republic. The groundwork for the US military occupation of 1916–1924 was laid on 13 May 1916, when the United States sent 700 US Marines to the Dominican Republic to restore order.[26] In the words of the leader of the US Marine expedition, Admiral W. B. Caperton:

It is not the intention of the United States Government to acquire by conquest any territory in the Dominican Republic nor to attack its sovereignty, but our troops will remain here until all revolutionary movements have been stamped out and until such reforms as are deemed necessary to ensure the future welfare of the country have been initiated and are in effective operation.[27]

Although the squabbling Dominican Congress eventually selected Foreign Minister Francisco Henríquez y Carvajal as provisional president on 25 July, the United States refused to recognize him until the new president accepted the reforms that they had tried to force on Jiménez. On 18 August 1916, the United States suspended the Dominican government's access to funds from the Customs Receivership when Henríquez "refused to meet the views of the United States in regard to the establishment of financial control and constabulary."[28]

Following continued pandemonium and fratricidal struggles for power among Dominican politicians, on 29 November 1916, Captain H. S. Knapp, the first US military governor, informed President Henríquez y Carvajal that the Dominican Republic was being placed under US military occupation and military government for an indefinite period of time. The proclamation stated:

This military occupation is undertaken with no immediate or ulterior object of destroying the sovereignty of the Republic of Santo Domingo, but, on the contrary, is designed to give aid to that country in returning to a condition of internal order that will enable it to observe the terms of the [1907] treaty aforesaid, and the obligations resting upon it as one of the family of nations.[29]

Although the proclamation claimed that the Dominicans had violated Article 3 of the 1907 US-Dominican Agreement by increasing their foreign debt without US permission, this was merely a legal pretext. The unstated strategic motive for the US occupation was the desire to protect the southern approaches to the United States and the Panama Canal from German aggression. President Wilson was concerned that hostile powers would seize on the Dominican Republic's chronic financial and political instability to the detriment of the US strategic position during World War I. According to Henríquez y Carvajal, "The United States having resolved to declare war on Germany anticipated the declaration by strengthening their position in the Caribbean in order to better guard the approaches to the Panama Canal and to prevent the establishment of submarine bases or the possibility of Germany's finding other aid in this region."[30] US Consul Clement S. Edwards confirmed Henríquez's contention by asserting, "In view of the tremendous magnitude of the issues at stake in the Great War, the United States may reasonably claim justification for their action."[31]

During its military occupation of the Dominican Republic, the United States attempted to bring a number of fundamental changes to the island nation's political, economic, and social life in the hope of creating a stable and cooperative neighbor that would safeguard US strategic and economic interests. Acknowledging that the 1907 Convention was merely a financial instrument whose success was impeded by its inability to forestall, avoid, or remedy violent political disturbances, the US Marines decided to disarm the Dominican citizenry. From a population of 750,000, US military forces confiscated 50,000 firearms and 200,000 rounds of ammunition.[32] The creation of a theoretically apolitical and professionalized National Guard was another attempt to impose order and guarantee democracy. In April 1917, the United States established a constabulary led primarily by US military officers. According to H. S. Knapp,

If the Guardia Nacional, now being organized, can be indoctrinated properly, and especially if it can be given the example of the United States Marines serving alongside it for a considerable period, there is hope that in the long run the people of Santo Domingo will appreciate so thoroughly the advantages of a stable condition of good order that, with the aid of the national police force, they will themselves not further permit the revolutionary movements that have done so much to retard the country's development.[33]

US policy makers were highly optimistic about the ability of the newly formed Guardia Nacional to defend democratic institutions. Believing that a well-trained police force was the panacea for restoring economic and political stability to the Dominican Republic, Knapp immediately disbanded the Dominican army, recruited 1,095 Dominicans for the Guardia Nacional, and initiated the training of Dominican officers and enlisted men by twenty-five US Marine Corps officers.[34]

Fiscal reforms implemented by the US military government ensured the regular dispersement of funds for salaries and services. Taxes on sugar and other agricultural exports from January to March 1920 were $1,661,000, as opposed to $976,067 for the same period in 1919. Rather than being wasted on civil war, Dominican revenues were funneled into a host of development projects. US Marines created the nation's first adequate road network, developed public health and sanitation projects, improved upon the postal and telegraph services, and encouraged the rapid expansion of the education system.[35] Although the US-imposed Dominican Customs Tariff of 1919, which allowed US-manufactured products unlimited entry into the Dominican market at a greatly reduced tariff, destroyed the small local industries that were unable to compete with the foreign products, the increased revenues generated from a greater flow of goods through the Dominican customs houses provided the government with ever increasing amounts of working capital.[36] Whereas the tariff was harmful to small businessmen, members of the oligarchy benefited handsomely.

The policies and regulations implemented by the US military government were also designed to promote US economic interests. The US military government encouraged and facilitated the expansion of US investment in the Dominican sugar industry, which, although increasing the nation's capacity to export sugar, deepened the dependency on a monocultural economy. During the US military occupation, 80 percent of the Dominican sugar industry came to be dominated by North American interests.[37] The US military government assured a safe environment for investment, while simultaneously enacting a variety of laws, such as the 1920 Land Registration Act, that facilitated the acquisition of land by US-owned sugar corporations. During the US military occupation, land under sugar cane production increased from 350,000 tareas in 1915 to 1 million tareas in 1923. Most of this land was taken by US sugar companies, who increased their land holdings by 89 percent during the occupation.[38] The 1920 Land Registration Act also benefited Dominican elites who incorporated community-owned lands into their own properties by obtaining legally recognized land titles from the US military government. Horacio Vásquez, who worked closely with the military government, used the 1920 Land Registration Act to gain land for the Horacistas at the expense of the Jimenistas. Modern Dominican dynasties—Barceló, Vicini, Espaillat, and Bermúdez—owe a large part of their current prosperity to the land that they acquired during the US occupation.[39]

Realizing increased wealth from US-implemented fiscal reforms and encouraged by the regular dispersement of funds for salaries and services, the Dominican oligarchy willingly cooperated with the US military government. Emilio Joubert, a high official of Horacio Vásquez's Partido Nacional Restaurador, expressed the sentiments of the Dominican oligarchy when he stated: "I have always been willing to give myself, body and soul, to the task of helping the Military Government or the State Department in any endeavor tending to promote the good of the Dominican Republic."[40] Although the conservative political elites had always wanted to collaborate with the United States, they were initially confined to government positions below the cabinet level. Regardless, members of several influential Dominican families, including Mario Fermín Cabral (a ranking member of the oligarchy and president of the Senate before the intervention), Francisco A. Herrera (an ex-chief of the Ministry of Treasury), Francisco J. Peynado (a prestigious lawyer for a foreign-owned sugar company), P. A. Ricart (the vice president of the Santo Domingo Chamber of Commerce), Arturo Fiallo Cabral (the superintendent general of public education), Horacio Vásquez (the leader of the Partido Nacional Restaurador), Federico Velázquez (the leader of the Partido Progresista), and Luis F. Vidal (the leader of the Partido Legalista), either offered their support or gave advice to the military government. In return for their services, these elites received lucrative jobs and contracts from the military government and the US-owned sugar companies. Not surprisingly, members of the Dominican elite clamored for greater amounts of US foreign investment so that they could expand the sugar industry and generate more revenue from the export of sugar.[41] In the words of historian Bruce Calder, these elites viewed the military government as "a patron—as a source of jobs, as a potential customer, as a possible sponsor for their favorite projects, or even an ally in settling grudges against other Dominicans."[42]

By 1920, however, many Dominicans began to fear that the United States never intended to restore the country's sovereignty and became openly antagonistic towards the military government. The obvious US penetration and control of the Dominican political economy also provoked nationalistic resentment among the masses.[43] At the same time, US government officials began to grow weary of expensive military occupations of Caribbean nations. On 4 December 1920, Admiral Snowden, the second military governor, announced: "The Government of the United States believes the time has arrived when it may, with a due sense of its responsibility to the people of the Dominican Republic, inaugurate the simple processes of its rapid withdrawal from the responsibilities assumed in connection with Dominican affairs."[44] Because of growing nationalist resentment, the military government invited its conservative political elite allies to participate in the development of a transition process. The nationalists, however, vehemently rejected this approach because it embraced the ratification of all legislation passed during the US military administration.

Nevertheless, on 30 June 1922, after months of negotiations, US Secretary of State Charles Evans Hughes and former Dominican Minister of Finance Francisco J. Peynado announced the so-called Hughes-Peynado Plan. In preparation for the 1924 presidential elections and the withdrawal of US troops, the plan called for the immediate naming of a provisional president. On 2 October 1922, a special committee appointed sugar baron Juan Bautista Vicini Burgos provisional president of the Dominican Republic.[45] Vicini Burgos's provisional government worked closely with the military government in order to assure an orderly transfer of power. US troops left Dominican soil in 1924, after Horacio Vásquez won the presidential elections and signed the 1924 Dominican-American Agreement, which guaranteed the Customs Receivership until the foreign debt was paid.

Although the US military occupation brought economic and political stability in the Dominican Republic, it accomplished little in terms of encouraging political modernization and institution building. Historians Richard Hillman and Thomas D'Agostino charge that the United States "failed to ameliorate the precise factor (the lack of established organizations and institutional processes) responsible for the anarchy and instability it sought to remedy through occupation."[46]

Ironically, the institution that the United States intended as the defender of constitutional democracy in the Dominican Republic became the vehicle for one of the twentieth century's most brutal and corrupt authoritarian regimes. As revolutionary activity threatened to topple the Vásquez government, US policy makers anxiously hoped that General Trujillo, the commander in chief of the US-created Guardia Nacional, would remain loyal to the government. Having affirmed his loyalty to the Vásquez regime on numerous occasions, US Minister Evan Young informed the State Department: "It is profoundly to be hoped that General Trujillo will abide, in the troubled days ahead, by the assurances which he has given the Legation."[47]   Trujillo, however, joined the movement that overthrew Vásquez in February of 1930. Trujillo's complicity in the overthrow of a democratically elected government was apparent to US diplomats in Santo Domingo. US Minister Curtis explained:

It is safe to say that if Trujillo had been truly loyal to the government, the revolution could not have succeeded and would probably not have broken out. Of the two principal causes of the revolution, one was basic, the other immediate. The basic cause was the economic depression now existing in this country; the immediate, the knowledge that the National Army would tacitly assist the revolutionaries.[48]

Trujillo's rise to power was the first test of Herbert Hoover's policy of non-intervention in Latin America. After the successful overthrow of Vásquez, US diplomats hoped that Trujillo and his troops would return to their barracks and turn over control of the government to civilians. US diplomats in Santo Domingo tried to discourage Trujillo from participating in the presidential elections scheduled for May of 1930.   Although they feared Trujillo's authoritarian potential, they conceded that "all legal and constitutional forms were strictly and willingly complied with."[49] On 19 March 1930, therefore, the State Department informed US Minister Curtis:

The Department hopes that you will be able to persuade Trujillo not to be a candidate, yet it realizes the great difficulty of bringing it about and should you not succeed and Trujillo be elected it is most important that you should not impair in any way your relations with him. For your strictly confidential information the Department desires you to know that it expects to recognize Trujillo or any other person coming into office as a result of the coming elections and will maintain the most friendly relations with him and his government and will desire to cooperate with him in every proper way.[50]

Trujillo, however, was determined to rule the Dominican Republic. On 19 May 1930, he was elected to the presidency with 223,851 votes—more than the number of eligible voters in the country.[51] Confronted with the reality of the situation, the State Department immediately accepted Trujillo as a guarantor of political and economic stability. In the words of the US minister in Santo Domingo:

Friendship for the United States in this country has increased rather than decreased as a result of the revolution. Not only did the United States indulge in no action distasteful to this Republic, but the services of the Legation in preventing bloodshed and acting as a mediator in the negotiations have received signal recognition, and the leaders on both sides have expressed their deep appreciation.[52]

Unlike traditional regional caudillos backed by armed civilians, Trujillo was supported by a well-trained and well-equipped constabulary with a virtual monopoly of power. The military, which became the strongest pillar in this corporatist society, was his main instrument of control. Between 1931 and 1933, 27 percent of the national budget was allocated to the military. US officials in Santo Domingo interested in protecting their strategic and economic interests considered these payments "absolutely necessary to preserve law and order."[53]

As soon as Trujillo took over he destroyed all political opposition and ensured that no future opposition would develop. Understanding that certain political structures, however, were necessary, he developed the Partido Dominicano to encourage the Dominican people to accept and support his regime.[54] An important function of the Partido Dominicano was to ensure nationwide support for his fixed elections. These elections were designed to prove to the United States that his regime, in addition to being stable, was also democratic. In the words of Trujillo: "Our Constitution guarantees a democratic and representative government, and I observe this as a sacred duty."[55] US policy makers were impressed by the fact that Trujillo held elections every four years for the duration of the Trujillo era. Trujillo, however, had already decided the winners of each presidential election in advance.

Trujillo continuously tried to convince US officials that he was the perfect leader for the Dominican Republic. He realized early in his career that his fortunes and those of the Dominican Republic rested with the United States. According to a US diplomat in Ciudad Trujillo: "Trujillo is a large frog in a little puddle. His cardinal policy is one of getting along with the United States."[56] Trujillo, therefore, worked to strengthen his power at home and revitalize the devastated Dominican economy by currying favor with the United States. The numerous friends he made in the US Marines during the military occupation served as valuable contacts. He believed it to be "the duty of any President of the Dominican Republic in the interests of his own country to maintain the most cordial relations with the United States."[57]

On 25 August 1931, Trujillo tactfully informed US President Herbert Hoover that the Dominican Republic found it necessary to suspend the amortization payments of the Dominican external debt in order to avoid a social revolution. According to Trujillo, "It has become daily more evident that, due to the existing worldwide economic depression, the Dominican Republic is making efforts to pay its foreign public debt to an extent exceeding its capacity to pay."[58] Impressed by Trujillo's attempts to maintain financial credit through the prompt payment of the service on his foreign debt, as well as his ability to maintain order, President Hoover informed Trujillo that the financial problems confronting the Dominican government would have "the sympathetic and prompt consideration of my government."[59] Concerned about order and stability, Hoover felt that Trujillo was the best leader available.[60]

Although Trujillo's debt payment suspension was contrary to the terms of the 1924 Convention, the US government offered no objections to his Emergency Law of October 1931, which placed a moratorium on payments on the Dominican foreign debt. Amortization payments on the foreign debt were deferred, although the interest payments were met. The US State Department was pleased. It explained: "The Dominican situation, all things considered, seems to be working along satisfactorily and we would like to be helpful and not do anything to destroy President Trujillo's morale or the present spirit which he is showing to cooperate in financial matters."[61] The Emergency Law, which remained in effect until 23 August 1934, granted Trujillo an extra $125,000 per month. Most of this money was used to purchase weapons for the military and build politically popular public works projects, both of which enhanced his hold over the Dominican political economy.[62]

THE GOOD NEIGHBOR POLICY AND US HEGEMONY, 1933–1945

Between 1933 and 1945, US hegemonic assumptions were veiled in the precepts of the Good Neighbor Policy.[63] A basic precept of the Good Neighbor Policy was the principle of US nonintervention in the internal affairs of Latin American nations. This policy was President Franklin D. Roosevelt's response to the criticisms of excessive US intervention—especially military occupations—in Latin America during the first three decades of the twentieth century. Although US foreign policy makers were interested in alleviating the domestic economic dislocation caused by the Great Depression, President Roosevelt's Good Neighbor Policy evolved during the 1930s into a mechanism to preserve national security from the Nazi threat.[64]

US policy toward the Trujillo regime during the Good Neighbor period, therefore, was part of a larger US policy. With Hitler on the rise, the United States needed stable, pro-US friends in the hemisphere. US policy makers recognized Trujillo as an authoritarian monster, yet they considered him useful for national security concerns.[65] In the words of Minister Arthur Schoenfeld, "In peace as in war the Dominican Republic under his Presidency [Trujillo's] would always be at the side of the United States."[66] US policy makers, therefore, consistently overlooked Trujillo's authoritarian excesses and maintained friendly diplomatic relations. When Trujillo massacred 12,000 Haitian cane cutters and their families in 1937, the official US reaction was merely a request that the Trujillo regime pay an indemnity of $270,000 to the families of the victims. US Marine Corps Commandant James Breckinridge's invitation to Trujillo to come to the United States in 1939 for an official visit was "a clear signal that the United States still backed him."[67]

In keeping with the economic recovery motives of the Good Neighbor Policy, the Roosevelt administration attempted to negotiate new commercial agreements with Latin America. It wanted to increase inter-American commerce hurt by the depression and confront an expanding German commercial presence in Latin

America. Increased German competition in the Dominican market resulted in a marked decline in US exports to the Dominican Republic of cotton textiles, cement, chemicals, and steel. The balance of trade in favor of the United States decreased from $4,177,867 in 1930 to $587,741 in 1935.[68]

US commercial interest greatly pleased Trujillo, who was campaigning for increased Dominican access to US markets, especially through the newly enacted US preferential sugar quota. In the words of the dictator: "The future of our relations with the people of the United States of America is a future of mutual benefit. Since our country lies within the Western Hemisphere, our interests are naturally tied to our great neighbor to the north. It is only natural that the United States import our exports."[69] Trujillo hoped that increased sugar sales would provide him with the needed funds to pay the nation's foreign debt. In the words of US Minister Arthur Schoenfeld:

Determined efforts have been made by the Dominican Government to enlist the cooperation of American sugar interests operating in this country in endeavoring to expedite Dominican debt negotiations with the United States by giving the companies assurance that [the] proposed levy of export tax on sugar will not be effective if they so cooperate.[70]

Consequently, in May of 1935, the State Department authorized Schoenfeld to begin exploratory negotiations with the Dominican government for a new Convention between the Dominican Republic and the United States. According to the State Department,

It is the desire of this government to strengthen in every possible way those close and friendly relations with the Dominican Republic which have happily existed during the past decade. It is also hoped that means may be found whereby the two governments may cooperate to their mutual advantage in developing commercial relations between them.[71]

Throughout the negotiations, Schoenfeld repeatedly assured Dominican policy makers that the US government's obligation towards the holders of Dominican external bonds and other holders of valid claims against the Dominican Government "remain secondary to the postulates of the so-called Good Neighbor Policy."[72]

Although he claimed that he had no wish to diminish the guarantees of payment offered to Dominican bond holders, Trujillo wanted to change the mechanism established for the payment of the debt so as to make it compatible with Dominican sovereignty. Trujillo felt that the presence of a US official performing the duties of the General Receiver of Dominican Customs, while simultaneously acting as a financial advisor to the Dominican president, was insulting to Dominican sovereignty.[73] According to Schoenfeld, Trujillo "feels he must have even greater freedom than at the present to manipulate the finances, aside from the conspicuous political triumph the conclusion of such an agreement would afford him."[74] Although Trujillo would surely benefit from a revised Convention, Dominican Minister to the United States Andrés Pastoriza pointed out: "The interest of the United States is just as great toward freeing itself from the embarrassing interference implied by the assistance which it agreed to lend to the Dominican Republic and which at any given moment may have been considered necessary."[75]

Trujillo, however, knew all along that Washington was primarily motivated by strategic impulses and the desire for hemispheric solidarity in the face of Nazi aggression. In a successful attempt to curry favor with Washington and obtain economic benefits, Trujillo's guiding principle in foreign policy was a tactic of adapting US hegemony for his own self-serving reasons. At the same time, US policy makers realized that Trujillo was using them just as much as they were using Trujillo. According to the US State Department research report:

As to the United States, he considers its good-will important for the prestige which he craves as well as for more material reasons, and he has from the beginning maintained a generally cooperative attitude in affairs concerning third countries and international organizations and conferences.[76]

On 4 December 1939, therefore, Trujillo graciously offered the United States the full use of its territory in order to ensure continental defense.[77]

Because of the new international environment brought about by World War II, as well as Trujillo's eagerness to cultivate US friendship, the Dominican dictator was able to negotiate the 1940 US-Dominican Convention, which abolished the General Receivership and relinquished customs collection by the United States. For Trujillo, this was a historic event because it constituted US recognition of Dominican financial independence.[78] Trujillo, elated with his personal triumph in the recovery of Dominican sovereignty, reiterated the special nature of US-Dominican relations. Trujillo boldly stated: "For the defense of the hemisphere and democratic traditions, the Dominican Republic is disposed to lend all its force in case the ambition for conquest which has been unchained in other countries brings war to these shores."[79] Not surprisingly, Trujillo was the first Latin American leader to declare war on the Axis powers.[80] The United States rewarded Trujillo for his support with a generous Lend-Lease Agreement in 1941: military equipment valued at $1.6 million.[81] Trujillo benefited enormously from his successful relations with the United States. US policy makers considered his regime an economic success story. In the words of US Ambassador Ellis O. Briggs, "The Trujillo dictatorship is the most efficient government the Republic has ever known, and more overall material progress has been achieved during the past 14 years than during the preceding 438 years since the discovery of the island by Columbus."[82]

THE COLD SHOULDER INTERLUDE AND US HEGEMONY, 1945–1947

After thirteen years of the Good Neighbor Policy, however, difficulties arose to disrupt the relationship of reciprocal manipulation between the United States and the Trujillo regime. The resignations of Secretary of State Cordell Hull and Assistant Secretary of State for Inter-American Affairs Sumner Welles in

1944—and the death of Roosevelt in 1945—provoked a major change in the personnel who would formulate US policy toward the Dominican Republic. Spruille Braden, who replaced Sumner Welles in 1945, had a different interpretation of the Good Neighbor Policy.

According to Braden, the principle of nonintervention in Latin American affairs was misguided. Braden contended: "Whatever we refrain from saying and whatever we refrain from doing may constitute intervention, no less than what we do or say."[83] Braden, who cherished the democratic idealism engendered by World War II, believed that the United States should only maintain friendly relations with democratic nations.[84] Reaffirming Braden's views, Ambassador George H. Butler contended: "The situation in the Dominican Republic is not a direct threat to world peace: but the cumulative effect of the undermining of democratic principles in many parts of the world does seem to be a serious threat to the national interests and security of the United States."[85]

Therefore, after the Nazi threat had been destroyed in 1945, and before the exact nature of the Soviet threat was revealed in 1947, the State Department distanced itself from Trujillo.[86] Rather than unabashed support of authoritarian dictators, the United States advocated the creation and defense of democratic traditions in the Western Hemisphere as vital to US national security. In December 1945, Secretary of State James Byrnes informed Ambassador Joseph F. McGurk that it was the department's policy "to oppose for political reasons the shipment of arms and ammunition to the Dominican Republic at this time."[87] According to Ambassador Ellis Briggs,

The fact that Trujillo has declared himself to be *on our side* in this war, and that he is collaborating with us in certain international matters, should not blind us to the realities of his domestic administration. We should not permit ourselves to be misrepresented as approving of the Trujillo dictatorship or of Trujillo's methods.[88]

Briggs further pointed out that "cordial official relations with the United States represent an important weapon in the arsenal whereby Trujillo maintains his dictatorship."[89] Ambassador Butler explained that Trujillo's self-proclaimed anticommunism was a ploy to curry favor with Washington. According to Butler,

President Trujillo is putting on a clever show of opposition to Communism in order to ride certain currents now becoming clearly noticeable in the United States. If this latter supposition is correct, the objective of the President is to use his anti-communist program as a basis for a fairly close *rapprochement* with the United States Government; without, however, his having to yield one inch of his arbitrary manner of ruling the Dominican Republic.[90]

Reacting to the new cold shoulder from the United States, in 1946 Trujillo, who claimed that he "could not make any substantial concessions to our concept of democracy and still retain power," complained that he was being "treated like a Hitler or a Mussolini."[91]

Conditions, however, soon changed. The 1947 appointment of conservative General George C. Marshall as Secretary of State, which coincided with the heating up of the Cold War and the resignation of Spruille Braden from the State Department's Latin American branch, provoked a radical change in US policy toward the Trujillo regime. The State Department's brief cold shoulder policy ended, and the dictator's regime became a welcome bastion of anticommunism in the Caribbean region. On 4 August 1947, the State Department informed the Dominican ambassador that his government could now request the renewal of the previously suspended arms export license.[92]

THE COLD WAR AND US HEGEMONY, 1948–1957

From 1948 to 1957, US policy toward the Dominican Republic was primarily motivated by an attempt to safeguard US hegemonic interests in the region from international communism. The policy designed to combat the communist menace was containment, a "relentless Cold War against communist expansion wherever it appeared in the back alleys of the world."[93] US support for Trujillo and other authoritarian leaders in the region created a virtual "coconut curtain" against communism in the Caribbean. According to John Foster Dulles, "Wherever a dictator is replaced in Latin America communism will triumph."[94]

Trujillo's national security needs also required the restoration of amicable relations between the United States and the Dominican Republic. He was especially concerned about the Dominican Republic's ability to increase sugar exports to the United States. Trujillo could not hope to obtain a generous preferential sugar quota without friendly relations with the United States. According to a US diplomat in Ciudad Trujillo, "Trujillo may honestly desire to maintain the closest possible relations with the United States, as he frequently alleges—but only on his own terms, including our acquiescence in his eventual absorption of most of the American capital invested here."[95] Therefore, in return for the dictator's support of US proposals and policies, the United States government did not protest Trujillo's attempts to buy out US sugar interests in the Dominican Republic and export greater amounts of sugar to the United States.[96]

Trujillo ingratiated himself with US policy makers by becoming the hemisphere's self-appointed bulwark against communist aggression. Trujillo's voting record in the United Nations and the Organization of American States, which paralleled that of the United States more closely than any other Latin American nation, illustrate the dictator's pragmatic foreign policy. What most concerned Trujillo and his cronies, however, was not communism per se—they knew that the Dominican communists, who numbered less than fifty, were disorganized university students and professors more adept at rhetoric than combat. Rather, Trujillo and his cronies, wallowing in the spoils of graft, feared change.[97] His government played on the US fear of communism and desire for stability and order to maintain the positions of privilege that came with the status quo. Trujillo frequently reversed the dependency process by using the US embassy for his own self-serving purposes. More often than not, US policy toward the Dominican Republic was a reaction to Trujillo's actions, rather than an initiative on the part of the Department of State.

The fact that the Dominican government was an authoritarian dictatorship did not prevent the United States from having normal relations with it. In general, most Latin American states were ruled by authoritarian dictatorships during the 1950s. In 1951, the US State Department's main goals in the Dominican Republic were:

1) To obtain the support of the Dominican government and people in efforts to promote inter-American and world-wide peace and prosperity; 2) building in the Dominican Republic an appreciation of the institutions and practices of representative government; 3) the economic development of the Dominican Republic and the promotion and protection of legitimate US business interests; and 4) the promotion of mutual understanding and friendship between the peoples of the Dominican Republic and the United States.[98]

US embassy officials, however, were quick to point out the numerous problems involved in negotiating with Trujillo. According to Ambassador William T. Pheiffer, "His unpredictability, vengefulness, pride, greed for praise, and worldly goods, complete identification of his opponents with the communists, wily maneuvering, propensity for intrigue, and lack of sense of proportion created an unrelieved atmosphere of uncertainty."[99]

Nevertheless, as the Cold War matured, the United States began to place greater emphasis on hemispheric solidarity against communism. As a result, the United States increased military aid programs to bolster Trujillo's regime. On 11 November 1950, Foreign Minister Virgilio Díaz Ordoñez informed the State Department that the Dominican government agreed to discuss the acquisition of sites in the Dominican Republic in connection with the operation of a Long Range Proving Ground (LRPG) for guided missiles. Dominican Ambassador Julio Ortega Frier claimed that Trujillo "was tickled to death at the opportunity thus afforded to participate in a joint defense project."[100] On 26 November 1951, the United States and the Dominican Republic signed an agreement allowing guided missiles to fly test flights from the US Air Force Missile Test Center at Cocoa Beach, Florida, through a portion of Dominican territory.[101] In light of the dictator's conciliatory gestures toward the United States, as well as his ability to maintain stability in an area considered strategically important to the United States, Washington policy makers continued to overlook his authoritarian abuses.[102]

According to the State Department, arms shipments to the Dominican Republic increased "the ability of the Dominican Republic to contribute to world and hemispheric defense against aggression."[103] The Mutual Security Act of 1951, for example, allowed Trujillo to receive over $6 million in military deliveries. On 6 March 1953, Trujillo and Dulles signed the Military Assistance Agreement, a bilateral military assistance agreement. Under the terms of the accord, the Dominican Republic agreed to prepare and maintain one aircraft fighter squadron and ten naval vessels for hemispheric defense purposes, which would be provided by the United States under the Grant Aid Program. In accordance with the provisions of the Military Assistance Agreement, the US Department of Defense recommended the establishment of a Military Assistance Advisory Group (MAAG) in the Dominican Republic, consisting of four officers and five enlisted men at a total cost of $108,000 for an eighteen-month period. As the United States pursued its policy of hemispheric solidarity in the face of international communism, Trujillo, who made his country the best armed Caribbean nation, increased his hold on the Dominican political economy with US arms purchases paid for with sugar revenues.[104]

Trujillo's carefully stagecrafted image as an ardent anticommunist earned him the reputation of an impassioned ally of the United States. Trujillo went to great pains and expense to build and cultivate this image. Writers were hired to produce pro-Trujillo literature.[105] As Dominican Ambassador Joaquín Eduardo Salazar told US officials:

As a result of the valiant and inflexible attitude of Generalissimo Rafael L. Trujillo Molina, a true pioneer of the anti-Communist struggle, Dominican foreign policy has been steadfastly directed toward combating, to the full extent of our capacity, all manifestations of the subversive and anarchistic seeds scattered in such unexpected ways by militant Marxism.[106]

In addition, Trujillo invested substantial sums of money to manipulate US public opinion in his favor. In a 6 January 1954 *New York Times* advertisement, Trujillo informed US readers:

The people of the United States have, and always had, in the Dominican Republic a true friend with a clear conception of the solidarity that ought to prevail between neighbors. Our country identifies itself with the United States and other free nations completely in the worldwide fight against communism.[107]

Trujillo also attempted to enhance his influence in the United States by bribing and blackmailing US congressmen and journalists. According to Dominican Consul in New York Arturo Espaillat, the dictator had price lists for the purchase of US congressmen: "An ordinary run-of-the-mill Representative would cost $5,000 or less. A few House Committee Chairmen could be had for about three times that much, depending on the committee. Senators came higher, of course."[108] Trujillo also used blackmail. Prominent US citizens were secretly photographed with Dominican prostitutes during all-expense-paid visits to Ciudad Trujillo.[109] Although the bribes, blackmail, and propaganda never won him the elusive preferential sugar quota of his dreams, they did result in pro-Trujillo speeches on the Senate floor.

By 1956, however, the friendly bilateral relationship between the United States and the Dominican Republic had begun to show signs of decay. Allegations that Trujillo's Servicio de Inteligencia Militar (SIM) agents kidnapped outspoken

Trujillo critic Jesús Galíndez Suárez on the streets of New York City produced an outpouring of US media and congressional attention. Also kidnapped was a young pilot from Oregon, Gerald Lester Murphy, who was suspected of flying the doomed Galíndez to Ciudad Trujillo. Murphy was probably murdered by SIM agents to keep him quiet. To cover up the execution, Trujillo's henchmen killed Octavio de la Maza Vásquez, a Dominican pilot and personal friend of Murphy. SIM agents forged de la Maza's suicide note, which claimed that de la Maza killed the US pilot and himself to end their homosexual love affair.[110]

Murphy's fate added to what was already a sensational story. Liberal US congressmen argued that the Galíndez-Murphy murders were examples of why the Eisenhower administration should withdraw support of Trujillo. Congressman Charles O. Porter (D-OR) requested that the United States bring the Galíndez-Murphy case before the Organization of American States. He also recommended that the United States eliminate the sugar quota and military assistance to the dictator.[111] The State Department, however, cited the "absence of firm evidence" and refused to officially accuse the Dominican government of complicity in the Galíndez-Murphy affair.[112] It was concerned that Trujillo might retaliate against US investment in the Dominican Republic or the guided missile testing facility, "which the Defense Department considers vital."[113]

Trujillo, however, was not without his defenders in the US Congress. Porter's criticism invited rebuttals from his colleagues, who praised Trujillo and insisted that the United States maintain amicable relations with the dictator. According to Senator George D. Aiken (R-VT), Trujillo "has cooperated fully with the United States leadership in world affairs and in the defense measures that the United States has urged in the Caribbean area.[114] Senator Olin D. Johnson (D-SC) argued that Trujillo's regime "has rendered a greater force in deterring the spread of communism in Latin America than any other country in the Caribbean area."[115] According to Senator Russell Long (D-LA), "It does not matter what type of government is maintained in Ciudad Trujillo, so long as it is not an atheistic, Communist government that could endanger our own safety and security. The Communists, therefore, are behind the present smear campaign of the Dominican Republic."[116]

Trujillo also attempted to counter the negative public relations resulting from the Galíndez-Murphy affair with larger bribes to influential US citizens. Trujillo spent $6 million on bribes and propaganda campaigns to create an image of innocence.[117] He enlisted the aid of the US sugar company directors and threatened them with higher taxes if they failed to help him regain popularity in the United States. As negative publicity over the Galíndez episode increased US public hostility toward the Trujillo regime, the mill owners increased their efforts to help Trujillo get a higher sugar quota. Advertisements in US and Dominican newspapers, paid for by the mill owners, praised Trujillo.[118]

Regardless of the tension caused by the Galíndez-Murphy affair, the Eisenhower administration continued to justify US relations with the Trujillo dictatorship. According to the Eisenhower administration, "While repressive methods of dictatorial power in the Dominican Republic are unsavory to the United States, the present government has brought stability and considerable progress to the country and Trujillo is a strong opponent of communism and a supporter of the United States in the United Nations."[119] Through 1957, the primary dynamic of US-Dominican relations continued to be a policy of amiable reciprocal manipulation.

NOTES

1. Richard M. Smith to the State Department, 16 November 1956; Extension Folder, Box 244; Dominican Republic, Narrative Reports, 1955–61; RR 166; NA.

2. Kenneth Coleman, "The Political Mythology of the Monroe Doctrine: Reflections on the Social Psychology of Hegemony," in *Latin America, the United States, and the Inter-American System*, ed. John Martz and Lars Schoultz (Boulder, CO: Westview, 1980), p. 95.

3. The region's strategic location—what José Martí called "the vortex of the Americas"—is especially favorable to transoceanic shipping. The United States developed a special set of security concerns that complemented its economic interests in the region. See Leslie Manigat, "Crisis, Ideology, and Geopolitics," in *The Caribbean and World Politics*, ed. Jorge Heine and Leslie Manigat (New York: Holmes & Meier, 1988).

4. Sumner Welles, *Naboth's Vineyard: The Dominican Republic, 1844–1924* (New York: Payson & Clarke, 1928), p. 925.

5. George R. Colton to the State Department, 31 March 1907; *FRUS 1907*, pp. 348–50.

6. Frank Moya Pons, *El Pasado Dominicano* (Santo Domingo: Fundación J. A. Caro Alvarez, 1986), p. 215. The US military occupation of the Dominican Republic guaranteed that US foreign relations with the Dominican Republic would overshadow any other diplomatic ties that the Dominicans would engage in.

7. See Robert Strausz-Hupé, *Democracy and American Foreign Policy: Reflections on the Legacy of Tocqueville* (New Brunswick, NJ: Transaction Books, 1994). Strausz-Hupé argues that since 1898 the United States has pursued the defense of Western civilization as a critical element of its own national security interest. He contends that the encouragement of democratic traditions everywhere in the Western Hemisphere has been perceived as vital to US national security.

8. Fredrick B. Pike, *The United States and the Andean Republics: Peru, Bolivia, and Ecuador* (Cambridge, MA: Harvard University Press, 1977), p. 303. Pike argues that US policy alternates between periods of defending its democratic institutions by trying to propagate them in foreign lands and of rejecting crusades for liberalism in order to remain liberal at home.

9. John Martz, "Democracy and the Imposition of Values: Definitions and Diplomacy," in *Latin America, the United States, and the Inter-American System*, ed. John Martz and Lars Schoultz (Boulder, CO: Westview, 1980), p. 157.

10. See Eric Paul Roorda, *The Dictator Next Door: The Good Neighbor Policy and the Trujillo Regime in the Dominican Republic, 1930–1945* (Durham, NC: Duke University Press, 1998). Roorda provides a detailed study of US reactions to the 1930, 1934, 1938, and 1942 Dominican presidential elections.

11. Rosario Espinal, *Autoritarismo y Democracia en la Política Dominicana* (San José: Centro de Asesoría y Promoción Electoral, 1987), pp. 15–23.

12. See David Healy, Drive to Hegemony: The United States in the Caribbean, 1898–1917 (Madison: University of Wisconsin Press, 1988). According to Healy, US hegemony in the Caribbean was the product of a remarkably consistent effort that ran uninterrupted from McKinley's administration forward.

13. Federico Gil, *Latin American-United States Relations* (New York: Harcourt Brace Jovanovich, 1971), p. 283. According to Gil, "The policy of the United States has had two unchanging objectives: to prevent the influence of extracontinental powers in the Western Hemisphere and to make Latin America a special sphere of influence of the United States, the latter to be accompanied by a variety of means, among which have been trade and investment, diplomacy, and military objectives."

14. *Listín Diario*, 15 June 1986.

15. Bruce Calder, The Impact of Intervention: The Dominican Republic during the US Occupation of 1916–1924 (Austin: University of Texas Press, 1984), p. xii.

16. John Hay to Commander Dillingham, 5 January 1905; *FRUS 1905*, pp. 300-1.

17. Thomas C. Dawson to the President, 1 July 1905; *FRUS 1905*, pp. 378–89.

18. Proclamation by the President, 25 July 1907; *FRUS 1907*, pp. 307–11.

19. William R. Russell to the State Department, 3 July 1912; *FRUS 1912*, pp. 359–60.

20. William R. Russell to the State Department, 13 November 1912; *FRUS 1912*, p. 375.

21. James M. Sullivan to the State Department, 18 December 1913; *FRUS 1913*, p. 448.

22. Welles, p. 761.

23. Michael Grow, *The Good Neighbor Policy and Authoritarianism in Paraguay* (Lawrence: Regents Press of Kansas, 1978), p. 117. According to Grow, "Factors of national economic self-interest shaped the actions of both sides in the inter-American equation and, if anything, a constant two-way flow of mutual opportunism and reciprocal exploitation lay at the core of the hemispheric relationship."

24. Howard J. Wiarda, *The Dominican Republic: A Nation in Transition* (New York: Praeger, 1969), pp. 216–17. The old oligarchy, based in Santiago and represented by the Vicini-Cabral, Bermúdez, and Barceló families, consistently engaged in a mutually self-serving symbiotic alliance with foreign capital.

25. Valentina Peguero, Vision General de la Historia Dominicana (Santo Domingo: Corripio, 1978), pp. 291–92.

26. Robert Lansing to William R. Russell, 7 May 1916; *FRUS 1916*, p. 225.

27. William R. Russell to the State Department, 26 June 1916; *FRUS 1916*, pp. 231–32.

28. Stabler to the State Department, 21 November 1916; *FRUS 1916*, p. 241.

29. Proclamation by H. S. Knapp, 29 November 1916; *FRUS 1916*, pp. 246–47.

30. Clement S. Edwards to the State Department, 23 March 1919; *FRUS 1916*, pp. 98–99.

31. Ibid.

32. US Military Government in Santo Domingo to the Secretary of the Navy; File 16870-47, Box 33; General Correspondence, Letters Sent, 1916–1924; General Records of the Army, Record Group 80 (RG 80, hereafter); NA.

33. Lieutenant Commander Belknap to the State Department, 8 August 1917; *FRUS 1917*, pp. 709–14.

34. Emelio Betances, *State and Society in the Dominican Republic* (Boulder, CO: Westview, 1995), pp. 83–84. Volunteers for the constabulary came from the poor, illiterate strata of Dominican society. By the time the Marines withdrew from the country in 1924,

the constabulary had a monopoly of power over all of Dominican society. The establishment of a National Guard made traditional regional caudillos obsolete and paved the road for a national military caudillo.

35. Thomas Snowden to the State Department, 1 April 1920; *FRUS 1920*, pp. 111–115.

36. Thomas Snowden to the Dominican Tariff Commission, 1 August 1919; *FRUS 1919*, pp. 166–67.

37. José A. Benítez, *Las Antillas: Colonización, Azúcar e Imperialismo* (Habana: Casa de las Americas, 1977), p. 260.

38. Rosemary Vargas-Lundius, *Peasants in Distress: Poverty and Unemployment in the Dominican Republic* (Boulder, CO: Westview, 1991), p. 90. The 1920 Land Registration Act, reinforcing previous but ineffectual land ownership laws, was designed to break up the community-owned lands and bring them into private ownership. The legislation drove many communal farmers off the land and added thousands of hectares to the sugar plantations.

39. James Ferguson, *Beyond the Lighthouse* (London: Latin American Bureau, 1992), p. 18.

40. Emilio Joubert to Samuel Robison, 17 May 1922, APG; PDN; SD. Like most Latin American elites, Joubert considered the well-being of the oligarchy and the well-being of the nation one in the same.

41. Angel Morales to Frank Kellogg, 14 October 1926; *FRUS 1926*.

42. Calder, *The Impact of Intervention*, pp. 28–30. Even some of the military occupation's most vocal opponents, frustrated with the nation's traditional political life, worked with the military government because they believed that it could bring the stability that Dominican governments had failed to achieve.

43. Vargas-Lundius, *Peasants in Distress*, p. 102. Gangs of gavilleros, bandits who lived at the margin of peasant society, were the only organized armed resistance to the US military occupation. These gangs grew by absorbing disillusioned peasants who had been deprived of their land by the big sugar companies.

44. State Department to William R. Russell, 4 December 1920; *FRUS 1920*, p. 145.

45. Peguero, *Vision General*, pp. 306–09. The committee was made up of Horacio Vásquez (Partido Nacional Restaurador), Federico Velázquez (Partido Progresista), Elías Brache, Francisco Peynado, and Monseñor Adolfo Nouel. Ramón Báez (Partido Liberal), the new leader of the Jimenistas, was not involved.

46. Richard S. Hillman and Thomas J. D'Agostino, *Distant Neighbors in the Caribbean: The Dominican Republic and Jamaica in Comparative Perspective* (New York: Praeger, 1992), p. 29.

47. Evan E. Young to Henry L. Stimson, 25 December 1929; *FRUS 1929*.

48. Charles B. Curtis to the State Department, 1 March 1930; *FRUS 1930*, vol. 2, p. 711.

49. Ibid., p. 716.

50. State Department to Charles B. Curtis, 19 March 1930; *FRUS 1930*, vol. 2, pp. 718–19. As long as there was no threat to US lives or property, the United States chose not to interfere.

51. Charles B. Curtis to the State Department, 19 May 1930; *FRUS 1930*, vol. 2, p. 723.

52. Charles B. Curtis to the State Department, 1 March 1930; *FRUS 1930*, vol. 2, p. 717.

53. Bernardo Vega, *Trujillo y El Control Financiero Norteamericano* (Santo Domingo: Fundación Cultural Dominicano, 1990), p. 83.

54. Robert D. Crassweller, *Trujillo: The Life and Times of a Caribbean Dictator* (New York: Macmillan, 1966), p. 116.

55. Lawrence de Besault, *President Trujillo: His Work and the Dominican Republic* (New York: Washington Publishing, 1936) p. 38. The quote comes from an interview the author conducted with Trujillo.

56. Robert Mills McClintock to Cordell Hull, 1 November 1938; Secret Reports Folder, Box 1; Dominican Republic, Miscellaneous Records; RG 84; NA.

57. Arthur Schoenfeld to the State Department, 21 May 1935; *FRUS 1935*, vol. 4, p. 504.

58. Rafael Trujillo to Herbert Hoover, 25 August 1931; *FRUS 1931*, vol. 2, pp. 110–11. In 1931, the Dominican Republic's foreign debt was $17 million. Dominican government revenues, which had been pledged under the 1924 US-Dominican Convention as security for payment of the bonds issued to cover the debt, had diminished to less than $7 million in 1931.

59. Herbert Hoover to Rafael Trujillo, 5 September 1931; *FRUS 1931*, vol. 2, pp. 117–18.

60. Ibid.

61. Harvey H. Bundy to Arthur Schoenfeld, 1 June 1932; *FRUS 1933*, vol. 5, p. 599.

62. Arthur Schoenfeld to Cordell Hull, 10 August 1934; Secret Reports Folder, Box 1; Dominican Republic, Miscellaneous Records; RG 84; NA.

63. Lloyd C. Gardner, *Economic Aspects of New Deal Diplomacy* (Madison: University of Wisconsin Press, 1964), p. 47. Gardner claimed that the Good Neighbor policy was "partly an admission that the United States should act more tactfully in its relations with weaker neighbors, and partly a realization that military intervention actually hindered the effective employment of American economic and military power."

64. See David Green, *The Containment of Latin America: A History of the Myths and Realities of the Good Neighbor Policy* (Chicago: Quadrangle Books, 1971). Green contends that the Good Neighbor Policy meant the containment of Latin America, a more or less conscious effort to maintain and strengthen US hegemony in the hemisphere by keeping Latin American nations economically and politically dependent, while undercutting revolutionary nationalism in the hemisphere.

65. See Eric Paul Roorda, "Genocide Next Door: The Good Neighbor Policy, the Trujillo Regime, and the Haitian Massacre of 1937," *Diplomatic History* 20 (summer 1996): 1–19.

66. Schoenfeld to the State Department, 21 May 1935, *FRUS 1935*, vol. 4, p. 504.

67. Betances, *State and Society*, p. 98. Betances explains that Trujillo tried to wipe out Haitian influence along the border. He argues that this was part of the dictator's drive to create a modern nation state obedient to his authority.

68. Cordell Hull to Arthur Schoenfeld, 29 October 1936; Sugar Folder, Box 13; Dominican Republic, General Records; RG 84; NA.

69. Rafael L. Trujillo Molina, "Discurso Nacional Frente al Congreso Nacional en Celebración del Día de la Independencía, 27 Febrero 1939," in *Discursos, Mensajes, y Proclamas*, vol. 9 (Ciudad Trujillo: Oficina Nacional del Presidente de la República Dominicana, 1948), pp. 34–35.

70. Arthur Schoenfeld to the State Department, 21 April 1934; *FRUS 1934*, vol. 5, p. 196. On 21 April 1934, Edwin I. Kilbourne of the West Indies Sugar Company flew to Washington to convey Trujillo's aspirations.

71. State Department to the Dominican Legation, 14 May 1935; *FRUS 1935*, vol. 4, p. 497.

72. Arthur Schoenfeld to the State Department, 17 June 1936; *FRUS 1936*, vol. 5, p. 448.

73. Arthur Schoenfeld to the State Department, 3 June 1933; *FRUS 1933*, vol. 5, p. 634. William E. Pulliam, the General Receiver of Dominican Customs since 1921, was not replaced when he resigned on 1 August 1938.

74. Arthur Schoenfeld to Sumner Welles, 23 February 1937; FRUS 1937, vol. 5, p. 452.

75. Andrés Pastoriza to the State Department, 19 May 1937; *FRUS 1937*, vol. 5, p. 462.

76. The Trujillo Regime in the Dominican Republic: An analysis of Trujillo's rule in the Dominican Republic during the Past Sixteen Years (Intelligence Research Report OCL-4190 prepared by the Division of Research for American Republics), 31 December 1946; *Declassified Documents Reference System: State Department Intelligence and Research Reports*, reel VIII, p. 50.

77. *El Caribe*, 4 December 1939.

78. Ellis M. Goodwin to the State Department, 9 February 1949; Sugar Folder, Box 197; Dominican Republic, General Records; RG 84; NA. In 1947, Trujillo gave the United States a check for $9,271,855.55 to pay the remaining foreign debt.

79. Wilson Scotten to the State Department, 20 October 1940; *FRUS 1940*, vol. 5, p. 830.

80. *Listín Diario*, 9 December 1941.

81. Lend-Lease Agreement Between the United States and the Dominican Republic, 2 August 1941; *FRUS 1941*, vol. 7, p. 253. Although the armaments were important, the agreement had a more important psychological impact—Dominicans were convinced that the United States supported the Trujillo regime.

82. Ellis O. Briggs to Cordell Hull, 5 July 1944; Secret Reports Folder, Box 1; Dominican Republic, Miscellaneous Records; RG 84; NA.

83. Spruille Braden, "Our Foreign Policy and Its Underlying Principles and Ideals," *Department of State Bulletin*, 24 February 1946, p. 295.

84. Spruille Braden to the State Department, 5 April 1945; Political Folder, Box 1; Dominican Republic, Confidential General Records; RG 84; NA. Not surprisingly, the United States only encourages democracy when there are no serious threats to US national security and economic interests.

85. George H. Butler to the State Department, 18 November 1946; *FRUS 1946*, vol. 11, p. 810.

86. Martz, "Democracy and the Imposition of Values: Definitions and Diplomacy," p. 157. This follows his belief that US policy makers actively encouraged democracy only when geopolitical security interests were not imperiled.

87. James Byrnes to J. F. McGurk, 16 November 1945; *FRUS 1945*, vol. 9, p. 987.

88. Ellis O. Briggs to the State Department, 3 January 1945; *FRUS 1945*, vol. 9, p. 981.

89. Ibid.

90. George H. Butler to the State Department, 12 June 1947; *FRUS 1947*, vol. 8, p. 638.

91. George H. Butler to the State Department, 30 October 1946; *FRUS 1946*, vol. 11, p. 806. Nevertheless, Trujillo claimed to be in complete accord with President Truman's views and stated: "We are still your friends, even though your mistreated friends."

92. State Department to Julio Ortega Frier, 24 October 1947; *FRUS 1947*, vol. 8, p. 658. The United States officially reinstated the arms export license a few days later.

93. US Senate, Committee on Foreign Relations, *Assumed Plots and Assassination Plots Involving Foreign Leaders*, Report No. 94-465, 20 November 1975, p. xiii.

94. Minutes from the 235th Meeting of the National Security Council, 3 February 1955; *Declassified Documents Reference System: Minutes of Meetings of the US National Security Council, Microfilm Collection*, reel 4, frame 843.

95. Richard A. Johnson to the State Department, 5 May 1954; Folder 739.00/5-554, Box 3384; Dominican Republic, Central Decimal Files, 1950–54; RG 59; NA.

96. H. S. Steele to the State Department, 19 April 1948; Communism Folder, Box 21; Dominican Republic, Confidential General Records; RG 84; NA.

97. Bertita Harding, *The Land that Columbus Loved* (New York: Gorden, 1979), p, 58. The earnings from the export of sugar at preferential prices provided great opportunity for corruption. Although Trujillo took the lion's share of the profits, the elites also benefited handsomely. According to Trujillo's Minister of the Economy, "If you owned a company that for years operated in the red, and you hired a manager [Trujillo] who made money for you year after year, would you fire him?"

98. Policy Statement Prepared in the State Department, 9 January 1951; Folder 611.39, Box 2766; Dominican Republic, Central Decimal Files, 1950–54; RG 59; NA.

99. William T. Pheiffer to the State Department, 1 March 1954; *FRUS 1952–1954*, vol. 4, p. 957.

100. Charles C. Hauch to the State Department, 9 April 1951; *FRUS 1951*, vol. 2, pp. 1367–68.

101. US Department of State, *Treaties and Other International Acts*, No. 2425.

102. Stephen G. Rabe, *Eisenhower and Latin America: The Foreign Policy of Anticommunism* (Chapel Hill: University of North Carolina Press, 1988), pp. 153–54. Trujillo consistently cooperated with and supported the policies of the United States throughout the Cold War, only turning against the United States in the late 1950s and early 1960s in retaliation for Washington's hostile actions.

103. Policy Statement Prepared in the State Department, 9 January 1951; Decimal File 611.39, Box 2766; Dominican Republic, 1950–54; RG 59; NA.

104. Memorandum of a Conversation between Rafael Trujillo and President Eisenhower in the White House, 6 March 1953; *FRUS 1952–1954*, vol. 4 pp. 936–38.

105. See Joaquín Balaguer, *Memorias de un Cortesano de la "Era de Trujillo"* (Santo Domingo: Corripio, 1989). Although his memory is selective, he recalls numerous anecdotes.

106. Translation of the Remarks of Dominican Ambassador Joaquín Eduardo Salazar Camarena upon the Occasion of the Presentation of his Letter of Credence, 6 July 1955; *President Dwight D. Eisenhower's Office Files, 1953–1961: Part 2–International Series*, reel 5 of 32, frame 364.

107. *New York Times*, 6 January 1954, p. 61.

108. Arturo Espaillat, *Trujillo: El Ultimo de los Césares* (Santo Domingo: Editora Nacional, 1963), p. 81.

109. Ibid.

110. Richard Rubottom to the State Department, 15 January 1957; *FRUS 1955–1957*, vol. 7, p. 887.

111. Charles O. Porter to John Foster Dulles, 18 July 1957; Decimal File 739.00/7-1857, Box 3096; Dominican Republic, 1950–54; RG 59; NA.

112. Richard Rubottom to the State Department, 20 February 1957; *FRUS 1955–1957*, vol. 6, p. 908.

113. Ibid.

114. US Congress, Committee on Foreign Relations, *Report of a Study Mission by George D. Aiken to the Caribbean in December 1957, to the Committee on Foreign Affairs*, 1958, p. 11.

115. *Congressional Record*, 85th Congress, 1st Session.

116. Russell Long to the US Senate, 1957; *Desenmascarando al Comunismo: Nueva Interpretación del Honorable Senador Long de Louisiana en la Cámara de Representantes de los Estados Unidos*; APG; PDN; SD.   Although it was never proven that these conservative senators accepted bribes from the Trujillo regime, it was a widely held belief at the time. They openly accepted Trujillo's all-expense-paid vacations in the Dominican Republic.

117. Bernard Diederich, *Trujillo: The Death of the Dictator* (Maplewood, NJ: Waterfront, 1990), p. 15.

118. *Listín Diario*, 24 March 1957.

119. Memorandum of Meeting in the White House, 20 November 1957; Folder 2, Box 42; Confidential File, White House Central Files (WHCF); Dwight D. Eisenhower Library (DDE, hereafter), Abilene, KS (KS, hereafter).

Chapter 3

US Sugar Legislation and Dominican Exports, 1900–1957

US-Dominican economic relations during this period reflect the efforts of Dominican elites to export sugar to the United States, while the United States, which had no real need for Dominican sugar, used sugar quota legislation as a foreign policy tool to manipulate Dominican responses to US hegemonic goals. Since taxes on sugar exports provided over 50 percent of the Dominican government's operating revenue, Dominican elites consistently defined Dominican national security in terms of their ability to obtain high prices for their sugar exports.[1]

Sugar, however, can be produced in virtually every country in the world. The Dominican Republic, therefore, was merely one of many foreign sources from which the United States could obtain sugar.[2] In fact, many US observers have argued that the US economy had no real need for Dominican sugar. According to political scientist Jerome Slater,

There is an oversupply of world sugar and should Dominican sources suddenly dry up—highly unlikely, in any event, no matter what the nature of Dominican politics, given the crucial role of sugar exports in the Dominican economy—the United States could easily allocate its quota to dozens of other countries which every year clamor to be let into the lucrative US market.[3]

US sugar legislation, therefore, offered an excellent foreign policy lever, whether for increased trade, economic penetration, or political conformity. A US diplomat in the Dominican Republic during the Trujillo era astutely pointed out that the Dominican Republic "will tag along like a tail to a kite insofar as sugar is concerned."[4] According to Howard Wiarda, US sugar quotas were "used as levers to manipulate Dominican politics."[5] On the other hand, Wiarda also explained that "adept Dominican politicians have learned to manipulate the United States just as the United States manipulates them."[6]

The international sugar trade was based on preferential marketing arrangements that grew out of the historical associations forged when the Caribbean sugar industries were largely foreign-owned, principally by the United States, France, the Netherlands, and the United Kingdom.[7] In 1903, the United States granted Cuba a 20 percent tariff reduction on sugar exports to US markets. This operated to the disadvantage of the Dominican sugar industry, which paid the full tariff on its sugar exports to the United States. When the US Congress promulgated the 1934 Sugar Act, Cuba's preferential position was reasserted, while sugar imports from the Dominican Republic and other full-duty countries were reduced.[8]

Since 1934, the principal Dominican interest in its economic relations with the United States has been a large-scale opening of the US sugar market to Dominican sugar. In the words of one US diplomat, "The foremost objective of Dominican foreign economic policy is to increase exports of sugar, primarily to the United States."[9] Although US capital controlled the majority of the Dominican sugar industry after the turn of the century, such control did not automatically lead to a large quota or preferential tariff treatment.[10] Able to meet most of its sugar needs from domestic sources and imports from Cuba, Puerto Rico, and the Philippines, the United States saw no need to grant the Dominicans a large preferential quota.

After World War II, however, when the threat of a communist challenge to US interests in Latin America convinced US policy makers that amicable relations with the Dominican Republic would be in the best interests of the United States, the US grudgingly allowed Trujillo to buy out US sugar interests in the Dominican Republic, and simultaneously increased the Dominican share of the US sugar quota, in return for Trujillo's international support. While Trujillo discerned that the United States was desperately trying to form a united hemispheric front against Soviet communist expansionism in the postwar years, US policy makers understood well that Trujillo was using the domination of the sugar industry as the base of his domestic political control. According to Robert Crassweller, Trujillo "saw in the entire economic process a source of dominion as potent as the Army."[11]

Dominican politicians and diplomats, therefore, were sensitive to the slightest movements on US sugar policy. According to US Ambassador John Bartlow Martin, "Sugar has always been the central economic force in the Caribbean. The price of sugar in the world market meant economic life or death."[12] Dominican elites, therefore, consistently clamored for an increased share of the preferential US sugar quota. They spent great amounts of time and money seeking to influence US policy makers, whose decisions on quantity and price could spell either prosperity or distress for the nation's economy.[13]

Dominican politician Joaquín Balaguer has argued that although the preferential sugar quota was extremely beneficial to the Dominican Republic, it was even more advantageous—in a strategic sense—to the United States. Increased sales of Dominican sugar to the United States funded an anticommunist government in the Dominican Republic. According to Balaguer,

The Dominican Republic constitutes a strategic point of the first order for the United States in the Caribbean area. The United States would be seriously threatened if this country were to fall into the hands of communism and follow the path of communism, linking up to extra-hemispheric systems and turning its back on obligations in the political and economic fields imposed by its membership in the inter-American regional system.[14]

Increased sales of Dominican sugar to the United States also allowed the Dominican Republic to increase imports, which were procured primarily from the United States. By 1924, 70 percent of all Dominican imports came from the United States.[15] According to former Secretary of Agriculture Henry Wallace,

The repeatedly unfortunate experiences of the United States have demonstrated that a decrease in imports from foreign countries unavoidably involves a decrease in the foreign markets for American exportable products, of which we have great surpluses. If the United States should undertake to reduce its imports of foreign sugar still further under the quota system it would also be necessary to decrease still further the production of our exportable products.[16]

An examination of US-Dominican economic relations between 1900 and 1957, therefore, reveals the centrality of sugar in the reciprocal manipulation fundamental to the two countries' bilateral relationship. An analysis of the goals and legislation surrounding the US sugar quota, an integral component of US-Dominican economic relations since the quota's inception in 1934, further reveals that the sugar quota was mutually useful to both the United States and the Dominican Republic. US and Dominican policy makers used the sugar quota in the pursuit of their respective self-interests.

US SUGAR LEGISLATION AND DOMINICAN SUGAR EXPORTS, 1900–1933

Since the colonial era, a large share of US sugar needs have been supplied by imports from various foreign countries.[17] Until 1934, sugar imports to the United States were governed by a series of tariffs. Beginning with the US tariff imposed on sugar in 1789, federal legislation regulating the production, importation, and marketing of sugar has governed the sugar economy of the United States. Until the 1920s, US sugar tariffs were low and did not inhibit the importation of Dominican sugar.

By 1888, the Dominican Republic was exporting over 16,000 tons of sugar to the United States annually.[18] Following an extended campaign conducted by Ulíses Heureaux's government to remove the US tariff on Dominican sugar, on 4 June 1891 the Dominican Republic signed a reciprocal trade agreement with the United States. In return for the export of Dominican sugar to the United States free of import duties, the US was granted the right to establish a coaling station at Samaná Bay. In addition, numerous manufactured products from the United States were put on the Dominican free list. In 1891, the Dominican Republic exported over 32,000 tons of sugar to the United States.[19]

The US-Dominican Reciprocity Treaty of 1891, however, irritated the

Europeans, especially the Germans. Germany had been the principal market for Dominican tobacco and hardwood exports. On 15 November 1891, Germany demanded that all German merchandise be granted the same preferential treatment accorded to US products. Unless granted, they promised to impose a retaliatory duty on Dominican tobacco, whose principal market was Hamburg.[20] On 13 January 1898, after years of frustrating negotiations with the Germans over the retaliatory tobacco duties, Heureaux unilaterally abrogated all treaties with the great commercial nations in order to free the Dominican Republic of the restrictive favored-nation clauses.

Although Heureaux had counted on negotiating a new commercial treaty with the United States, the Spanish-American War had an unforseen impact on sugar exports to the United States. The US victory provided the United States with secure, cheap sources of sugar from Spain's former colonies. Tariff barriers were immediately removed from sugar shipments coming from Puerto Rico and the Philippines. In 1903, after the United States granted Cuba its independence, Cuban sugar was given a 20 percent tariff reduction. Dominican sugar, by contrast, remained subject to the full tariff. Nevertheless, Dominican sugar was still competitive in the US market because the use of cheap Haitian labor lowered the cost of production for Dominican sugar.

Although the new commercial treaty signed by the United States and the Dominican Republic in 1900 made no provision for a reduced tariff on Dominican sugar exports to the United States, the US hoped to maintain cordial diplomatic and commercial relations with the Dominican Republic. According to US Minister Powell:

I trust that the cordial relations that have existed for so long between our respective countries will continue to exist, and be strengthened as time rolls on. I can assure you of the warm feeling that exists toward the people of this Republic, and the desire on the part of one and all to see your avenues of commerce opened and your roadsteads filled with ships freighted with the rich products of your Republic.[21]

In response to Minister Powell's letter, Dominican Foreign Minister Henríquez y Carvajal replied: "We look upon the great country you represent as the one to whom we may appeal in time of need for succor and assistance. We also trust that the prosperity that exists in your country will attend us, and that our products may continue to reach your markets in the future as they have in the past."[22]

In 1903, Minister Powell reiterated his government's commitment to continued economic ties between the United States and the Dominican Republic. According to Powell: "It is the great desire of Mr. Roosevelt, the President, that the closest friendship shall exist between the two sister Republics, each being allied to the other by strong commercial ties."[23]

In 1906, in an effort to strengthen US-Dominican commercial ties, Dominican President Cáceres stated:

The relations of the Republic with foreign nations are those of the sincerest cordiality.

Paying its debts, respecting foreign rights, defending our own rights with firmness and discretion, the Republic will live in peace with all nations. To attain the maximum of economic power is the ambition of all great peoples. The conquest of world markets is the fight in which the productive races are expending their energies. The Republic ought to take advantage of this conflict of interests to make treaties which will enable us to dispose of our products with positive advantages.[24]

In an attempt to stimulate Dominican sugar exports, on 20 April 1906 the Dominican Congress passed a law exempting sugar from all internal taxation. In response, US sugar barons expanded sugar production, and the Dominican government increased its revenues. In 1906, 53,375 tons of Dominican sugar—virtually the entire sugar crop—were sold to the United States.[25] President Cáceres was committed to expanding the Dominican sugar industry with US capital. In the words of President Cáceres, "In the future the administration over which I preside will devote itself principally to the encouragement of agriculture. It is my most firm conviction that only the development of our agricultural resources will make the peace lasting. In agriculture lies the welfare for which we long."[26] Nevertheless, although sugar taxes were the major source of revenue for the Dominican government, Dominican sugar exporters were unable to achieve significant tariff reductions from the United States.

World War I greatly disrupted the Dominican Republic's traditional trade patterns. As Table 3.1 shows, Dominican-German trade collapsed and Dominican-US trade rapidly increased. Because of the British naval blockade of German ports, Dominican coffee, tobacco, and hardwood exports unable to reach Hamburg were sold to an eager market in the United States.[27] In addition, US sugar corporations in the Dominican Republic, whose domination of the Dominican sugar industry was greatly enlarged during the US military occupation of the island nation (1916–1924), increased production to supply the demand caused by the destruction of the European sugar beet fields. As Table 3.2 shows, Dominican sugar exports to the United States rapidly increased after the passage of the Underwood Tariff in 1914 reduced the US tariff on sugar.

Table 3.1
Dominican Exports to the US and Germany, 1911–1916

	1911	1912	1913	1914	1915	1916
United States	52%	59%	54%	81%	79%	81%
Germany	27%	14%	20%	8%	--	--

Source: H. Hoetink, "The Dominican Republic, 1870–1930," in *The Cambridge History of Latin America*, vol. 5, ed. Leslie Bethell, p. 302.

Although the US corporations increased Dominican sugar production during World War I, after the war ended they were unable to convince US policy makers to guarantee the Dominican Republic a sizable portion of the US sugar market.[28]

With Cuba, the Philippines, Puerto Rico, and Hawaii, the United States was able to satisfy most of its sugar needs and limit its market to all other sugar producers via the 1921 Fordney-McCumber Tariff.[29]

Table 3.2
Dominican Sugar Exports to the US, 1912–1919

Year	Exports (in pounds)	Value (in dollars)
1912	17,681,938	524,190
1913	2,670,630	67,275
1914	4,316,282	86,761
1915	86,188,211	2,891,076
1916	107,503,110	4,384,695
1917	114,367,301	5,242,515
1918	14,395,335	709,349
1919	7,989,541	706,347

Source: Quarterly Report of the Military Governor of Santo Domingo, 2 January 1921; *FRUS 1920*, vol. 2, p. 158.

Nevertheless, as part of the agreement to remove the US Marines from the Dominican Republic, the newly elected Horacio Vásquez government was required to sign the 1924 US-Dominican Agreement. In addition to guaranteeing the US Customs Receivership until the foreign debt was paid, it also granted most-favored-nation status to all products imported from the United States. In return, the United States promised to extend the same benefits to Dominican products, with the important exception of sugar. As Table 3.3 shows, Dominican sugar exports to the United States were virtually eliminated. As US Secretary of State Charles Evans Hughes pointed out:

The principal export of the Dominican Republic is sugar. Owing to the fact that Porto Rico is able to import sugar into the United States free of all duty and that Cuba is enabled to import sugar into the United States with a preferential rate of 20%, Dominican sugar is unable to compete in the United States market with the sugar produced in either of these two islands, and consequently, all sugar exported from the Dominican Republic is sold either in Europe or Canada.[30]

Although the Dominican Republic continued to buy most of its imports from the United States, during the 1920s most Dominican sugar was exported to the United Kingdom. By the end of the 1920s, the United Kingdom imported more than 75 percent of all Dominican sugar produced, while the United States imported less than 2 percent.[31]

The Great Depression devastated the Dominican sugar industry. In 1927, the Dominican Republic exported 295,896 tons of sugar for $16,668,385. In 1930, sugar exports increased to 345,930 tons but only generated $9,910,289 in revenue.[32]   General Rafael Trujillo, who realized that his political hold would remain tenuous unless he was able to improve the failing economy, wanted a secure market in the United States for a substantial quantity of Dominican sugar. He also wanted greater liberty to control his own tariff policy with a view to the negotiation of reciprocal trade agreements, especially with Europeans, who took the bulk of his exports.[33]   According to Dominican Minister Arturo Despradel, during the depression additional funds were also needed for "practical agricultural relief in order to bring about an increase in the volume of our products, thus offsetting as much as possible the low commodity prices now prevailing and limiting the country's purchasing power."[34]

Table 3.3
Dominican Sugar Exports to the US, 1920–1933

Year	Exports (in kilos)	Value (in dollars)
1920	151,108,000	43,348,301
1921	145,761,512	12,007,981
1922	48,370,811	2,646,751
1923	56,285,236	6,039,597
1924	50,778,540	5,517,193
1925	6,267,161	364,384
1926	3,569,963	168,555
1927	3,753,143	196,560
1928	1,886,976	96,512
1929	3,191,800	102,500
1930	6,516,856	200,631
1931	16,264,410	363,266
1932	2,896,569	51,184
1933	11,192,285	223,279

Source: James W. Gantenbein to the State Department, 16 October 1934; Decimal File 611.3931/10-1634, Box 3151; Dominican Republic; RG 59; NA.

Given the importance of sugar revenues to the Dominican government, and the negative effect that the economic depression was having on those revenues, in 1933 the US minister reported the seriousness of the Dominican economic crisis to the US State Department. In the words of Arthur Schoenfeld,

The present limitation of the European market for Dominican sugar, chiefly to Great Britain and France, exposed the Dominican economy to the hazards of arbitrary action by either of these two countries, with results that might be disastrous to the agricultural industry in this country. Since American investments in the Dominican agricultural industry are very large, such arbitrary action on the part of England or France would involve catastrophe for these American interests under these conditions.[35]

Responding to the severity of the international economic crisis, at the end of 1933 the US Tariff Commission reached the conclusion that tariffs could not be raised fast enough to keep abreast of falling sugar prices. The time had come to institutionalize the sugar trade. In 1934, the chairman of the Tariff Commission recommended a quota system that attacked the price problem by restricting foreign supplies and providing direct payments to domestic producers.[36]

US SUGAR LEGISLATION AND DOMINICAN SUGAR EXPORTS, 1934–1947

Insisting that the tariff system had failed to protect the domestic and Cuban sugar industries from foreign competition, in 1934 President Franklin D. Roosevelt decided to replace the tariff system with a sugar quota.[37] In the words of Secretary of Agriculture Henry Wallace,

The program, as outlined in the President's message and implemented by pending legislation, recognizes a duty to stabilize the price and production of sugar for the benefit of the continental producers and the industry of the insular possessions. It also takes into account the obligations of the United States towards Cuba as implied by the Monroe Doctrine and specified in the Platt Amendment.[38]

On 9 May 1934, therefore, Roosevelt signed the Jones-Costigan Amendment to the 1933 Agricultural Adjustment Act.[39] The 1934 Sugar Act, as it came to be called, provided an entirely new method of regulating the sugar industry. Sugar imports were limited by a quota that specified the amount of sugar that each foreign nation could export to the United States.[40]

The Sugar Act required the Secretary of Agriculture to estimate the annual consumption of sugar in the United States. Once consumption requirements were determined, the quantity of sugar needed was divided among the domestic areas and foreign countries supplying sugar to the United States by assigning a quota to each. In the event that any area, domestic or foreign, was unable to fulfill its quota, the Secretary reallocated the deficit to foreign areas that were able to take up the slack, and thus maintain an even flow of sugar to consumers. The US sugar market was divided among producers down to the last spoonful: so much for domestic cane and beet producers, and so much for each of the foreign governments that curried favor with the US Congress.[41] Initially, 48 percent of the sugar consumed in the United States was domestically produced, 48 percent came from Cuba and the Philippines, and 4 percent was allotted to other foreign sugar exporters.[42]

Although fundamentally a piece of domestic legislation, the Sugar Act eventually became a valuable tool of US foreign policy. According to Harold Cooley, chairman of the House Agriculture Committee during the 1950s, "Quotas should be treated like rewards and should be based on who are our friends and who are not."[43] It was an instrument to promote US trade abroad, as well as a vehicle to reward foreign nations for adhering to US guidelines. Dominican historian José Madruga contends that "the most effective weapon that the United

States has against monoculture economy Caribbean states is the ability to increase and decrease the export quotas to the United States."[44]   Political, rather than economic, considerations, therefore, determined which countries received the greatest preferential access to US markets.

The principal economic effect of the Sugar Act was to separate sugar prices in the United States from those in the rest of the world. When the US domestic sugar industry was protected only by a tariff, the difference between the price of raw sugar in the United States and other countries tended to equal the difference in import duties plus the differences in the cost of transporting the sugar from the exporting country to the importing country. With the establishment of quotas that limited the quantity of sugar that could be imported or marketed from domestic production in any year, US sugar prices became independent of those in other countries.[45]   Foreign suppliers who were granted access to the preferential US market enjoyed prices that were often two cents per pound higher than prices in the world market.[46]   Many US policy makers, therefore, looked on the sugar quota as a form of economic assistance advancing the goals of the Good Neighbor Policy.[47]

Initially, the amount of sugar that a foreign nation could export to the United States was roughly based on previous sugar exports to the United States in the years immediately prior to the enactment of the Sugar Act.   Although the Dominican Republic exported 145,000 tons of sugar to the United States in 1921, in 1933 the Dominican Republic only exported 11,000 tons of sugar to the United States.   In October 1934, therefore, the United States granted the Dominican Republic its first sugar quota at preferential prices—a mere 2,067 tons. This tiny amount provoked an angry reaction in the Dominican press. Luis F. Vidal, who represented the Casa Vicini sugar interests, called the quota "simply ridiculous."[48] In Washington, Dominican Ambassador Rafael Brache explained to President Roosevelt that the Dominican Republic also needed a New Deal, but that they would be unable to fund it without a large preferential sugar quota.[49]

As Table 3.4 shows, in 1935, the United States greatly increased its imports from the Dominican Republic.   Fearful of Nazi Germany's expanded economic presence in Latin America, the United States took 27 percent of all Dominican exports, against 20 percent in 1934.   Sugar accounted for $1,581,935 of total dutiable Dominican exports to the United States valued at $1,607,904, leaving to other dutiable exports a negligible value of $25,969.[50]   Nevertheless, the Dominican government continued to argue that they were not able to negotiate successful reciprocal trade agreements with other nations because of the restrictive clauses in the 1924 US-Dominican Agreement.[51]   The Dominican Republic's preferential sugar quota in 1936 was still a paltry 3,334 tons.[52]

In a further attempt to increase the trifling Dominican quota, in 1936 Dominican Foreign Minister Ernesto Bonetti Burgos suggested that a 300,000-ton sugar quota would enable his nation to withstand Japanese and German pressures for closer political and economic affiliation.[53]   Trujillo was playing the United States off against the Axis powers for his own self-serving reasons. According to

Bonetti Burgos: "The preferential treatment accorded Cuba in the existing Cuban-American trade agreement, and otherwise, was in effect discriminating against the Dominican Republic in view of the abrogation of the Platt Amendment and the cessation of special political relations between the United States and Cuba."[54] The Department of State responded that the United States still maintained special political relations with Cuba and that it would be impossible to grant the Dominican Republic a greatly increased quota in 1936.[55] The State Department did, however, hint at the possibility of greatly increased sugar quotas in the future. A few days later, therefore, Bonetti Burgos acknowledged the special relationship between Cuba and the United States when he informed Schoenfeld that he understood that the moment was not at hand for an increased quota for the Dominican Republic.[56]

Table 3.4
US Trade with the Dominican Republic, 1930–1935

Year	US Exports (in dollars)	US Imports (in dollars)
1930	8,545,988	4,368,121
1931	5,882,655	3,427,767
1932	4,595,541	1,907,992
1933	5,384,858	1,928,170
1934	6,016,165	2,613,741
1935	4,742,192	4,154,451

Source: Arthur Schoenfeld to the State Department, 13 October 1936; *FRUS 1936*, vol. 5, p. 413.

Trujillo, however, did not have to wait long for an expanded sugar quota. In 1937, responding to the expanded Nazi economic presence in Latin America, President Roosevelt petitioned Congress for larger quota allotments to facilitate reciprocal trade agreements with Latin American nations.[57] Although the Sugar Act of 1937 continued to favor Cuba and the Philippines, unused portions of the Philippine quota were reserved exclusively for foreign countries other than Cuba.[58] The inability of the Philippines to fulfill its quota meant that 86,805 tons were reallocated. In 1937, therefore, the Dominican Republic, which was allotted 25,000 tons from the redistributed Philippine quota, exported 31,668 tons of sugar to the United States.[59] According to Schoenfeld, "Although the increase recently granted to the Dominican Republic is very small in comparison with the nation's total sugar production, the precedent established is of the greatest importance and may well give rise to events of greater consideration."[60]

Although the increased sugar quota gave a boost to the Dominican economy and the dictator's prestige at home and abroad, in 1938 Trujillo asked for parity of tariff treatment with Cuba. In response to the Dominican petition, the US Department of State once again stated that the US-Cuban Trade Agreement made it impossible for the United States to grant parity of treatment for Dominican products.[61] Trujillo, nevertheless, was grateful for his recently expanded sugar quota. This was reflected in a speech before the Dominican Congress on 27 February 1939, in which the dictator praised the United States for the special allotment.[62]

In 1940, Roosevelt urged the House Committee on Agriculture to refrain from recommending "any bill that would impair the foreign outlets for our surplus products, run counter to the Good Neighbor Policy, discriminate among various groups of domestic producers and processors, or increase the burden on our consumers and taxpayers."[63] Trujillo, however, was busy squeezing the Dominican sugar industry for his own financial purposes. In early 1942, Trujillo passed a law that compelled the foreign-owned sugar corporations to pay a 20 percent tax on all earnings over $1.50 per hundred-pound bag. US policy makers did not object, because they considered the maintenance of friendly relations with the Trujillo regime essential during World War II. The owners of the sugar mills were not upset either, because they did not believe that the prices would go much higher.[64] The destruction of the European sugar beet crop, however, caused sugar prices to shoot up to $2.65 per hundred pounds. In 1942, the British Food Ministry agreed to purchase 400,000 tons of Dominican sugar with US Lend-Lease funds.[65]

Table 3.5
Total Dominican Imports and Exports, 1941–1947

Year	Imports (in dollars)	Exports (in dollars)
1941	11,739,000	17,124,000
1942	11,481,000	20,057,000
1943	14,361,000	36,205,000
1944	18,525,000	60,269,000
1945	18,126,000	43,564,000
1946	27,664,000	66,689,000
1947	53,448,000	83,206,000

Source: Richard H. Stephens to the State Department, 2 July 1957; Economic Conditions Folder, Box 244; Dominican Republic, Narrative Reports, 1955–61; RG 166; NA.

As Table 3.5 shows, World War II was an economic bonanza for Dominican agricultural exporters. Dominican sugar sales to the United Kingdom were rapidly increased and Trujillo took full credit for negotiating the deal with the United Kingdom.[66] On 10 December 1943, therefore, Trujillo asked the Sugar Producers' Association for a $1 million donation to the celebration of the Dominican Centennial. On 4 January 1944, the South Porto Rico Sugar Company, which accounted for 41 percent of Dominican sugar production, announced that it refused to participate in the donation.[67] In retaliation for the South Porto Rico

Sugar Company's failure to cooperate, on 6 January 1944, Trujillo increased sugar export taxes from $.23 to $.35 per hundred pound bag. In 1944, the Dominican government earned $4,497,442 from sugar taxes.[68]

Trujillo's expanded sugar exports at extraordinary prices, however, were limited to the duration of the war. As early as 1943, US diplomats in Ciudad Trujillo pointed out that "the lack of a ready market in the United States" discouraged the expansion of the Dominican industry.[69]   F. B. Adams, the president of the West Indies Sugar Corporation, also mentioned the possibility for growth in the Dominican sugar industry. Regarding the potential of the US sugar quota in the post-World War II world, in 1944 Adams pointed out: "The amount of money involved in this affair is small; the opportunity for using it to strengthen, as nothing else could, the cordial relations between the US and the DR is great."[70]

In an attempt to persuade the United States that he deserved a generous postwar quota, Trujillo tried to convince the United States that he was Latin America's most ardent anticommunist by enlisting the support of the US sugar mill directors to combat communism. On 17 November 1945, Dominican Foreign Minister Peña Batlle and Trujillo met with Edwin Kilbourne from the West Indies Sugar Company, W. T. Hennessey from the South Porto Rico Sugar Company, and W. L. Fox from the Boca Chica Sugar Company to discuss how they could act as intelligence agencies that would report communist activities directly to Trujillo, who would pass on the information to Washington.[71] In addition, on 11 December, Dominican Foreign Minister Peña Batlle warned the US embassy that without increased sugar revenues the Trujillo government "would fall" to communism.[72]

In 1945, however, the Department of State was not interested in strengthening relations with the Trujillo regime. Quite the contrary. Beginning in 1945, the Department of State began to distance itself from Latin American dictatorships.[73] In 1946, the US Legation in Ciudad Trujillo warned against raising the Dominican share of the US sugar quota. In the words of US diplomat George Scherer:

Politically, I must recommend against an increase in the Dominican quota, as long as Trujillo is in power, since it would play directly into his hands. First, the President would make certain to receive all credit for accomplishing the increase and in addition he would make it appear to come as a result of close friendship between the US and this Republic. Second, he would probably use the allocation of quotas among the various mills to serve his own political purposes. Third, if the quota were to result in a greater sugar income for the Republic, he would be tempted to siphon off in taxes the increase in income.[74]

By 1947, however, the realities of the Cold War convinced the State Department to end its cold shoulder treatment toward the Trujillo regime. Ambassador George Butler recommended an expanded sugar quota for the Dominican Republic. According to Butler:

An increased share in the United States sugar market would provide a more stable market for Dominican sugar producers, mostly American interests, and would make them less dependent on the fluctuation of the world sugar prices. Undoubtedly, the Dominicans should be given some consideration for their cooperation during the war, even though it was profitable for them to cooperate.[75]

Although international sugar prices remained high in the postwar period, Trujillo was interested in the possibility of a greatly expanded quota in the secure, preferential US market.[76]

US SUGAR LEGISLATION AND DOMINICAN SUGAR EXPORTS, 1948–1957

The Sugar Act of 1948 regulated US sugar imports during the first decade of the Cold War. Although it retained the basic features of the Sugar Act of 1937, the new legislation, which Senator William J. Fulbright (D-AR) called a "complex, crazy quilt maze of regulations," included a new proviso designed to safeguard US economic interests.[77] Section 202(e) of the new act read as follows:

If the Secretary of State finds that any foreign country denies fair and equitable treatment to the nationals of the United States, its commerce, navigation, or industry, the Secretary of Agriculture shall have authority to withhold or withdraw any increase in the share of the domestic consumption requirements provided for such country by this Act as compared with the share allowed under Section 202(b) of the Sugar Act of 1937.[78]

Although the new act still favored Cuba and the Philippines, other foreign countries were rewarded with expanded quotas. In 1948, the Dominican Republic received an 8,133-ton quota.[79] This was good news for Trujillo.

Beginning in 1948, Trujillo launched a personal assault on the sugar industry. He began to build new sugar mills and purchase foreign-owned mills in order to consolidate his economic and political control over the island. Using a combination of chicanery and intimidation, Trujillo adroitly convinced US sugar mill owners that the most advantageous path to follow was one that was not inimical to his course.[80] Editorials capitalizing on nationalistic rhetoric against the immense control exerted by foreign interests in the Dominican sugar industry appeared in the government-controlled press. Referring to the US-owned South Porto Rico Sugar Company as the "sugar octopus," one editorial claimed: "In the Dominican Republic the sugar octopus is at present stronger and more powerful than at any other time."[81]

At the same time, however, Trujillo praised US leadership in the Americas and promised full support for US plans "to stop Soviet expansion."[82] US Ambassador Ralph Ackerman believed that an increased sugar quota was a small price to pay for Trujillo's support in the global struggle against communism. Ambassador Ackerman contended: "Sympathetic consideration should be given to the Dominican plea for a worth-while participation in the American market and I strongly feel that it will pay dividends in the long run."[83] Confident that Trujillo planned to adequately compensate the sugar mill owners, US policy makers acceded to Trujillo's plan to dominate the Dominican sugar industry. In addition, they continuously increased Trujillo's share of the preferential quota. According to the State Department,

The Dominican Government regards our policy towards its desire for a larger share of the US sugar market as the basic yardstick for measuring our willingness to take positive steps to cooperate with it in economic matters. The principal Dominican interest in its economic relations with the United States is a large scale opening of the United States market to Dominican sugar, the country's largest export.[84]

In 1951, the Dominican share of the preferential quota was increased to 12,389 tons. In addition, a large portion of the unfilled Philippine quota was granted to the Dominican Republic.[85] Nevertheless, by 1953 the basic Dominican sugar quota was still a paltry 27,037 tons.[86] Trujillo was especially envious of the advantageous sugar quota that the US allotted to the Cubans. In order to convince the US that his country was more deserving of the privileged sugar quota allotted to Cuba, Trujillo overemphasized the anticommunist nature of his regime and the bonds of friendship between the Dominican Republic and the United States. According to Trujillo, "To unite with, to unify purposes, and to fight all together in a communion of ideals with the invincible bulwark of American democracy—the United States of America—should be the firm purpose of all the Governments and peoples of this Hemisphere."[87]

Table 3.6
Total Dominican Imports and Exports, 1948–1957

Year	Imports (in dollars)	Exports (in dollars)
1948	65,329,000	82,801,000
1949	46,014,000	73,749,000
1950	42,985,000	83,515,000
1951	48,236,000	108,455,000
1952	79,390,000	115,015,000
1953	81,626,000	118,449,000
1954	82,827,000	119,727,000
1955	98,456,000	114,860,000
1956	108,278,000	124,559,000
1957	129,500,000	136,600,000

Source: Richard H. Stephens to the State Department, 2 July 1957; Economic Conditions Folder, Box 244; Dominican Republic, Narrative Reports, 1955–61; RG 166; NA.

As Table 3.6 shows, throughout the 1950s, the Dominican Republic maintained a favorable balance of international trade. Four agricultural crops—sugar, coffee, cacao, and tobacco—made up over 90 percent of Dominican exports.[88] In 1952, for the first time during the Trujillo era, Dominican exports to the United States had a greater combined value than exports to the United Kingdom.

Table 3.7
Total Dominican Exports by Destination, 1951–1962

Year	UK	US	Year	UK	US
1951	50.3%	36.0%	1957	34.7%	41.7%
1952	37.1%	44.7%	1958	22.5%	53.9%
1953	21.0%	46.2%	1959	14.6%	53.9%
1954	20.6%	56.6%	1960	12.3%	53.0%
1955	21.8%	52.6%	1961	10.0%	58.6%
1956	24.7%	46.3%	1962	.4%	81.9%

Source: Richard H. Stephens to the State Department, 2 July 1957; Economic Conditions Folder, Box 244; Dominican Republic, Narrative Reports, 1955–61; RG 166; NA.

As Table 3.7 shows, during the 1950s Dominican exports to the United States increased and the Dominican Republic became increasingly dependent upon the US market.[89] This rising dependency on US markets was not, however, viewed with apprehension by Trujillo, who never expected that political considerations would eventually turn this dependency into a serious threat against his regime. In 1951, exports to the United States, primarily coffee, cacao, and tobacco, were valued at $53,329,000, while exports to the United Kingdom, primarily sugar, were valued at $41,782,000.[90] Nevertheless, the Dominican government's revenue continued to rely primarily on sugar export taxes. In 1951, the Dominican government earned $22,022,960 from taxes on sugar exports.

Since the majority of Dominican imports came from the United States, Trujillo argued that the United States should open its market to Dominican sugar. The State Department surmised Trujillo's predicament in the following passage:

Because Dominican sugar has traditionally found a market in Great Britain and because the war stimulated a boom in world demand for sugar, the Dominican sugar export situation has been favorable in recent years. However, the increasing production of sugar in the British Empire, as well as with the Dominican realization of dependence on the US as the supplier of about 75% of Dominican imports, there has been a concerted effort to obtain a fundamental change in our sugar policy, so that the Dominican Republic will ultimately be able to dispose of a good share of its sugar output in the US market.[91]

Trujillo, who maintained that Dominican sugar was being discriminated against in the US market, claimed that the United States only absorbed 40 percent of Dominican exports.[92] Consequently, in 1953 US and Dominican businessmen were instructed to place the following legend on international correspondence:

Due to US quota restrictions, only 3.7% of Dominican Sugar Exports were imported by the United States in 1952. Sugar represents 60% of total Dominican Exports. 75% of Dominican Imports in 1952 came from USA. Any increase or reduction of our purchases in the US will depend on the correction of this unjust status.[93]

Trujillo wanted to establish "real reciprocity, commercially and otherwise," between the Dominican Republic and the United States.[94] In 1954, therefore, the Dominican government hired Surrey, Karasik, Gould & Efron, a Washington, DC law firm, to organize a publicity campaign in the United States to increase the Dominican sugar quota.[95] Describing Trujillo's propaganda campaign, a US embassy official in Ciudad Trujillo reported:

The economic arguments for a greater share of the US sugar market are the familiar ones, but when political support for these arguments is sought an appeal is made to the value which the United States places upon effective opposition to Communism in this hemisphere. According to the Dominican government, the United States discriminates against its firmest friend and the only country in America where Communism simply does not exist by forcing it to sell its sugar in the sterling bloc while making 70% of its purchases in the United States. The failure of the US government to reward the Dominican government presents not only a historic example of ingratitude but also a dangerous example of crass stupidity.[96]

The US sugar quota, however, was not designed as a means of largesse for Dominicans. The US sugar program was developed, first and foremost, for the protection of domestic interest groups. Domestic US producers, although unable to supply the entire US market themselves, were politically powerful enough to make certain that they were not excluded from the market by more cheaply produced foreign sugar. According to the Sugar Division of the US Department of Agriculture, "Under free market conditions, where market forces are at work, a major part of our national sugar industry would not survive."[97] According to Harold Cooley (D-NC), the chairman of the House Agriculture Committee, the sugar program has "operated so well and so smoothly that the average housewife is not aware that we have a sugar program. Even the average Congressman is unaware of the fact that we have a sugar program."[98] Cooley once remarked:

We know—all of us know—that sugar can be produced in offshore areas at far less cost than we produce it here. All of us know that this program is saturated with subsidy and control and regimentation and all of these unholy and un-American things that we have been told of from day to day. You fix the amount that a man can grow, the amount that he can market, the amount to be refined, and you pay a tremendous subsidy to the producers. Here is a bill that has all of the things that [Secretary of Agriculture] Benson has been denouncing. Yet, I am for it. He is for it. The President is for it.[99]

In 1955, domestic sugar growers and their lobbyists were determined to enlarge their quotas at the expense of offshore producers. Cane men from Florida and Louisiana; beet growers from the West; representatives from the US refineries; lawyers from Puerto Rico, Hawaii, and the Philippines; lobbyists from the Dominican Republic, Mexico, and Cuba; manufacturers of candy, alcohol, soft drinks, and ice cream; foreign investors; shipping companies; and labor leaders all made their pleas before the House Committee on Agriculture preceding the introduction of sugar legislation in 1956.[100] When the US Congress adjourned for

Easter recess, Trujillo sponsored a Caribbean holiday for members of the House
Agricultural Committee and their families. Throughout the all-expense-paid
festivities, the Dominicans campaigned for a larger sugar quota. Although Cooley
was not present, his sister, son, and daughter-in-law had a fantastic time carousing
in the Dominican Republic. Congressman W. R. Poage (D-TX), the senior
committeeman on the junket, was impressed by Trujillo's pro-US, anticommunist
rhetoric. Poage, therefore, subsequently endorsed a more generous quota to the
Dominican Republic.[101]

Table 3.8
Basic US Sugar Quota for Dominican Republic, 1948–1957

Year	Quota (in tons)	Year	Quota (in tons)
1948	8,133	1953	27,037
1949	11,975	1954	28,015
1950	12,052	1955	30,058
1951	12,389	1956	34,441
1952	16,008	1957	42,489

Source: Richard H. Stephens to the State Department, 2 July 1957; Economic Conditions Folder, Box 244;
Dominican Republic, Narrative Reports, 1955–61; RG 166; NA.

As Table 3.8 shows, the new sugar legislation increased the basic Dominican
sugar quota to 34,441 tons. In 1956, although the Dominican Republic exported
42,091 tons to the United States at preferential prices, it exported 410,878 tons to
the United Kingdom, 77,472 tons to Japan, 43,093 tons to the Netherlands, and
48,110 tons to West Germany at world market prices.[102] Whereas Dominican
sugar exports earned $56,234,938 in 1956, Trujillo hoped to increase his profits
by securing a larger share of the US sugar market.[103] Nevertheless, the US-
Dominican sugar connection remained a mixed blessing for Trujillo. On the one
hand, income generated from sugar sales allowed the dictator to tighten his grip
on the Dominican political economy and engage in public works programs that
fueled his megalomania. On the other hand, Trujillo had to maintain good
relations with the Eisenhower administration to obtain larger sugar quotas.

NOTES

1. Federico García Godoy to Max Henríquez Ureña, 27 June 1938; Sugar Folder, Box
33; Dominican Republic, General Records; RG 84; NA.

2. See Grupo de Países Latinoamericanos y del Caribe Exportadores de Azúcar, *Report
on United States Sugar Policy and its Effects Toward the Economy of GEPLACEA's
Member Countries* (Mexico City: GEPLACEA, 1984). The Vatican City and Iceland,
however, are completely dependent on sugar imports.

3. Jerome Slater, *Intervention and Negotiation: The United States and the Dominican
Republic* (New York: Harper & Row, 1970), p. 47.

4. Jack Neathery to Hector Adam, 27 April 1947; Sugar Folder, Box 189; Dominican Republic, General Records; RG 84; NA.

5. Howard Wiarda, *The Dominican Republic: A Nation in Transition* (New York: Praeger, 1969), p. 134.

6. Howard Wiarda and Michael Kryzanek, *The Dominican Republic: A Caribbean Crucible* (Boulder, CO: Westview, 1982), p. 68.

7. Abdessatar Grissa, *Structure of the International Sugar Market and Its Impact on Developing Countries* (Paris: Development Centre of the Organization for Economic Co-Operation and Development, 1976), p. 18.   Sugar has been sold profitably almost exclusively in these preferential markets.

8. Reference is to PL 213, approved 9 May 1934, which amended the Agricultural Adjustment Act of 12 May 1933 to include sugar beets and sugar cane as basic agricultural commodities and establish import quotas for these products.   See House, Committee on Agriculture, *Sugar Beets and Sugarcane as Basic Agricultural Commodities*, House Report 1109, 73rd Congress, 2nd Session, 1934, *House Reports*, Serial 9775, p. 1; *Congressional Record*, 73rd Congress, 2nd Session, 1934, Vol. 78, pp. 5797–6020.   The preferential sugar quota authorized by the Sugar Act of 1934 was in effect until 1974.   President Ronald Reagan revived the Sugar Act in 1982 as part of his Caribbean Basin Initiative.

9. Richard C. Desmond to the State Department, 21 March 1955; Economic Conditions Folder, Box 244; Dominican Republic, Narrative Reports, 1955–61; RG 166; NA.

10. Thomas J. Hetson, *Sweet Subsidy: The Economic and Diplomatic Effects of the US Sugar Acts, 1934–1974* (New York: Garland, 1987), p. 57.   Until 1914, the British imported over 50 percent of their sugar from Germany and Austria-Hungary.   Cut off from those supplies, the British turned to Cuba and the Dominican Republic.

11. Robert D. Crassweller, *Trujillo: The Life and Times of a Caribbean Dictator* (New York: Macmillan, 1966), p. 123.

12. John Bartlow Martin, *US Policy in the Caribbean* (Boulder, CO: Westview, 1978), p. 14.   Few commodities raised more complex economic, political, and social issues during the Cold War than sugar.   Because of its past associations with slavery, the Dominican sugar industry carried much ideological baggage.

13. Ilse Mintz, *US Import Quotas: Costs and Consequences* (Washington, DC: American Enterprise Institute for Public Policy Research, 1973), p. 33.   Highly paid lobbyists played an important role in deciding the allocation of foreign quotas.

14. Joaquín Balaguer, "Presidential Speech at the Annual Luncheon of the US Chamber of Commerce of Santo Domingo in the Hotel Embajador," unpublished document, 30 April 1971, p. 3.

15. Harry Hoetink, "The Dominican Republic, 1870–1930" in *The Cambridge History of Latin America*, vol. 5, ed. Leslie Bethell (London: Cambridge University Press, 1984), p. 300–3.

16. Henry A. Wallace to Robert J. Buckley, 1 March 1938; Cited in Myer Lynsky, *Sugar Economics, Statistics, and Documents* (New York: US Cane Sugar Refiners' Association, 1938), pp. 17–18.

17. James Bovard, *The Farm Fiasco* (San Francisco: Institute for Contemporary Studies, 1991), p. 62.   On 14 April 1789, the House of Representatives adopted a levy of one cent per pound on raw sugar and three cents per pound on refined sugar.   The Senate concurred on 11 June, and the new tariff went into effect on 1 August 1789.

18. Oficina Nacional de Estadística de la República Dominicana, *La Industria Azucarera en Marcha* (Ciudad Trujillo: Oficina Nacional de Estadística de la República Dominicana, 1955).

19. Thomas C. Dawson to the Secretary of State, 18 October 1906; *FRUS 1906*, p. 587.

20. Ibid. This demand greatly alarmed the Heureaux government. Tobacco, the most important export crop of the Cibao, was the second most important export from the island.

21. W. F. Powell to Francisco Henríquez y Carvajal, 16 January 1900; *FRUS 1900*, p. 426.

22. Francisco Henríquez y Carvajal to W. F. Powell, 16 January 1900; *FRUS 1900*, p. 426.

23. W. F. Powell to Alejandro Woss y Gil, 22 October 1903; *FRUS 1903*, p. 395.

24. Thomas C. Dawson to the Secretary of State, 7 March 1907; *FRUS 1907*, pp. 568–69.

25. Fenton R. McCreery to the Secretary of State, 19 September 1907; *FRUS 1907*, pp. 320–21.

26. Fenton R. McCreery to the Secretary of State, 1 July 1908; *FRUS 1908*, p. 257.

27. Hoetink, "The Dominican Republic, 1870–1930," p. 302.

28. Quarterly Report of the Military Governor of Santo Domingo, 2 January 1921; *FRUS 1920*, vol. 2, p. 158.

29. Frank Báez, *Azúcar y Dependencia en la República Dominicana* (Santo Domingo: Universidad Autónoma de Santo Domingo, 1986), p. 63. The Fordney-McCumber Tariff placed a tariff of 2.2 cents per pound on all sugar imports.

30. Charles Evans Hughes to President Coolidge, 20 June 1924; *FRUS 1924*, vol. 1, p. 666.

31. James W. Gantenbein to the State Department, 16 October 1934; Decimal File 611.3931/10-1634, Box 3151; Dominican Republic; RG 59; NA.

32. C. B. Curtis to the State Department, 2 June 1931; Sugar Folder, Box 154; Dominican Republic, Narrative Reports, 1904–39; RG 166; NA. In 1930, sugar sold for less than one cent per pound.

33. Arthur Schoenfeld to Cordell Hull, 10 August 1934; Secret Reports Folder, Box 1; Dominican Republic, Miscellaneous Records; RG 84; NA.

34. Arturo Despradel to the Secretary of State, 24 December 1932; *FRUS 1933*, vol. 5, p. 622.

35. Arthur Schoenfeld to the Secretary of State, 18 September 1933; *FRUS 1933*, vol. 5, pp. 649–50.

36. Douglas Cater and Walter Pincus, "Our Sugar Diplomacy," *The Reporter* 24, no. 8 (13 April 1961), p. 25.

37. Karaim Reed, "What Do Cory Aquino, Cocaine Addicts, and American Consumers Have in Common?," *The Washington Monthly* (November 1987): 18–20. The sugar price had to be kept artificially high because the United States is not a very suitable place to grow sugar. The climate in most of the country can only accommodate sugar beets, which have to be chopped up and cooked to make sugar, costing almost 40 percent more than milling sugar cane. US sugar beet growers could not compete with cane growers in the Dominican Republic in a free market economy.

38. US Senate, Committee on Finance, *To Include Sugar Cane and Sugar Beets as Basic Agricultural Commodities*, Hearings, 73rd Congress, 2nd Session, 1934.

39. Reducing the Tariff on Sugar, Proclamation No. 2985, 9 May 1934; *Statutes at Large*, vol. 48, part 2, pp. 1742–1743.

40. US Cuban Sugar Council, *Sugar: Facts and Figures, 1952* (Washington, DC: US Cuban Sugar Council, 1953), p. 70. A quota is a maximum limitation, specified in either monetary value or physical units, on imports of a product for a given period. Control over foreign suppliers was relatively simple because customs officers could turn back over-quota

sugar at US ports, and also prevent the entry of sugar from countries that did not have quotas. In the Dominican Republic, the government distributed the sugar quota among the various sugar producers.

41. US Senate, Committee on Finance, *To Include Sugar Cane and Sugar Beets as Basic Agricultural Commodities*, Hearings, 73rd Congress, 2nd Session, 1934, pp. 7–8. Sugar quotas were increased annually to meet expanded domestic consumption.

42. Eduardo LaTorre, *Sobre Azúcar* (Santo Domingo: Instituto Technológico de Santo Domingo, 1988), p. 42.

43. *The Washington Post*, 3 April 1961. Congressman Cooley (D-NC), who came to Congress in 1934, was chairman of the House Agriculture Committee from 1950 until 1966, when he lost his bid for reelection.

44. José Manuel Madruga, *Azúcar y Haitianos en la República Dominicana* (Santo Domingo: Amigo del Hogar, 1986), p. 38.

45. Organization of American States, *Marketing Problems of Sugar at the Hemisphere and World Levels* (Washington, DC: Organization of American States, 1964), p. 7.

46. US Department of Agriculture, *A History of Sugar Marketing* (Washington, DC: Government Printing Office, 1971). In 1958, the world market comprised one-tenth of the sugar trade and for most producers constituted a residual outlet after domestic requirements and exports to preferential markets had been fulfilled. Since the market price was near the cost of production, it was essentially a dumping price.

47. US House, Committee on Agriculture, *The Development of Foreign Sugar Quotas*, 1965, p. 6. The report specified numerous criteria to be used in assigning quotas, such as "the economic need of the country for a US quota and the relative value of a quota to such a country."

48. James W. Gantenbein to the State Department, 16 October 1934; Decimal File 611.3931/34, Box 3151; Dominican Republic; RG 59; NA. Vidal insinuated that the failure to achieve a substantial preferential sugar quota might result in the growth of extremist political factions in the Dominican Republic.

49. Rafael Brache to Rafael Trujillo, 18 October 1934; File 30330; APG; PND; SD.

50. Arthur Schoenfeld to the State Department, 13 October 1936; *FRUS 1936*, vol. 5, p. 413.

51. Arthur Schoenfeld to the State Department, 8 January 1936; Sugar Folder, Box 13; Dominican Republic, General Records; RG 84; NA.

52. Arthur Schoenfeld to the State Department, 13 October 1936; *FRUS 1936*, vol. 5, p. 413. The British continued to purchase the lion's share of Dominican sugar exports.

53. Arthur Schoenfeld to the State Department, 11 March 1936; Sugar Folder, Box 13; Dominican Republic, General Records; RG 84; NA. Bonetti Burgos contended that the 300,000-ton quota would be of the utmost importance to the Dominican economy while, at the same time, it would only be of slight importance in relation to the total sugar imports into the United States from foreign countries.

54. Arthur Schoenfeld to the State Department, 3 November 1936; *FRUS 1936*, vol. 5, p. 457.

55. Franklin B. Atwood to Cordell Hull, 2 December 1936; Sugar Folder, Box 13; Dominican Republic, General Records; RG 84; NA.

56. Ernesto Bonetti Burgos to Arthur Schoenfeld, 8 December 1936; Sugar Folder, Box 13; Dominican Republic, General Records; RG 84; NA.

57. Franklin Roosevelt to Congress, 1 March 1937; *Congressional Record*, 75th Congress, 1st Session, 1937, Vol. 81, p. 1661.

58. Cordell Hull to Arthur Schoenfeld, 8 September 1937; Sugar Folder, Box 24; Dominican Republic, General Records; RG 84; NA. The Sugar Act of 1937 did not drastically change the Sugar Act of 1934. The new act allocated 1,004,903 tons to the Philippines and 1,939,546 tons to Cuba.

59. Franklin B. Atwood to Joaquín Balaguer, 11 September 1937; Sugar Folder, Box 24; Dominican Republic, General Records; RG 84; NA.

60. Arthur Schoenfeld to Cordell Hull, 9 January 1937; Sugar Folder, Box 24; Dominican Republic, General Records; RG 84; NA.

61. Sumner Welles to Arthur Schoenfeld, 22 April 1938; Sugar Folder, Box 33; Dominican Republic, General Records; RG 84; NA.

62. Rafael L. Trujillo Molina, "Discurso Nacional Frente al Congreso Nacional en Celebración del Día de la Independencía, 27 Febrero 1939," in *Discursos, Mensajes, y Proclamas*, vol. 9 (Ciudad Trujillo: Oficina Nacional del Presidente de la República Dominicana, 1948), pp. 34–35.

63. Samuel Rosenman, ed., *The Public Papers and Addresses of Franklin Roosevelt*, vol. 9, (New York: Random House, 1941), p. 229.

64. Robert McGregor Scotten to the State Department, 12 February 1942; Sugar Folder, Box 91; Dominican Republic, General Records; RG 84; NA.

65. Edward R. Stettinius Jr. to R. H. Brand, 12 March 1942; Sugar Folder, Box 91; Dominican Republic, General Records; RG 84; NA. World War II brought an economic bonanza to the Dominican sugar industry and the Dominican government because of the special tax imposed by Trujillo. In 1942, the Dominican government earned $2.8 million from export taxes on sugar.

66. US Embassy to the State Department, 12 September 1945; Sugar Folder, Box 157; Dominican Republic, General Records; RG 84; NA.

67. A. M. Warren to the State Department, 13 January 1944; Sugar Folder, Box 216; Dominican Republic, Narrative Reports, 1942–45; RG 166; NA.

68. George F. Scherer to the State Department, 4 September 1945; Sugar Folder, Box 216; Dominican Republic, Narrative Reports, 1942–45; RG 166; NA.

69. Don V. Catlett to Edward P. Lawton, 29 January 1943; Sugar Folder, Box 216; Dominican Republic, Narrative Reports, 1942–45; RG 166; NA.

70. F. B. Adams to Cordell Hull, 8 March 1944; Sugar Folder, Box 140; Dominican Republic, General Records; RG 84; NA.

71. George F. Scherer to the State Department, 19 November 1945; *FRUS 1945*, vol. 9, p. 989.

72. George F. Scherer to the State Department, 11 December 1945; *FRUS 1945*, vol. 9, p. 992.

73. Spruille Braden to the State Department, 5 April 1945; Political Folder, Box 1; Dominican Republic, Confidential General Records; RG 84; NA.

74. George F. Scherer to the State Department, 31 May 1946; Sugar Folder, Box 10; Dominican Republic, Confidential General Records; RG 84; NA.

75. George H. Butler to the State Department, 24 June 1947; Sugar Folder, Box 671; Dominican Republic, Narrative Reports, 1946–49; RG 166; NA.

76. Dale E. Farringer to the State Department, 14 January 1948; Sugar Folder, Box 196; Dominican Republic, General Records; RG 84; NA. In 1947, Trujillo collected $16,169,063 from taxes on sugar exports. This enabled him to cancel the remaining foreign debt owed to the United States and end the US Customs Receivership that had been in place since 1905.

77. *Congressional Record*, 7 February 1956, p. 2202.

78. Sugar Act of 1948; *Statutes at Large*, vol. 1, part 1, section 202(e), p. 924. In 1960, this proviso enabled President Eisenhower to suspend Cuba's participation in sugar quota.

79. Ellis M. Goodwin to the State Department, 5 November 1949; Sugar Folder, Box 671; Dominican Republic, Narrative Reports, 1946–49; RG 166; NA.

80. Stanley G. Slavens to the State Department, 7 May 1951; Foreign Trade Folder, Box 127; Dominican Republic, Narrative Reports, 1950–54; RG 166; NA.

81. *La Nación*, 25 May 1948.

82. H. S. Steele to the State Department, 19 April 1948; Communism Folder, Box 21; Dominican Republic, Confidential General Records; RG 84; NA.

83. Ralph H. Ackerman to the State Department, 18 May 1951; Decimal File 839.2351/5-1851, Box 4747; Dominican Republic, 1950–54; RG 59; NA.

84. Policy Statement Prepared in the State Department, 9 January 1951; Decimal File 611.39/1-951, Box 2766; Dominican Republic, 1950–54; RG 59; NA.

85. US Embassy in Ciudad Trujillo to the State Department, 7 February 1951; Economic Conditions Folder, Box 127; Dominican Republic, Narrative Reports, 1950–54; RG 166; NA.

86. John E. Montel to the Department of Agriculture, 1 August 1956; Sugar Folder, Box 246; Dominican Republic, Narrative Reports, 1955–61; RG 166; NA.

87. Richard A. Johnson to the State Department, 3 July 1953; Decimal File 611.39/7-353, Box 2766; Dominican Republic, 1950–54; RG 59; NA.

88. Richard H. Stephens to the State Department, 2 July 1957; Economic Conditions Folder, Box 244; Dominican Republic, Narrative Reports, 1955–61; RG 166; NA.

89. Ibid. The decline in the importance attached to United Kingdom markets was a phenomenon experienced throughout Latin America, not only the Dominican Republic. After World War II, the United States had clearly overshadowed the United Kingdom as the world's strongest economic entity.

90. William Belton to the State Department, 30 April 1952; Sugar Folder, Box 129; Dominican Republic, Narrative Reports, 1950–54; RG 166; NA.

91. Policy Statement Prepared in the State Department, 9 January 1951; Decimal File 611.39/1-951, Box 2766; Dominican Republic, 1950–54; RG 59; NA.

92. Rafael L. Trujillo Molina, "Message before the Dominican National Congress, 27 February 1951," in *Discursos, Mensajes y Proclamas*, vol. 10 (Ciudad Trujillo: Oficina Nacional del Presidente de la República Dominicana, 1952). Between 1950 and 1954, the United Kingdom purchased 75 percent of all Dominican sugar exports. The United Kingdom bought 458,574,319 kilograms for $57,988,346 in 1951, and 444,226,878 kilograms for $42,553,890 in 1952.

93. Stanley G. Slavens to Secretary of State, 4 September 1953; Sugar Folder, Box 128; Dominican Republic, Narrative Reports, 1950–54; RG 166; NA. Although most firms complied with the request, letters without the legend were routinely lost or delayed by the Dominican postal service.

94. Richard A. Johnson to the State Department, 29 September 1953; Decimal File 611.39/9-2953, Box 2766; Dominican Republic, 1950–54; RG 59; NA.

95. William T. Pheiffer to Secretary of State, 30 November 1954; Sugar Folder, Box 128; Dominican Republic, Narrative Reports, 1950–54; RG 166; NA. For several years, Walter Surrey and Monroe Karasik were US State Department officials.

96. William C. Affeld to the State Department, 4 September 1956; Sugar Folder, Box 246; Dominican Republic, Narrative Reports, 1955–61; RG 166; NA.

97. Organization of American States, *Marketing Problems of Sugar at the Hemispheric and World Levels*, p. 8.

98. *Congressional Record*, 30 July 1955, p. 10632.

99. US House Committee on Agriculture, *Amendments to the Sugar Act of 1948*, Hearings, 84th Congress, 2nd Session, 1955, p. 55.

100. James Fred Rippy, "Sugar in Inter-American Relations," *Inter-American Economic Affairs* 9, (spring 1956): 60. Felipe Vicini, a lobbyist for the powerful Vicini family, argued that the Dominican Republic must be given a larger share of the US sugar market in order to prevent the spread of communism.

101. US House Agricultural Committee, *Amendments to the Sugar Act*, Hearings, 1955, p. 14. Poage took over as chairman of the House Agricultural Committee in 1966.

102. Francis L. Spalding to the State Department, 20 May 1957; Decimal File 839.00/5-2057, Box 4382; Dominican Republic, 1950–54; RG 59; NA.

103. Francis L. Spalding to the State Department, 25 April 1957; Decimal File 839.2351/4-2557, Box 4384; Dominican Republic, 1950–54; RG 59; NA.

Chapter 4

Eisenhower and Trujillo, 1958–1960

During the first six years of the Eisenhower administration (1953–1960), the United States publicly and privately supported Trujillo in an attempt to maintain US hegemony in the Dominican Republic. Authoritarian dictators were perceived as efficient obstacles against the spread of communism. As late as 1958, a US diplomat in Ciudad Trujillo stated:

The Dominican Republic has been consistent in its support of United States policies and objectives in the United Nations and other international agencies. Its opposition to the efforts of international communism has been militant and effective. By virtue of its geographic location, it is a potential strong point in the control and defense of the Caribbean area.[1]

Since access to US markets for Dominican sugar, coffee, tobacco, and cacao exports was essential to the Dominican political economy, Trujillo remained a strong advocate of friendly US-Dominican relations. He maintained fifty-four consulates in the United States, more than any other nation. These consulates planted stories with friendly journalists in US newspapers to remind US citizens that the Dominican Republic was a bastion of anticommunism and worthy of receiving a preferential sugar quota.[2] Bernard Diederich asserts that Trujillo spent over $6 million during the 1950s to create a positive image.[3] In 1958, thanks in part to Trujillo's campaigning, the Dominican Republic obtained a basic sugar quota of 58,000 tons.[4]

By 1958, however, Trujillo's attempts to strike at exiled dissidents in the United States, and the improper activities of Dominican agents and officials in the United States, had caused a visible strain in US-Dominican relations. More than any other incident, the Galíndez-Murphy affair had turned Trujillo into an embarrassing political liability for the Eisenhower administration.[5] Whereas the

Galíndez case had lost most of its momentum by the end of 1956, the disappearance (and presumed death) in Ciudad Trujillo in December of Gerald Lester Murphy, the US pilot from Oregon who had flown the doomed Galíndez to the Dominican Republic, created a situation that was difficult for the dictator to rectify with propaganda.[6]

Although the assassination of exiled dissidents (such as Galíndez) was generally accepted, the US public frowned upon the assassination of US citizens overseas. Murphy's parents were "tireless in their demands for justice," and two congressmen from Murphy's home state—Senator Wayne Morse and Representative Charles Porter, who brought the story to major US newspapers—criticized the Eisenhower administration's support of Trujillo.[7] Although the Eisenhower administration felt no desire to change its warm relations with Trujillo, the pressure applied by a large sector of the press and public opinion forced it out of its apathy. On 24 March 1957, therefore, the US government gently pressed Dominican officials for a "truthful account of what happened to Gerald L. Murphy."[8]

Notwithstanding Trujillo's denial of participation in the deaths of Galíndez and Murphy, a series of trails and investigations revealed illegal activities committed by some of Trujillo's agents and public relations men in the United States. US State Department investigations of the Galíndez-Murphy case pointed to the involvement of General Arturo Espaillat, former Dominican Consul in New York City. In addition, John Frank was tried and convicted in November 1957 for failure to register as a Dominican agent.[9] As a result of the Galíndez-Murphy affair, therefore, Trujillo's prestige suffered a heavy blow in the United States, and the Eisenhower administration felt pressure to cool its relations with Trujillo.

During the second half of 1957, therefore, the Eisenhower administration refused or hesitated to act favorably on such normally routine matters as requests for technical assistance, visits by Dominican officials to the United States, and export licenses for military equipment. On 17 January 1958, Trujillo, who was piqued by this cool treatment, indicated to Ambassador Joseph S. Farland that "despite his long-standing friendship he could not continue to cooperate as fully with the United States as in the past" unless the United States was willing to clarify its relationship with the Dominican Republic. As an indication of what this would mean, Trujillo informed Ambassador Farland that the Dominican Republic did not plan to attend February's Law of the Sea Conference in Geneva.[10]

In early 1958, therefore, the Eisenhower administration examined its cool treatment policy toward the Trujillo regime. Although it recognized that Trujillo was an authoritarian thug, the State Department wanted amicable relations with the Dominican Republic because Trujillo permitted a guided missile tracking station on his territory and publicly supported the US in the Cold War. The State Department also came to the conclusion that Trujillo's departure from the Dominican political scene without adequate preparation could cause a political breakdown and run contrary to US hegemonic interests in the Dominican Republic. Thus, the State Department decided: "It is in our interest to carry on normal cooperative relations with the Dominican Republic in as many fields as, and to the extent that, such cooperation can be effectively and mutually beneficial within a framework of mutual respect."[11]   In late 1957, therefore, the State Department authorized Ambassador Farland to discuss the normalization of US-Dominican relations with Trujillo.[12] On 12 February 1958, Farland reported back to the State Department that Trujillo was greatly interested in normalizing US-Dominican relations.[13]

Although the US press and certain US government officials continued to disparage the dictator, Trujillo stated that "he could not and would not in any way alter his friendship and affection toward the United States.[14] Nevertheless, on 18 June, the Dominican Congress passed a resolution asking President Héctor Trujillo to terminate all military cooperation between the United States and the Dominican Republic.[15] Trujillo took this course of action to show his displeasure over the decision of the Command and General Staff College at Fort Leavenworth not to grant a diploma to his son, Rafael Leonidis Trujillo Martínez (Ramfis), because of excessive absences and a low grade point average.[16] Trujillo contended that the United States was intentionally disrupting the relationship that had been the basis of US-Dominican foreign relations since the turn of the century. Ambassador Farland astutely pointed out: "Trujillo's unhappiness is more deeply rooted than simply the trouble involving Ramfis. Trujillo privately has indicated his desire to cooperate fully on all military matters with the United States but feels that we are not reciprocating his desire for cooperation."[17]

US-Dominican relations, however, had weathered worse storms. If nothing else would have occurred to disrupt US-Dominican relations, it is more than likely that the backlash of the Galíndez-Murphy and Ramfis-Leavenworth affairs would have died down and US-Dominican relations would have returned to their habitual warmth. By August 1958, however, events elsewhere challenged the Eisenhower administration's traditional policy toward authoritarian dictators in general, and Trujillo in specific. Liberal democrats were replacing authoritarian dictators throughout Latin America. Venezuela's Rómulo Betancourt, Colombia's Alberto Lleras Camargo, Brazil's Juscelino Kubitschek, and Costa Rica's José Figueres criticized the Eisenhower administration's close relationships with authoritarian dictators, especially Trujillo.[18] In addition, liberal Democrats in the US Senate, including Frank Church, Hubert Humphrey, and John F. Kennedy, argued that the unconditional support of authoritarian dictators was earning the enmity of Latin America's newly elected liberal democrats and endangering US interests in Latin America. When Vice President Richard M. Nixon's motorcade was attacked by an angry mob of demonstrators in Caracas, Venezuela, in May, US policy makers were convinced that something was drastically wrong with US policy in the region.[19] The Eisenhower administration reluctantly began to realize that its support of authoritarian dictators might threaten US interests and possibly produce a potential breeding ground for communism.[20]

Parallel to the Eisenhower administration's halfhearted change in attitude toward the Dominican Republic was Trujillo's growing resentment against the

United States. Trujillo blamed the declining performance of the Dominican economy on the failure of the Eisenhower administration to grant him a greatly expanded sugar quota. Sugar prices, the main source of foreign revenue, plummeted and undermined the economic foundation of the nation. Beginning in 1956, international sugar prices had begun to fall. Although sugar exports increased by 3.5 percent annually between 1955 and 1959, the value of these exports only grew by 1.6 percent.[21] Although Dominican products continued to generate income, the real purchasing power of Dominican exports abroad declined. Foreign deficits for 1956, 1957, and 1958 were $6.6 million, $5.8 million, and $3 million respectively.[22] Since Dominican imports from the United States exceeded Dominican exports to the United States, Foreign Minister Herrera Báez argued that this disequilibrium should be corrected by giving the Dominican Republic a larger sugar quota. In the words of Herrera Báez, "Favorable action by the United States on this proposal would not only equalize the trade situation but would provide positive evidence that matters of inter-American economic cooperation are receiving the attention they deserve."[23] Assistant Secretary of State Rubottom, however, politely informed the Dominicans that although he recognized the importance to the Dominican government of sugar exports, there was nothing that the executive branch could do at the moment to increase the Dominican sugar quota. According to the State Department,

Action to amend the US Sugar Act is solely within the province of the Congress of the United States; the current Sugar Act does not expire until 31 December 1960, but when Congress is ready to consider the Act, the Department of State will be glad to consider the views of the Dominican Government in preparing recommendations for the Congress.[24]

Throughout the rest of 1958, Trujillo did nothing to further annoy the Eisenhower administration. On 7 November, Herrera Báez told Secretary of State Dulles that his government "has traditionally followed a policy of close and friendly cooperation with the United States and that it wished to continue these policies in the future."[25] Thus, although the Eisenhower administration was slowly coming to the conclusion that unconditional support of authoritarian dictators was not in the best interests of the United States, it had not yet devised a policy for dealing with the Trujillo dictatorship. Trujillo, nevertheless, continued to encourage his subjects to believe that he had the complete support of the United States. Farland explained:

It is also believed that the Generalissimo's recent affirmation of warm friendship for the United States is prompted by a desire not to alienate that Government. The Dominican leader undoubtedly realizes now that his defensive position, both psychological and real, would be weakened by outward evidences of loosened Dominican-United States ties.[26]

US-Dominican Foreign Relations, January–December 1959

The political turmoil in the Caribbean region that gathered momentum with the removal of Venezuela's Marco Pérez Jiménez on 23 January 1958 and climaxed with Fidel Castro's overthrow of Fulgencio Batista on 1 January 1959 generated an atmosphere of anxiety and tension in the Dominican Republic.[27] Trujillo, who suddenly found himself one of the few remaining authoritarian dictators in the region, feared an invasion of Dominican exiles supported by Venezuela or Cuba. This atmosphere of insecurity led to increased military expenditures, efforts to purchase military hardware abroad, and the calling up of increasing numbers of men for military service. In addition to a 1959 military budget of $38.7 million, Trujillo committed an extra $50 million for the immediate purchase of arms and the maintenance of a 25,000-man army. Since this was more than 50 percent of the nation's 1959 budget, it exerted a powerful strain on the national economy, which was already suffering from low sugar prices.[28]

Fidel Castro's victory also had a profound impact on the Eisenhower administration. In the aftermath of the Cuban revolution, the United States altered its views on the nature of communism in Latin America. After years of supporting dictators as the best defense against communism, Eisenhower concluded that authoritarian dictators created Batista-like conditions that threatened US hegemony in the region. Eisenhower came to view Trujillo with increasing distaste, "an embarrassment, an awkward inheritance from an earlier time, now lingering too long and imperiling the future and unwittingly preparing the way for Castroism."[29] In the words of Rubottom: "When dealing with Dominican matters, we must always keep in mind our national security interests. Hispaniola plays an important part in our defense strategy of the Western Hemisphere. However, we must avoid giving the impression that the United States favors dictatorships in Latin America."[30] Terrified that the Cuban revolution might become the model for revolution in the Dominican Republic, Eisenhower decided to explore democratic alternatives to authoritarian dictatorship in the Dominican Republic.[31]

The fact that friendly advice did not convince Batista to relinquish the reins of government until it was too late was not lost on the Eisenhower administration. Since the US supplied Batista's army, the Cuban revolutionaries blamed the US for the Batista army's atrocities. In February 1959, therefore, the State Department suspended military aid to the Dominican Republic. According to the State Department,

Export licenses for combat equipment, military weapons and ammunition, spare parts for combat equipment, combat aircraft, military trainer aircraft and armed patrol vessels will continue to be withheld except for reasonable amounts of necessary spare parts for all types military aircraft now in possession of Dominican and Cuban air forces.[32]

Believing that it could reason with the Trujillo regime, the Eisenhower administration remained unwilling to play either of its two most powerful potential trump cards in its relationship with the dictator—the famous *cuota y flota* (quota and flotilla) threats. Washington's most powerful tactics of persuasion with the Trujillo regime were the threats of a suspended sugar quota and US military intervention. Instead, US policy makers believed that other, more subtle, methods (such as secret diplomatic visits) could be employed to achieve US policy goals. In addition, congressional legislation (not executive decisions) determined the sugar quota. It was unlikely that Eisenhower would have been able to push anti-Trujillo sugar legislation through a Democratic-controlled congress filled with the dictator's supporters and beneficiaries.[33] Apprehensive policy makers also feared that if they tinkered with the sugar quota, Trujillo would force the removal of the US guided missile tracking station in Sabana de la Mar, which they considered a strategic military asset.[34] A National Intelligence Estimate explained: "While Trujillo remains in power, no major opposition to the present US military arrangements is likely, although Trujillo, as in the past, will probably use the military facilities issues as a bargaining tool for gaining US cooperation in other fields."[35]

Trujillo, therefore, was confident that the United States would not reduce his preferential sugar quota as long as the Eisenhower administration considered the guided missile tracking station a strategic military interest. Nevertheless, he was incensed by Eisenhower's refusal to sell him all of the weapons that he desired. Trujillo had purchased military equipment at favorable prices from the United States for years. After Eisenhower limited weapons sales to Trujillo, he purchased them at inflated prices on the European market.[36] On 16 March, Manuel de Moya, who complained bitterly to Farland about the suspension of military aid to the Dominican Republic, "reiterated the fact of Dominican friendship for the US, but made note of his government's growing concern over lack of reciprocity therein."[37]

By this time, however, the Eisenhower administration desperately needed regional allies in its struggle against Castro. In the name of anti-Castroism, the Eisenhower administration began to woo Betancourt and the Latin American liberal democrats. The price of obtaining the support of Betancourt, Figueres, and other Latin American liberals against Castro was an anti-Trujillo foreign policy. Within a year, Eisenhower asserted: "I would be willing to trade several military bases for a strong OAS determined to hang together" against Castro.[38] The Eisenhower administration, therefore, continued its cold shoulder treatment toward the Trujillo regime.

In June, as Trujillo hammered away with his incessant demands for a larger sugar quota, the situation in the Dominican Republic became more complicated. On 14 June, fifty-six Dominican exiles led by Enrique Jiménez Moya invaded the Dominican Republic at Constanza, Maimón, and Estero Hondo by air. The insurgents, who had the material and moral support of the Cuban and Venezuelan governments, came from Cuba on planes chartered in Miami. Since the Dominican *campesinos* (rural folk) gave "full support and allegiance to Trujillo," the invasion failed and Trujillo's forces quickly rounded up the rebels.[39] Facing hostility from Venezuela and Cuba, and the cold shoulder from the United States,

Trujillo expanded his ruinously expensive campaign of arms procurement from Europe to bolster his hold on power. In the words of Ambassador Farland:

Failure to find some economic solution may lead the GODR [Dominican government] into the disastrous temptation of a resort to external military action against its area opponents, not only to remove what it considers the threat to its own continued existence, but also as a means of relieving itself of the economic and financial strains of continued and costly military preparedness.[40]

Farland believed that tension and unrest would continue in the Caribbean region.

Reacting to the turmoil in the Caribbean, on 12 August 1959, the Foreign Ministers of the Western Hemisphere met at Santiago, Chile, where they adopted a resolution calling on all Latin American governments to guarantee a system of social justice and human rights for their citizens. The Declaration of Santiago stated that "the perpetuation of a dictatorship in power is incompatible with the establishment of democracy in Latin America."[41] Within days, however, new turmoil broke out in the Caribbean. In retribution for Castro's participation in the June invasion, Trujillo sponsored an invasion of Cuban exiles at Trinidad, Cuba. Trujillo looked ridiculous, however, when it turned out that his so-called Cuban exiles were actually Castro's agents. Trujillo's failure at Trinidad, the invasion at Constanza, Maimón, and Estero Hondo, and the wave of democratization in Latin America stimulated more dissent against the Trujillo dictatorship. By September, internal clandestine opposition against Trujillo was greater that at any previous time.[42]

In September, faced with a difficult international situation and a deteriorating internal situation, Trujillo once again tried to improve his relations with the United States. In an effort to curry favor with the Eisenhower administration, Trujillo promised that the US military missions would never be expelled from the Dominican Republic. By the end of the month, however, when Trujillo learned that the United States had supplied Betancourt's Venezuela with a new submarine, while maintaining the arms embargo against the Dominican Republic, he suspended his financial support of the US military missions in Ciudad Trujillo. Trujillo believed that the United States was intentionally thwarting his efforts to improve the Dominican Republic's defensive position in the face of international threats.[43]

Meanwhile, the Eisenhower administration continued to distance itself from the Trujillo regime. In order to protect US national security interests, the State Department decided to maintain official contacts with Trujillo's government at "their present almost minimal level" while discreetly making contact with dissident elements.[44] Ambassador Farland was informed to be cool and correct in his dealings with Trujillo, but to keep in touch with the dissidents. Farland, who believed that Trujillo would never leave the island voluntarily and that the dictator's death was a precondition for any change of government, contended that the search for viable democratic alternatives to the Trujillo regime was not going to be easy.[45] Although most Dominican campesinos supported Trujillo or were apolitical, many members of the gente de la segunda supported Trujillo because their wealth and association with the Trujillo regime tied them irrevocably to the Trujillo era.[46] In the words of US Chargé d'Affaires Harry Lofton,

The majority of commercial and professional Dominicans probably harbor no personal love for Trujillo as there are few that the 29-year Era has not touched in some manner. They are, however, quick to emphasize that their economic well-being derives from the Trujillo regime and openly state that they would be most reluctant to move against it or effect drastic changes, even after Trujillo's demise.[47]

Farland pointed out, however, that some professionals and members of the gente de la primera represented opposition groups that were anticommunist and pro-US.[48]

In November 1959, the Eisenhower administration decided that it would have to take a more active position regarding the formation of the post-Trujillo period. It argued that, by eliminating and weakening the moderate, pro-US political opposition at home, Trujillo was providing a breeding ground for communism.[49] Therefore, in the words of Rubottom:

In view of a distinct possibility that the Government of Generalissimo Rafael Trujillo might face a crisis or fall before the end of 1960, it is of great importance that the United States work, without exposing itself to charges of violation of non-intervention commitments, towards insuring insofar as possible that any successor government is reasonably friendly to the United States and in harmony with US objectives.[50]

The year 1959, then, ended with US-Dominican relations full of tension and uncertainty.

US-Dominican Foreign Relations, January–June 1960

In early 1960, the Eisenhower administration decided that US interest demanded Trujillo's removal. On 14 January 1960, the National Security Council, although not directly calling for participation in the overthrow of Trujillo, emphasized the need to promote and stimulate a new civilian or military leadership in the Dominican Republic that would be prepared to take power upon the disappearance of Trujillo.[51] US policy sought to ensure, in the event of Trujillo's downfall, that the successor regime would be friendly to US interests. Although the State Department advocated the maintenance of official contacts with the Dominican government, it discreetly encouraged the formation of noncommunist business, professional, and academic opposition groups. In early February, President Eisenhower asked the Special Group, his select clique of national security advisors, to consider covert aid to Trujillo's enemies.[52]

Meanwhile, Trujillo cracked down on his opponents, charging that they were engaged in a conspiracy to overthrow his government. A notable change in the nation's political atmosphere developed as members of almost every prominent

Dominican family were seized, in many cases with great brutality, and subjected to heavy fines and jail sentences. For example, Ramfis's brother-in-law, Guido d'Alessandro, was among the fifteen hundred people arrested and charged with plotting against Trujillo. The rising tide of discontent that spread throughout the Dominican Republic's influential commercial, professional, and intellectual classes was enhanced by an economic crisis caused by low export prices for sugar and the tremendous drain on foreign exchange caused by vast arms purchases. This was the first time that Trujillo had encountered anything other than sporadic opposition to his regime from this segment of the population.[53]

Because of the growing political and economic crisis faced by the dictator, especially the loss of US patronage, Trujillo tried to reinforce his hold on power by searching for support from the Roman Catholic Church, one of his traditional corporatist pillars of support. Trujillo demanded that the Church grant him the title Benefactor of the Dominican Church, but the bishops refused.[54] On 31 January, a pastoral letter from the nation's six Roman Catholic bishops was read in all Dominican churches. This letter, which reaffirmed basic human rights, stressed the Church's determination to alleviate the suffering of the Dominican people and urged Trujillo to end the violence that plagued the nation. The increasing enmity of the Catholic clergy—many of whom were Spanish or US citizens—convinced Trujillo that repressive measures also needed to be taken to control the Catholic Church. This break between the Church and the Trujillo government allowed opponents of the Trujillo regime to organize within the Church.[55]

The Eisenhower administration was alarmed by Trujillo's crackdown on dissidents. The members of the commercial, professional, and intellectual classes arrested were the very people that the State Department had pinned its hopes on for a noncommunist government after Trujillo's departure. Eisenhower feared that if the arrests continued, any successor to the Trujillo regime might resemble the Castro regime in Cuba. In the words of Under Secretary of State for Political Affairs Livingston Merchant:

We viewed the situation in the Dominican Republic with concern because Trujillo had put in jail a large number of the moderate element. It was from this moderate, liberal element that we hoped a successor to Trujillo would come. If this element were eliminated and Trujillo disappeared from the scene, it was possible that some Castro-like solution would be forthcoming.[56]

Disturbed by the situation in the Dominican Republic, on 9 February 1960, the Eisenhower administration sent a secret mission led by Senator George Smathers (D-FL) to Ciudad Trujillo to discuss with Trujillo the prospects for stepping down and permitting free elections. Smathers arrived in Ciudad Trujillo with William Pawley, an intimate friend of Eisenhower and Trujillo, and Charles "Bebe" Rebozo, a bosom buddy of Vice President Nixon. This was the first of three clandestine efforts to convince Trujillo to resign and leave the country voluntarily. During the meeting, Smathers asked Trujillo "to arrange while still alive for transition to moderate democratic government."[57]   Trujillo unconvincingly responded that he would hold free and democratic elections. Nevertheless, since no reference to the content of the conversation between Smathers and Trujillo appeared in the Dominican press, most Dominicans had the impression that Trujillo was receiving public support from a prominent US politician, precisely at a difficult moment. After the meeting, Trujillo ushered everyone into the National Palace's Chapel and had photos taken of himself accompanied by Smathers, Rebozo, and Dearborn. In the words of Dearborn, "the purpose was to publish pictures showing Trujillo, United States, and Catholic Church as happy triumvirate."[58]

The Eisenhower administration and the Organization of American States (OAS), however, were not fooled by Trujillo's antics. According to Dearborn, who doubted Trujillo's promise to hold free and democratic elections, the central issue in US policy toward the Dominican Republic came down to "whether we need Trujillo's help against international communism sufficiently to support a regime characterized by such unsavory practices."[59] Meanwhile, Venezuelan Ambassador Marcos Falcón Briseño, who thought that the Trujillo regime had no redeeming qualities, demanded an official investigation of flagrant human rights abuses in the Dominican Republic. On 16 February, the OAS passed a resolution to send an Inter-American Peace Committee to investigate Venezuela's accusations. The Dominican government, however, announced that it would not allow the committee to visit the Dominican Republic. Dominican representative Virgilio Díaz Ordóñez called the decision "the official end of the principle of non-intervention."[60] Trujillo obviously felt that he had been abandoned by the United States and the OAS. An editorial in El Caribe reported: "[US Secretary of State] Herter has become just as intolerable as Betancourt. The only thing that the United States has not done to us yet is drop an atomic bomb on our country."[61]

Realizing that the Smathers mission had failed to impress upon Trujillo the urgency of resigning and instituting the democratization process, on 26 March, Eisenhower sent a second clandestine mission headed by retired General Edwin Norman Clark, who was Eisenhower's aide during World War II. Although the conversations between Clark and Trujillo were amiable, Clark was unable to convince the dictator of the importance of instituting a genuine democratization process. Realizing that his mission was a failure, Clark recommended that Eisenhower initiate a more aggressive policy to overthrow Trujillo and replace his regime with a democratically elected government.[62] Herter, who agreed with Clark, informed Eisenhower:

There may not be time quietly to encourage a moderate, pro-United States leadership among the civilian and military dissident elements to take over in the event of the flight, assassination, death, or overthrow of Trujillo—as was visualized in the existing Dominican Republic contingency plan discussed with you and with the National Security Council on 14 January.[63]

The National Security Council endorsed the proposal. Treasury Secretary

Douglas Dillon explained: "If Trujillo could be removed from power in the Dominican Republic, while pro-Castro elements were prevented from seizing power in that country, our anti-Castro campaign throughout Latin America would receive a great boost."[64] Vice President Richard Nixon, however, reminded everyone that anticommunism had a higher priority than democracy. The primary US concern in the Dominican Republic was to prevent pro-Castro groups from seizing power.[65] As political scientist Piero Gleijeses has effectively pointed out: "The Americans wanted anti-Communist stability more than democracy in the Dominican Republic as well as in the rest of the hemisphere."[66]

On 25 April 1960, therefore, Clark, Herter, and Eisenhower discussed the possibility of a "plan for removing Trujillo from control of the country, and to establish in his position a controlling junta which would immediately call for free elections and make an attempt to get the country on a truly democratic basis."[67] Farland was instructed to make contact with moderate dissident elements and offer them immediate diplomatic recognition and US military assistance should they come to power. A few days later, Farland made his initial contacts with a moderate, pro-US group of dissidents, led by disgruntled elite Juan Tomás Díaz, that had solicited rifles with telescopic sights. Farland was aware that these conspirators planned to assassinate Trujillo and he approved.[68] According to the Church report, "Increasing American awareness of Trujillo's brutality and fear that it would lead to a Castro-type revolution caused United States' officials to consider various plans to hasten his abdication or downfall."[69]

Reacting to increased US hostility and internal dissent, Trujillo employed a variety of schemes, ploys, and tricks to convince the United States that his regime was moving along the path toward democracy, while simultaneously warning Farland that the Eisenhower administration's hostility toward the Trujillo regime could force the Dominican Republic into the Soviet camp.[70] In March, as part of his vociferous effort to persuade the United States that he was liberalizing his regime, Trujillo freed the surviving invaders from the Constanza, Maimón, and Estero Hondo fiasco. Six days later, he announced that state lands would be distributed to the peasants. On 2 April, he resigned as leader of the Partido Dominicano and announced that he would welcome the formation of opposition political parties.[71] On 7 April, he announced that he would guarantee free national elections in 1962.[72]

Playing on US fears of communism, Trujillo consistently argued that the only alternative to authoritarian rule in the Dominican Republic was communism.[73] In order to convince the Eisenhower administration that the only organized opposition was communist, Trujillo allowed Máximo Antonio López Molina and Andrés Ramos Peguero, the exiled leaders of the Marxist-inspired Movimiento Popular Dominicano (MPD), to return to the Dominican Republic and hold political rallies.[74] He also instructed Radio Caribe, his state-controlled news service, to institute broadcasts that were pro-Soviet and anticlerical in nature. Trujillo replaced United Press International (UPI) news releases on Radio Caribe with Tass news releases. In addition, Trujillo insinuated that he would give his country to the Soviets and Cubans if the United States broke diplomatic relations and joined the other Latin American states in collective action against his country.[75] Trujillo, however, had no intention of turning the Dominican Republic over to anybody. It was merely a bluff.

Trujillo's threats and deceptions, however, backfired. By linking the problems in Cuba and the Dominican Republic, Trujillo had reinforced Eisenhower's opinion that a solution to the Castro problem was linked to the Trujillo problem. Considering Castro and Trujillo, Eisenhower stated that he wanted "to see both of them sawed off."[76] According to Eisenhower, "If a solution can be found to the emotionally-charged problem in the Dominican Republic, whose regime is universally hated in Latin America, there is room for hope that we will get some support in facing up to the Castro dictatorship."[77] Eisenhower, therefore, believed that the findings of the special OAS Committee on Inter-American Peace would assist US policy in Latin America by providing the impetus for a similar finding against the Castro regime.[78]

On 8 June, the OAS Committee on Inter-American Peace accused the Trujillo regime of gross human rights violations and blamed Trujillo for a significant amount of the tension in the region. Many of the fifteen hundred people arrested and charged with plotting against Trujillo in January 1960 had been repeatedly tortured. One of the Trujillo regime's most popular torture devices was the *pulpo* (octopus), an electrical apparatus with long tentacles that were attached to all parts of the body and a leather cap that was attached to the skull by means of screws.[79]

In an attempt to counteract the negative publicity, Trujillo invited a group of international law experts to the Dominican Republic. The group was led by ex-President Emilio Portes Gil of Mexico, a close friend of Vice President Joaquín Balaguer. On 21 June, the group of legal experts decided that the OAS committee had exceeded its mandate and had criticized the Dominican government unjustly.[80] Realizing too late that his communist scare tactics and blackmail attempts were having the opposite of their intended effect, Trujillo abandoned his overtly belligerent policy.

Trujillo's inconsistent policy toward the United States needs to be explained. In the words of a US diplomat in Ciudad Trujillo, "Most of Trujillo's behavior can be explained as an over-reaction to a severe inferiority complex. Because of his compulsive need to attain greater and greater heights (vicious cycle) he is very sensitive to criticism and is frequently prone to be impatient with obstacles in his path, which results in the frequent use of force to achieve his ends."[81] The problem, however, was more complicated than a severe inferiority complex. Trujillo's inconsistent policy was also the result of two conflicting and ideologically antagonistic sets of advisors: Balagueristas, led by Vice President Joaquín Balaguer, who advocated reconciliation with the Catholic Church and the United States; and Espaillatistas, led by Servicio de Inteligencia Militar (SIM) director Arturo Espaillat, whose ideas stimulated local and international violence as well as verbal attacks against the United States and the Roman Catholic Church.[82]

One of Trujillo's most significant miscalculations resulted from an incomplete blending of ideas from the two factions. By June 1960, Trujillo, following the advice of the Balagueristas, desperately wanted to restore friendly relations with the United States. He mistakenly believed, however, that Rómulo Betancourt's condemnation of his regime was responsible for the Eisenhower administration's hostility toward his regime. Trujillo, therefore, believed that Betancourt's immediate removal from the Caribbean political spectrum would improve his chances of restoring amicable relations with the United States. On 24 June, Trujillo's agents attempted to assassinate Betancourt by planting a bomb near his car in Caracas. Ironically, Trujillo's blundered effort to improve relations with the United States served to further damage US-Dominican relations and increase Venezuelan condemnation of Trujillo's regime in the OAS.[83]

US-Dominican Foreign Relations, July–August 1960

On 6 July, in a bid to punish Fidel Castro, the US Congress amended the Sugar Act of 1948 to permit the President to determine the sugar quota for Cuba. Eisenhower immediately canceled Cuba's quota.[84] This amounted to virtually complete economic sanctions against Cuba. The Eisenhower administration blocked the world's largest sugar producer from access to the world's largest consumer market. This meant that the United States had to find other sources for the approximately three million tons of sugar that Cuba had provided annually. The Sugar Act authorized the redistribution of the former Cuban quota, the so-called Cuban windfall, among the other sugar exporting nations already partaking of the sugar quota. By law, the President was forced to allocate a share of the Cuban windfall to the Dominican Republic, but delayed authorizing its purchase.[85] Policy revolving around the sugar quota once again took center stage in US-Dominican relations.

The suspension of Cuba's quota was a very forceful reminder to Trujillo of the potential power that the United States could wield over another nation's political economy. Nevertheless, Trujillo stood to gain an economic bonanza because of the redistribution of the Cuban sugar quota. In 1960, the Cuban windfall added 321,857 tons to Trujillo's basic quota of 130,000 tons.[86] Under different circumstances, the Dominican Republic would have been the perfect new supplier; after all, in 1957 the Dominican Republic had been described as the *isla del azúcar* (sugar island).[87] For Eisenhower, who was trying to achieve OAS unity against Cuba, it was particularly embarrassing to be compelled by US congressional legislation to provide a sugar bonus worth more than $30 million in 1960 and $140 million in 1961 to a country in which Trujillo owned more than 60 percent of the sugar production.

Thus, the Eisenhower administration was faced with a serious dilemma. How could it justify increased US sugar purchases from Trujillo, while at the same time eliminating Castro from the US sugar market? The State Department wanted to change the legal requirement for the purchase of sugar from the Dominican Republic. According to Herter, the United States would "lose prestige if we bought sugar from the Dominican Republic after refusing to buy it from Cuba."[88] Fearing that the OAS member states would perceive the reallotment of a large portion of the Cuban quota to the Dominican Republic as indicative of US support of the Trujillo regime, at one point (in a fit of rage) Eisenhower said that if the law was not changed, he would "simply refuse to buy Dominican sugar."[89] He claimed that even if impeachment proceedings were brought against him, they would take longer than his term had to run.[90]

Trujillo's domestic political allies in the US Congress, however, fought Eisenhower's campaign to deny the Dominican Republic its legal allotment of the Cuban windfall. Trujillo had numerous supporters—many of whom he had bribed—among the conservative, democratic, southern congressmen who were deeply involved in agricultural matters. According to Dominican Minister of the Interior General Arturo Espaillat: "Many of the North American Congressmen were provided with female companionship during their visits to the Dominican Republic. Senator Ellender entered into a relationship with one of Trujillo's prostitutes, who was promptly dispatched to the Dominican embassy in Washington so that she might be more accessible to the Senator."[91] Congressman Harold Cooley (D-NC) claimed that the Department of Agriculture's failure to authorize the purchase of Dominican sugar was "a direct flaunting of the will of the Congress."[92] Senator Allen J. Ellender (D-LA), the chairman of the Senate Agricultural Committee, claimed that the attempt to deny the expanded sugar quota to Trujillo was a deliberate attack, completely without justification, on a friendly government. He called the State Department's policy "putrid."[93] Since Eisenhower knew that Trujillo had bribed the key legislators on the agricultural committees, he eventually tried to circumvent their authority.[94]

Although obviously playing from a weaker hand, Trujillo intensified his vigorous propaganda campaign to secure his portion of the windfall quota. On 3 August, in an attempt to convince the Eisenhower administration that he was moving the Dominican Republic along the path toward democracy, Trujillo's brother Héctor resigned the presidency and Vice President Joaquín Balaguer, an intellectual, became president.[95] Trujillo believed that Balaguer would provide an appropriate image for the liberalization of the regime. According to Balaguer, however,

This was the saddest and most graceless moment of my political career. I made no effort to obtain the presidency, which I received not as a reward for my political labors, but rather as a transitory and dubious compromise imposed on the Trujillo regime because of the severity of the international repudiation of the Trujillo regime caused by its numerous errors.[96]

In an attempt to convince the US policy makers that Trujillo was about to abandon the country, Balaguer named Trujillo Dominican Ambassador to the United Nations. In an effort to further the impression that no members of the Trujillo family were running the country, General José García Trujillo was replaced as Minister of War by General José René "Pupo" Román Fernández. Behind the scenes, however, Trujillo remained in control.[97] According to a US diplomat in Ciudad Trujillo, these changes were merely "a desire on the part of the GODR to make it appear Trujillo's influence is on the wane in order to influence the San José MFM [Meeting of Foreign Ministers] not to impose sanctions against it."[98] When Eisenhower later recalled this incident, he sarcastically remarked, "Who does he [Trujillo] think that he is kidding."[99]

The perplexity of US sugar quota legislation, however, was intensified at the Sixth Meeting of Foreign Ministers in San José, Costa Rica, when Venezuelan Foreign Minister Marcos Falcón Briseño strongly recommended suspending diplomatic and economic relations with the Dominican Republic. Although he did not want to go as far as suspending diplomatic and economic sanctions, on 19 August, Secretary of State Herter informed CIA Director Allen Dulles, "If the United States continued to oppose breaking off relations, we would run the risk of becoming isolated in the Western Hemisphere and give the impression that we were playing ball with the dictators."[100] Meanwhile, Dominican Foreign Minister Herrera Báez left the OAS conference early. Herrera Báez declared: "We are shocked by the indifference to the spread of communism in the Caribbean in countries where liberty had been a cherished asset. The measures taken against us are illegal, unless they receive authorization from the United Nations."[101]

Nevertheless, on 20 August, the OAS voted unanimously to impose diplomatic and economic sanctions against the Dominican Republic. Trujillo's regime was energetically condemned for acts of hemispheric aggression. All OAS-member states were obliged to break diplomatic relations with the Dominican Republic and impose economic sanctions.[102] On 26 August, the United States formally broke diplomatic relations with the Dominican Republic. It was the first time in more than forty years that the United States had broken relations with a Latin American nation. The State Department contended that the unanimous decision in the OAS to impose diplomatic and economic sanctions on the Dominican Republic would facilitate the possibility of imposing similar sanctions on the Castro regime.[103]

The economic sanctions proposed by the OAS, however, posed a greater problem for the United States. No specific reference was made to sugar at the San José Conference. In San José, the only economic sanctions discussed were arms exports. Regardless, the reduction of the Dominican sugar quota could only be achieved by congressional approval. On 23 August, therefore, Eisenhower asked Congress for authority to obtain sugar from suppliers other than the Dominican Republic, pointing out that the legally mandated new Dominican quota "would give that country a large sugar bonus seriously embarrassing to the United States in the conduct of our foreign relations throughout the Hemisphere."[104] Eisenhower also wanted to prohibit nations that received US aid from purchasing Dominican sugar.[105]

Eisenhower's message provoked a heated debate between the Eisenhower administration and Trujillo's friends in Congress. On 25 August, Senator Ellender criticized the State Department for delaying purchases of Dominican sugar. Warning that this attitude would create a second Cuba, Ellender claimed that the

United States would benefit from "a Trujillo in all of the South and Central American countries."[106] Another friend of Trujillo, Senator Olin Johnson (D-SC), claimed that the United States had stabbed Trujillo in the back. According to Johnson: "Stupidity and idealism have forced us to turn our backs on the anti-communists and support forces that want to overthrow governments that have been very friendly toward the United States."[107] The administrator of the US-owned Central Romana sugar mill, C. Douglas Debevoise, publicly came out in support of Trujillo. He claimed that the communists would take power in the Dominican Republic if the US Congress refused to grant the Trujillo regime its share of the Cuban windfall. He urged Congress to refuse Eisenhower's proposal, saying that to accept it would cause economic chaos in the Dominican Republic.[108] Trujillo's supporters were strong enough to ensure that the sugar issue would not be resolved before Congress adjourned on 1 September. Congressional inaction left standing a law requiring the purchase of 451,857 tons of Dominican sugar at preferential prices in 1960. Given the difficulty Eisenhower had in trying to exclude Trujillo from the windfall quota, it is no wonder that he never tried to seize Trujillo's basic quota. Because of congressional legislation, Eisenhower's hands were tied.

US-Dominican Foreign Relations, September–December 1960

Without a doubt, one of the most important pending matters affecting US-Dominican relations at the beginning of September was the allocation of the 322,000 tons of windfall quota sugar assigned to the Dominican Republic. Nobody was sure when the Dominican Republic would be able to ship its sugar to the United States. Because of the suspense surrounding the issue, the US consul in Ciudad Trujillo speculated about Trujillo's thoughts concerning the matter. What follows is the consul's piquant rendition of Trujillo's thoughts.

This thing is more serious than I suspected. Despite all the time and money devoted to the "progressive democratization" theme, the conciliatory words and proposals I gave the San José Conference through Herrera Báez, and the inside conciliatory efforts of the Paraguayan and Brazilian Foreign Ministers, the 6th MFM broke diplomatic relations with me. However, my friends in Congress were able to forestall a serious loss in the US sugar market. The propaganda campaign I entrusted to Radio Caribe to make it appear I would go Communist out of spite backfired. I'm still not positive I'm going to get the sugar but it appears President Eisenhower will be forced to permit me to sell it to the US. My ability to achieve this victory over Ike has enhanced my prestige. While all of this is going on if I can just unseat those bastards Betancourt, Lleras, and Duvalier all will be well. If in fact I do sell the sugar maybe things will get back on the tracks. If not, I'll really pull the plugs on American enterprises here and dispose of my enemies at the same time. I'll sell the Dominicans on the theory we can live without the Americans and try to put the blame on them for the unprofitable economic and political pressures.[109]

After weeks of speculation, on 26 September, the Eisenhower administration grudgingly accepted the reality (and legality) of US sugar quota legislation and officially authorized the purchase of the Dominican Republic's share of the windfall quota. Irritated, but not defeated, by executive decree Eisenhower imposed a $0.02 per pound special tax on the Dominican windfall quota, which was equal to the US premium. In the fourth quarter of 1960, this action deprived Trujillo of $13 million at a time when the economy was in a sharp decline; moreover, it struck directly at Trujillo's personal financial base.[110] According to the State Department, "Depriving the Dominican Government of the US premium price would be in accord with the spirit of the San José Meeting of Foreign Ministers and would, we believe, be well received in most of the Latin American countries."[111] It also exacerbated Trujillo's economic woes and proved to have a powerful psychological effect on the dictator. According to Howard Wiarda, Eisenhower's failure to concede the economic benefits of the greatly expanded sugar quota "was the proverbial straw which broke the back of the Trujillo regime."[112] The sugar tax, plus the cold shoulder treatment from the Eisenhower administration and the Latin American nations, severely weakened Trujillo's legitimacy and cast him in the role of Caribbean desperado.

Trujillo was infuriated by Eisenhower's circumvention of sugar quota legislation. During his remaining nine months in power, Trujillo's foreign policy was dominated by attempts to remove the diplomatic and economic sanctions, especially the punitive tax on the Dominican share of the windfall quota. Heavy pressure was placed on US businessmen working in the Dominican Republic to verbally support Trujillo.[113] In a futile attempt to improve his image and bolster his grip on power, Trujillo continued to spend millions of dollars on bribes and propaganda campaigns.[114] According to a US diplomat: "That the breaking of diplomatic relations was a severe psychological jolt to him is quite evident from the extraordinary homage ceremonies he has engaged in the DR to save his wounded ego."[115] Trujillo anxiously awaited a Kennedy victory in the November presidential elections in the mistaken belief that a Democratic victory at the polls would produce a friendlier US foreign policy toward his regime.[116]

Regardless, Trujillo continued to export sugar to the United States. As Table 4.1 shows, even after paying the $0.02 per pound fee, the rise in world sugar prices helped foreign exchange earnings. Consequently, the continued purchase of Dominican sugar hurt US relations with Venezuela. In the words of Weikko Forsten, a US diplomat in Caracas, "The truth and reason for the purchase is not being comprehended."[117] Although the $0.02 per pound tax ensured that Trujillo would not gain additional profit from preferential sugar sales, Falcon Briseño pointed out that Trujillo had won a psychological victory. He claimed that the purchase of Dominican sugar, albeit without the preferential differential, was in violation of the spirit of the San José Resolution. On 1 October, therefore, Venezuela asked for an immediate vote in the OAS to expand the economic sanctions against the Dominican Republic.[118] When Eisenhower eventually met with Falcón Briseño, the president expressed his unhappiness that congressional legislation required continued Dominican sugar purchases.[119] In an attempt to justify US policy, Dillon explained that the United States did not want to take "concrete moves against the Dominican Republic just at present, since no successor to Trujillo is ready to take power, and the result might be to bring an individual of the Castro stripe into power there."[120]

Table 4.1
Dominican Sugar Production and Exports, 1958–1960

Year	Production (in tons)	Exports (in tons)	Value (in dollars)
1958	690,792	651,500	54,500,000
1959	694,177	626,000	45,700,000
1960	1,099,129	1,060,000	85,200,000

Source: John Hugh Crimmins to Robert Woodward, 6 March 1962; Decimal File 839.235/3-662, Box 2459; Dominican Republic, 1960–63; R. 59; NA.

Therefore, on 26 October, Eisenhower decided to send his third emissary, William Pawley (a former diplomat, prominent businessman, and Trujillo's friend), to Ciudad Trujillo to convince Trujillo to resign.[121] Pessimistic about Pawley's ability to convince Trujillo to resign, on 29 October, Assistant Secretary of State for Latin American Affairs Thomas Mann asked Henry Dearborn for his opinion about removing Trujillo from power. The Deputy Chief of Mission's candid response was as follows:

I believe the only reason the Generalissimo might leave is fear of imminent death—and this is not certain. For this reason I think the Dominicans themselves have got to do the persuading. We can help them do it in a number of ways, some of which are probably not legally possible for us. It would be better for the United States, the OAS, and the Dominican Republic if the Dominicans could execute Trujillo before he can leave the island. With his millions, Trujillo could dedicate the rest of his life to destabilizing the Dominican government, assassinating his enemies, and causing untold chaos in the Caribbean basin. If I were a Dominican, and thank God I'm not, I would consider the assassination of Trujillo as the first step toward a democratic government and would consider it my Christian duty to kill Trujillo. If you remember the tale of Dracula, you will remember that it was necessary to drive a stake through his heart to stop him from committing further crimes.[122]

Dearborn believed that the best solution to the problem was Trujillo's assassination. As long as Trujillo remained in the Dominican Republic and maintained his economic domination, Dearborn concluded that Trujillo will "continue his political domination whether he is President or dogcatcher."[123]

Eisenhower, however, still hoped that Trujillo could be convinced to resign. Unfortunately, Pawley, who conducted his visit in mid-November after Kennedy won the presidential election, was unable to convince Trujillo to resign. Trujillo told Pawley: "You can come in here with the Marines, and you can come in here with the Army, and you can come in here with the Navy or even the atomic bomb, but I'll never leave here unless I go on a stretcher."[124] Pawley's attempt to convince Trujillo to resign, just like the previous Smathers and Clark visits, was a complete failure. Believing that he had brought his nation great material progress, a Dominican Republic without his leadership was inconceivable to the aging dictator. According to Trujillo: "*Yo lo hice todo solo, todo solo* (I did it alone, all alone)."[125]

Following Kennedy's narrow victory on 7 November and Pawley's disappointing mission, all plans regarding Trujillo and Castro were put on hold until the Democratic Party's transition team could evaluate the situation. Although Trujillo held municipal elections on 14 December, hardly anybody in the State Department believed that the elections were free and democratic. At the same time, Trujillo continued full speed ahead with his authoritarian and insidious practices to maintain control.[126] The arms embargo did not deny Trujillo the weapons he desired. The majority of arms that Trujillo purchased continued to arrive from Europe, and Trujillo had his own arms factories in the Dominican Republic. According to a US diplomat, "The purely economic and financial effect of the limited US embargoes imposed as a result of the decisions taken at the VI MFM in San José, Costa Rica in August of 1960 has been very slight and has done very little if any damage to the economy. However their political and psychological value has been of quite considerable importance."[127]

As the Dominican political economy began to deteriorate at a more rapid pace, both Dominican and US policy makers became increasingly jittery. The Trujillo family was losing confidence in its ability to hang on to the reins of power. By the end of 1960, the Trujillos had smuggled over $135 million out of the country. They were using their earnings from the sugar industry to convert their vast fortune into dollars.[128] An open letter to Trujillo from Partido Revolucionario Dominicano (PRD) leader Juan Bosch, dated 27 February 1961, epitomized the new mood in the Dominican Republic. Bosch explained that Trujillo's days in power were limited because Castro's victory irrevocably changed the political climate in the Caribbean. Bosch wrote:

In this historical moment, your life can be compared to that of a strong, agile, aggressive, ferocious shark accustomed to being the terror of the seas for many years. An unexpected cataclysm has changed the sea water to sulfuric acid and now the shark can no longer continue living. If you admit that the political climate in Latin America has changed, and that in this new environment there is no place for you, and you emigrate to waters that closer approximate your personality, then our country can celebrate the next twenty-seventh of February in peace and harmony. If, however, you do not admit the change in the political climate, and you continue your tyranny, the next anniversary of the country's independence day will be filled with blood and chaos.[129]

Although Trujillo clung tenaciously to the reins of power at the end of 1960, both Bosch and Eisenhower sensed that the dictator was losing control.

NOTES

1. Henry S. Hammond to the State Department, 10 March 1958; Decimal File 839.00/3-1058, Box 4382; Dominican Republic, 1955–59; RG 59; NA.

2. Arturo Espaillat, *Trujillo: El Ultimo de los Césares* (Santo Domingo: Editorial Nacional, 1963), p. 81.

3. Bernard Diederich, *The Death of the Dictator* (Maplewood, NJ: Waterfront, 1990), p. 15.

4. Henry S. Hammond to the State Department, 10 March 1958; Decimal File 839.00/3-1058, Box 4382; Dominican Republic, 1955–59; RG 59; NA.

5. Diederich, *The Death of the Dictator*, p. 5. The incident began on 12 March 1956 when Jesús Galíndez, a Basque exile who had previously lived in Ciudad Trujillo, disappeared from Manhattan. Only ten days earlier he had presented his doctoral dissertation, a well-documented analysis of Trujillo's dictatorship, to his oral defense committee at Columbia University. All evidence indicated that Trujillo ordered his kidnapping, had him flown to the Dominican Republic, and there had him killed.

6. R. Richard Rubottom to Robert D. Murphy, 15 January 1957; *FRUS 1955–1957*, vol. 7, p. 887. Murphy was probably murdered by SIM agents to keep him quiet.

7. Robert D. Crassweller, *Trujillo: The Life and Times of a Caribbean Dictator* (New York: Macmillan, 1966), p. 314.

8. *Washington Post*, 24 March 1957.

9. Bill Wieland to Richard Rubottom, 30 January 1958; Decimal File 611.39/1-3058, Box 2475; Dominican Republic, 1955–59; RG 59; NA. The Galíndez-Murphy case, however, was never officially solved.

10. Ibid.

11. Ibid.

12. John Foster Dulles to Porfirio Herrera Báez, 7 November 1958; *FRUS 1958–1960*, vol. 5 (microfiche supplement), document 5.

13. Joseph S. Farland to the State Department, 12 February 1958; Decimal File 611.39/2-1258, Box 2475; Dominican Republic, 1955–59; RG 59; NA.

14. Joseph S. Farland to the State Department, 21 May 1958; Decimal File 611.39/5-2158, Box 2475; Dominican Republic, 1955–59; RG 59; NA.

15. Francis L. Spalding to the State Department, 25 June 1958; Land Policy Folder, Box 246; Dominican Republic, Narrative Reports, 1955–61; RG 166; NA. This would have included the Military Assistance Agreement, the Naval Mission, and the Long Range Proving Ground. Merely a scare tactic, the resolution was rescinded by Trujillo in September.

16. Richard Rubottom to the State Department, 26 June 1958; *FRUS 1958–1960*, vol. 5 (supplement), pp. 84/1455.

17. Memorandum of Discussion at a Department of State-Joint Chiefs of Staff Meeting, 27 June 1958; *FRUS 1958–1960*, vol. 5 (supplement), pp. 84/1457. Trujillo was especially upset that the Cubans received a larger sugar quota.

18. Bernardo Vega, *Eisenhower y Trujillo* (Santo Domingo: Fundación Cultural Dominicana, 1991), pp. 1–3. In addition, the Roman Catholic Church, which had been a bastion of support for authoritarian dictators for decades, began to back away from unabashed support of authoritarian dictators during the tenure of Pope John XXIII.

19. Dempster McIntosh to the State Department, 6 December 1957; *FRUS 1955–1957*, vol. 7, pp. 1164–67. The demonstrators criticized the US for supporting Latin America's dictators.

20. Memorandum of Discussion of the 366th Meeting of the National Security Council, 22 May 1958; *FRUS 1958–1960*, vol. 5, p. 244.

21. Frank Moya Pons, *El Pasado Dominicano* (Santo Domingo: Fundación J. A. Caro Alvarez, 1986), pp. 333–335. It should be pointed out that similar circumstances befell coffee, cacao, and tobacco exports.

22. Oficina Nacional de Estadística de la República Dominicana, *Comercio Exterior de la República Dominicana* (Ciudad Trujillo: Oficina Nacional de Estadística de la República Dominicana, 1960).

23. Henry S. Hammond to the State Department, 31 July 1958; Decimal File 839.2351/7-3158, Box 4384; Dominican Republic, 1955–59; RG 59; NA.

24. Richard Rubottom to John Foster Dulles, 6 November 1958; Decimal File 611.39/11-658, Box 2475; Dominican Republic, 1955–59; RG 59; NA.

25. Memorandum of Conversation between Porfirio Herrera Báez and John Foster Dulles, 7 November 1958; *FRUS 1958–1960*, vol. 5 (supplement), pp. 84/1462.

26. Joseph S. Farland to the State Department, 31 December 1958; Decimal File 739.00/12-3158, Box 3096; Dominican Republic, 1955–59; RG 59; NA.

27. Ronald A. Webb to the State Department, 23 March 1959; Decimal File 839.00/3-2359, Box 4383; Dominican Republic, 1955–59; RG 59; NA.

28. Joseph S. Farland to the State Department, 17 July 1959; Decimal File 839.00/7-1759, Box 4383; Dominican Republic, 1955–59; RG 59; NA. Trujillo had the largest military in the Caribbean.

29. Crassweller, *Trujillo*, p. 421.

30. Richard Rubottom to the State Department, 13 March 1959; Decimal File 739.00/3-1359, Box 3099; Dominican Republic, 1955–59; RG 59; NA.

31. Allen Dulles to Richard Rubottom, 15 April 1959; *FRUS 1958–1960*, vol. 5, p. 372. The CIA was instructed to make preliminary contact with the various Dominican exile groups in the United States.

32. State Department to Certain Diplomatic Missions, 14 October 1959; *FRUS 1958–1960*, vol. 5, p. 408.

33. Joseph S. Farland to the State Department, 14 January 1959; Decimal File 839.00/1-1459, Box 4383; Dominican Republic, 1960–63; RG 59; NA.

34. Henry Dearborn to the State Department, 18 October 1959; Decimal File 739.5-MSP/11-1859, Box 3099; Dominican Republic, 1955–59; RG 59; NA.

35. Threats to the Stability of the US Military Facilities Position in the Caribbean Area and in Brazil, 10 March 1959, *FRUS 1958–1960*, vol. 5, p. 367.

36. Joseph S. Farland to the State Department, 17 July 1959; Decimal File 839.00/7-1759, Box 4383; Dominican Republic, 1955–59; RG 59; NA.

37. Joseph S. Farland to the State Department, 17 March 1959; Decimal File 739.5-MSP/3-1759, Box 3099; Dominican Republic, 1955–59; RG 59; NA.

38. Memorandum of Discussion of 437th Meeting of the National Security council, 17 March 1960; *FRUS 1958–1960*, vol. 5, p. 429.

39. Joseph S. Farland to the State Department, 26 June 1959; Decimal File 739.00/6-2659, Box 3099; Dominican Republic, 1955–59; RG 59; NA.

40. Joseph S. Farland to the State Department, 17 July 1959; Decimal File 839.00/7-1759, Box 4383; Dominican Republic, 1955–59; RG 59; NA.

41. Organization of American States, *Declaration of Santiago* (Washington: DC, Organization of American States, 1959.

42. Vega, *Eisenhower y Trujillo*, p. 7.

43. Henry Dearborn to the State Department, 14 October 1959; Decimal File 739.562/10-1459, Box 3100; Dominican Republic, 1955–59; RG 59; NA.

44. Richard Rubottom to the State Department, 10 December 1959; *FRUS 1958–1960*, vol. 5 (supplement), pp. 84/1476–79.

45. Joseph S. Farland to the State Department 17 July 1959; Decimal File 839.00/7-1759, Box 4383; Dominican Republic, 1955–59; RG 59; NA.

46. Ibid.

47. Harry M. Lofton to the State Department, 26 May 1959," *FRUS 1958–1960*, vol. 5 (supplement), pp. 84/1471.

48. Joseph S. Farland to the State Department 17 July 1959; Decimal File 839.00/7-1759, Box 4383; Dominican Republic, 1955–59; RG 59; NA.

49. Rubottom to Herter, 10 November 1959; *FRUS 1958–1960*, vol. 5 (microfiche supplement), document 9.

50. Richard Rubottom to the State Department, 10 December 1959; *FRUS 1958–1960*, vol. 5 (supplement), pp. 84/1476–79.

51. Memorandum from the 432nd Meeting of the National Security Council, 14 January 1960; *FRUS 1958–1960*, vol. 5 (supplement), p. 84/1480–83.

52. Diederich, *Trujillo*, pp. 40–41. Born in 1955, the Special Group was responsible for authorizing covert CIA operations. It was a subcommittee of the National Security Council.

53. Henry Dearborn to the Secretary of State, 29 January 1960; Decimal File 739.00/1-2960, Box 1636; Dominican Republic, 1960–63; RG 59; NA.

54. Joseph S. Farland to the State Department, 25 January 1960; Decimal File 739.00/1-2560, Box 1636; Dominican Republic, 1960–63; RG 59; NA. Relations between Trujillo and the Vatican were cemented by the 1954 Concordat, which made Roman Catholicism the official Dominican religion.

55. Joseph S. Farland to the Secretary of State, 31 January 1960; Decimal File 739.00/1-3160, Box 1636; Dominican Republic, 1960–63; RG 59; NA.

56. Livingston Merchant to the State Department, 8 February 1960; Decimal File 739.00/2-860, Box 1636; Dominican Republic, 1960–63; RG 59; NA.

57. Henry Dearborn to the State Department, 9 February 1960; Decimal File 739.00/2-960, Box 1636; Dominican Republic, 1960–63; RG 59; NA.

58. Ibid.

59. Henry Dearborn to the State Department, 11 February 1960; *FRUS 1958–1960,* vol. 5 (supplement), p. 84/1490.

60. Virgilio Díaz Ordóñez to Tulio Franco, 19 March 1960; File 30390; APG; PND; SD.

61. *El Caribe*, 27 March 1960.

62. Edwin Clark to the President, 21 April 1960; *FRUS 1958–1960*, vol. 5 (supplement), pp. 84/1508.

63. Christian Herter to the President, 14 April 1960; Decimal File 739.00/4-1460, Box 1636; Dominican Republic, 1960–63; RG 59; NA.

64. Memorandum from the 441st Meeting of the National Security Council, 14 April 1960; *FRUS 1958–1960*, vol. 5 (supplement), pp. 84/1506.

65. Ibid. Assessments of communism in the Dominican Republic were based on fears and dubious historical analogies rather than on concrete studies.

66.Piero Gleijeses, *The Dominican Crisis: The 1965 Constitutional Revolt and American Intervention* (Baltimore, MD: The Johns Hopkins University Press, 1978), p. 284.

67. Memorandum of a Meeting in the White House, 25 April 1960; *FRUS 1958–1960*, vol. 5 (supplement), pp. 84/1508.

68. US Senate, *Alleged Assassination Plots Involving Foreign Leaders*, 1975, p. 192.

69. Ibid., p. 191. The chair of the investigative committee was Senator Frank Church, hence the Church Report. Trujillo's brutality was nothing new, but an "increasing awareness" of it by Eisenhower was.

70. C. A. Saillant, "Letter to the Editor," *El Caribe*, 21 July 1962, p. 18. Saillant was Ramfis's personal secretary.

71. *Miami Herald*, 2 April 1960.

72. *Miami Herald*, 7 April 1960.

73. John D. Barfield to the State Department, 17 April 1961; Decimal File 739.00/4-1761, Box 1637; Dominican Republic, 1960–63; RG 59; NA.

74. John D. Barfield to the State Department, 15 August 1960; Decimal File 739.00/8-1560, Box 1637; Dominican Republic, 1960–63; RG 59; NA.

75. Memorandum of Conversation with Virgilio Díaz Ordoñez, 13 June 1960; Decimal File 739.00/6-1360, Box 1637; Dominican Republic, 1960–63; RG 59; NA. Herrera Báez claimed that Trujillo received two Soviet emissaries who communicated Nikita Khrushchev's desire to visit Ciudad Trujillo during his next official visit to Cuba.

76. Memorandum of a Conference with President Eisenhower, 13 May 1960; *FRUS 1958–1960*, vol. 5 (supplement), pp. 84/1514.

77. Eisenhower to Harold MacMillan, 11 July 1960; *FRUS 1958–1960*, vol. 5, p. 1004.

78. Douglas Dillon to the President, 20 May 1960; Dominican Folder, Box 4; Confidential Files, White House Central Files; DDE; KS.

79. Howard Wiarda, *Dictatorship and Development: The Methods of Control in Trujillo's Dominican Republic* (Gainesville: University of Florida Press, 1968), p. 57.

80. Emilio Portes Gil to Rafael Trujillo, 23 June 1960; File 15141; APG; PND; SD.

81. John D. Barfield to the State Department, 17 April 1961; Decimal File 739.00/4-1761, Box 1637; Dominican Republic, 1960–63; RG 59; NA.

82. C. A. Saillant, *El Caribe*, 21 July 1962, p. 18.

83. John D. Barfield to the State Department, 15 August 1960; Decimal File 739.00/8-1560, Box 1637; Dominican Republic, 1960–63; RG 59; NA.

84. Memorandum of a Discussion in the White House, 6 July 1960; *FRUS 1958–1960*, vol. 6, p. 979. Unlike Trujillo, Castro had few friends in the US Congress. As a result, Castro nationalized all US enterprises in Cuba.

85. John Hugh Crimmins to Robert Woodward, 6 March 1962; Decimal File 839.235/3-662, Box 2459; Dominican Republic, 1960–63; RG 59; NA. Prior to 1960, Cuban sugar sales to the United States averaged three million tons annually.

86. *El Caribe*, 24 July 1960.

87. José Vicini, *La Isla del Azúcar* (Ciudad Trujillo: Editora Dominicana, 1957), p. 2.

88. Memorandum of the Discussion at the 453rd Meeting of the National Security Council, 25 July 1960; *FRUS 1958–1960*, vol. 6, pp. 1028–30.

89. Ibid.

90. Ibid. Since he eventually authorized Dominican sugar purchases, apparently Eisenhower was just ranting.

91. Espaillat, *Trujillo*, p. 87.

92. Thomas C. Mann to the State Department, 23 July 1960; Decimal File 839.235/7-2360, Box 2459; Dominican Republic, 1960–63; RG 59; NA.

93. Edwin M. Martin to the State Department, 9 August 1960; Decimal File 839.235/8-960, Box 2459; Dominican Republic, 1960–63; RG 59; NA.

94. Memorandum of Conversation between President Eisenhower and Secretary Herter, 30 August 1960; Office of the Staff Secretary, Subject Series, State Department Subseries, Box 4, Folder State Department 8/60 to 9/60; DDE; KS.

95. Henry Dearborn to the State Department, 4 August 1960; Decimal File 739.11/8-460, Box 1642; Dominican Republic, 1960–63; RG 59; NA.

96. Joaquín Balaguer, *Memorias de un Cortesano de la "Era de Trujillo"* (Santo Domingo: Corripio, 1989), p. 144.

97. *El Caribe*, 7 August 1960. Román Fernández, who was married to a daughter of Trujillo's sister, eventually took part in the assassination plot that killed Trujillo in 1961.

98. John D. Barfield to the State Department, 15 August 1960; Decimal File 739.00/8-1560, Box 1637; Dominican Republic, 1960–63; RG 59; NA.

99. Dwight D. Eisenhower, *Waging Peace, 1956–61* (Garden City, NY: Doubleday, 1965), p. 537.

100. Christian Herter to Allen Dulles, 19 August 1960; Telephone Calls 7/1/60–8/31/60, Box 13; Christian Herter Papers; DDE; KS. Dulles was worried that the recall of US diplomats from Ciudad Trujillo would weaken his contacts with dissident elements in the Dominican Republic. Regardless, the US was left with three consulates filled with CIA operatives.

101. *Miami Herald*, 20 August 1960.

102. *New York Times*, 9 September 1960. Haiti was the last American nation to break diplomatic relations.

103. Charles L. Hodge to the State Department, 29 May 1961; Decimal File 839.00/5-2961, Box 2457; Dominican Republic, 1960–63; RG 59; NA.

104. President Eisenhower to Congress, 23 August 1960, House Document 451, 86th Congress, 2nd Session, 1960, *House Documents*, Serial 12269, pp. 1–2.

105. Ibid.

106. *New York Times*, 25 August 1960.

107. G. Pope Atkins and Larman C. Wilson, *The United States and the Trujillo Regime* (New Brunswick, NJ: Rutgers University Press, 1972), p. 114.

108. *New York Times*, 25 August 1960. At the beginning of August, Debevoise had send a letter to all stockholders in the Central Romana stating that the State Department was violating the law by not allowing the reallocation of a part of the Cuban windfall to the Dominicans.

109. John D. Barfield to the State Department, 22 September 1960; Decimal File 839.235/9-2260, Box 2459; Dominican Republic, 1960–63; RG 59; NA.

110. John Hugh Crimmins to Robert Woodward, 6 March 1962; Decimal File 839.235/3-662, Box 2459; Dominican Republic, 1960–63; RG 59; NA. This amount would have canceled out the $28 million deficit from 1959.

111. Douglas Dillon to the President, 20 September 1960; Decimal File 839.235/10-2060, Box 2459; Dominican Republic, 1960–63; RG 59; NA.

112. Wiarda, *Dictatorship and Development*, p. 160.

113. Charles L. Hodge to the State Department, 13 October 1960; Decimal File 839.00/10-1360, Box 2457; Dominican Republic, 1960–63; RG 59; NA.

114. Gustavo Segundo Volmar, "The Impact of the Foreign Sector on the Domestic Economic Activity of the Dominican Republic from 1950 to 1967," p. 213.

115. John D. Barfield to the State Department, 17 April 1961; Decimal File 739.00/4-1761, Box 1637; Dominican Republic, 1960–63; RG 59; NA.

116. *El Caribe*, 3 October 1960.

117. Weikko Forsten to the State Department, 7 October 1960; Decimal File 839.235/10-760, Box 2459; Dominican Republic, 1960–63; RG 59; NA.

118. Thomas C. Mann to the State Department, 6 October 1960; Decimal File 839.235/10-660, Box 2459; Dominican Republic, 1960–63; RG 59; NA.

119. Memorandum of a Conversation between Eisenhower and Falcon Briseño, 3 November 1960; Staff Notes Folder, Box 54; Ann Whitman File, Papers as President of the United States; DDE; KS. Significantly, Eisenhower failed to mention his earlier pledge to prohibit Dominican sugar imports at the risk of impeachment. As a consolation, Eisenhower agreed to go along with Venezuelan attempts to expand the economic sanctions against the Dominican Republic. On 4 January 1961 the OAS voted to include an embargo on the export of petroleum and trucks to the Dominican Republic.

120. Memorandum of a Conference in the White House, 13 October 1960; *FRUS 1958-1960*, vol. 6, p. 1084.

121. Christian Herter to Thomas Mann, 26 October 1960; Telephone Calls 9/1/60–1/20/61, Box 12; Christian Herter Papers; DDE; KS.

122. Henry Dearborn to Thomas Mann, 27 October 1960; *FRUS 1958–1960*, vol. 5 (supplement), p. 84/1529.

123. Ibid. On 26 October 1960, Trujillo announced that he was resigning from the military and running for Governor of Santiago. Hence, Dearborn's comment.

124. Pawley, William; Oral History, p. 33; Herbert Hoover Library, West Branch, Iowa.

125. Bernardo Vega, *Trujillo y el Control Financiero Norteamericano* (Santo Domingo: Fundación Cultural Dominicano, 1990), p. 610.

126. Henry Dearborn to the State Department, 29 November 1960; Decimal File 739.00/11-2860, Box 1637; Dominican Republic, 1960–63; RG 59; NA. For example, on 25 November, Patria, Minerva, and María Teresa Mirabal, the famous Mirabal sisters, members of the Dominican oligarchy and outspoken critics of the Trujillo regime, were assassinated on their way home from visiting their husbands in jail. Although there is no documentation to prove that Trujillo authorized the killing, most Dominicans believed "El Jefe" was responsible.

127. Charles L. Hodge to the State Department, 29 May 1961; Decimal File 839.00/5-2961, Box 2457; Dominican Republic, 1960–63; RG 59; NA.

128. John Bartlow Martin to the President, 25 September 1961; Folder 9, Box 115A; Country Series, President's Office Files; JFK; MA.

129. *El Caribe*, 27 February 1961.

Chapter 5

Kennedy and Democratization Efforts, 1961–1962

President John F. Kennedy inherited two policies toward the Trujillo regime: one clandestine and the other public. The clandestine policy toward Trujillo included contact with dissident elements in the Dominican Republic and secret visits to Ciudad Trujillo by US emissaries to convince Trujillo to resign. Striving to maintain US political and economic hegemony in the Dominican Republic, US diplomat Henry Dearborn argued:

I wish to emphasize that Trujillo is a short-term proposition in the Dominican Republic, that future US interests lie in building goodwill among moderate elements of dissidents, and that if USG gives slightest indication of softening toward Trujillo US security and business interests in Dominican Republic will suffer consequences for years to come.[1]

As a result, in February 1961, CIA operatives were authorized to deliver small arms and sabotage equipment to the dissidents in Ciudad Trujillo.[2]

The public policy toward Trujillo included supporting the spirit of the decisions taken by the OAS at San José in 1960 and the $0.02 per pound tax on the Dominican share of the Cuban windfall. This fee was increased to $0.025 per pound during the first quarter of 1961 to bring the net price paid to the Dominican Republic more in line with the world market price. Although Trujillo had a personal fortune estimated at $800 million, the tax on Dominican sugar caused the dictator financial hardship because most of his wealth was tied up in Dominican real estate.[3] The Dominican share of the Cuban windfall—322,000 tons in 1960 and 202,000 tons in the first quarter of 1961—would have brought a premium of $22.6 million over the world market price. Since Trujillo owned over 60 percent of the Dominican sugar industry, a large part of the windfall would have ended up in Trujillo's pocket. The punitive tax on Dominican sugar exports, therefore, was a vehicle of economic coercion to push Trujillo out of power.[4]

Kennedy came into office as a sharp critic of Eisenhower's sympathetic policy toward Latin American dictatorships and anticommunist military authoritarianism. He was, however, susceptible to prevailing anticommunist sentiment and anxious to respond to the Cuban challenge. The basis of Kennedy's policy toward Latin America was the Alliance for Progress, a $20 billion, ten-year program designed to promote economic development and political democracy in the hemisphere, and provide military aid to defeat communist insurgents.[5] The Alliance called for economic progress and social justice within a North American framework of democratic reforms and procedures.[6] Kennedy envisaged the stimulation of democratic reforms as serving the national interest in providing a counterweight to the radical solutions being advanced by Castro.[7] The Alliance was a device for containing Castroism. Secretary of State Dean Rusk explained that the Alliance and military aid were two facets of the same policy. Rusk explained that the Alliance was the best way of attacking the long-run sources of communist appeal, such as poverty and injustice, but that military aid would be used to ward off the short-run communist tactics of disruption and subversion. In the words of Rusk, "Vitamin tablets will not save a man set upon by hoodlums in an alley."[8] For Kennedy, the success of the United States in preventing a second Cuba rested on the defeat of dictators and the triumph of democracy.

Kennedy immediately focused on the Dominican Republic as an area where the goals of the Alliance could be successfully implemented.[9] He believed that replacing Trujillo with pro-US, moderate, democratic reformers was indispensable to maintaining US strategic and economic hegemony in the Dominican Republic. Kennedy's State Department explained US interest in the Dominican Republic as follows:

The paramount interest of the US is to prevent Castro-Communist or other unfriendly elements from taking control and to insure that Trujillo is succeeded by a friendly, democratic government. These objectives can best be achieved by cooperation with and encouragement of those elements in the Dominican Republic and elsewhere who share them and oppose Trujillo.[10]

Given the Dominican Republic's geographic proximity to Cuba, Kennedy hoped that the Dominican Republic might eventually become a showcase for democracy—proof that the Alliance could achieve stability and progress in Latin America.[11] Kennedy promised that the Dominican Republic could join the Alliance and reap the benefits of economic development as soon as it "rejoined the society of free men."[12]

Thus, believing that Eisenhower's tax on Dominican sugar did not go far enough, the Kennedy administration immediately adopted a position against Trujillo's participation in the Cuban windfall. Kennedy requested changes in sugar quota legislation from Congress that would allow him to suspend the Dominican share of the Cuban windfall.[13] US diplomat John D. Barfield contended: "If windfall sugar sales are denied it would constitute the first actually imposed major sanction on Dominican exports yet taken against Trujillo and could well denote the end for Trujillo."[14] Deputy Director of the CIA Richard Bissel also argued that the outcome of the sugar legislation that came up for renewal in the

US Congress was exceptionally important to the future of US-Dominican relations. Bissel explained: "The Trujillo government cannot last another six months if they do not get their share of the Cuban windfall sugar. If Congressional action is favorable to Trujillo, it is probable that he will continue to rule uneasily for an indefinite period unless material outside pressure is brought to bear against him."[15]

The President's proposal to deny the Dominicans their share of the Cuban windfall met fierce resistance in Congress.[16] Members of the US business community in Ciudad Trujillo were coerced into helping the dictator overcome unfavorable US press and to pressure the US Congress in his favor.[17] In addition, it was estimated that Trujillo spent over $3 million in bribes to politicians, newspapermen, diplomats, and other influential people to lobby the US Congress to reinforce his standing.[18]

Among those suspected of accepting bribes was Harold Cooley (D-NC), the chairman of the House Agriculture Committee throughout the 1950s and early 1960s. In 1961, Representative Cooley introduced a bill to extend the Sugar Act of 1948 to 31 December 1962 without changing the allocation system, a proposal that would have assured the Dominican Republic its share of the Cuban windfall. Cooley, who argued that "quotas should be treated like rewards and should be based on who are our friends and who are not," contended that Trujillo was the only dictator being denied the benefits of the Cuban windfall.[19] Dominican Ambassador Manuel de Moya begged Cooley for a larger share of the sugar quota and asked the congressman what he could do to prove Dominican friendship toward the United States. Cooley replied that he did not know what the Dominicans could do, but that he "hated like hell to see a country trying to be friendly get kicked in the teeth."[20]

While Congress debated whether to grant or deny a large chunk of the Cuban sugar quota to the Dominican Republic, on 22 March the Dominican government purchased a half-page advertisement in the *Washington Post* attacking the "vermin" in the State Department who sought to apply more sanctions against Trujillo.[21] US social columnist Igor Cassini, who used the pseudonym Cholly Knickerbocker, was also on Trujillo's payroll to portray the Dominican regime positively in the US press.[22] A few days after Kennedy's inauguration, Cassini had met with the president's father in West Palm Beach, Florida and informed him that it was quite possible that a "leftist revolution" could spread through the Dominican Republic unless the United States resumed diplomatic relations with the Trujillo regime and eliminated the special tax on Dominican sugar exports. Cassini argued that the Trujillo regime would be replaced by a communist government if the United States were to completely eliminate the Dominican sugar quota. Cassini suggested that Joseph Kennedy Sr. convince his son to send a secret emissary to speak with Trujillo to avoid this cataclysm.[23]

After speaking with his father, the President accepted Cassini's suggestion that it might be useful to send an emissary to Ciudad Trujillo to discuss ways to avoid a potential leftist takeover. The State Department recommended sending Robert D. Murphy, a retired foreign service officer, to visit Trujillo.[24] On 11 March, before going to Ciudad Trujillo, Murphy secretly met with Rafael Leonidis Trujillo Martínez (Ramfis) in New York. Murphy told Ramfis to instruct his father to "build an elaborate smoke-screen around the dictatorship to convince the North Americans that the Trujillo regime was the safest route to democracy."[25] Murphy also discussed the problem of the Dominican sugar quota, reassuring Ramfis that the special tax would be removed as soon as the Trujillo regime developed a thicker veneer of democracy. Murphy contended that it was essential for Trujillo to divest himself of his huge economic holdings, especially the sugar mills. That way, Murphy argued, the United States would more quickly lift the special tax on the Dominican sugar quota, since one of the biggest complaints against lifting the special tax on Dominican sugar was that Trujillo would personally benefit.[26]

On 29 March, the US Congress approved a law that extended the Sugar Act of 1948 through 30 June 1962. The new legislation also granted the Executive Branch discretion over purchases of non-quota sugar from any country with which the United States did not maintain diplomatic relations. Kennedy had specifically requested this authority in order to avoid further US purchases of the Dominican Republic's portion of the Cuban windfall. Such purchases, as required by the old legislation, would have required the purchase of 396,000 additional tons of Dominican sugar during the last nine months of 1961. Although this action denied the Dominican Republic its share of the Cuban windfall for the last nine months of 1961, it did not affect the basic sugar quota of the Dominican Republic, which in 1961 amounted to 111,157 tons.[27] In the words of Philip W. Bonsal, US Representative to the OAS:

In this manner the United States Government, continuing its policy of fidelity to the spirit and purposes of the Sixth Foreign Ministers Meeting, has prevented access by the Dominican Republic for the rest of the present year to a share of the United States sugar market which would have been several times its share of that market under its present basic quota allocation.[28]

On 15 April 1961, Murphy met with Trujillo, President Balaguer, and Herrera Báez in Ciudad Trujillo. On the following day, Murphy sent a lengthy letter detailing the meeting to McGeorge Bundy, Kennedy's national security advisor. The so-called Murphy Report asserted that Trujillo was moving along the path toward democracy and planning to hold presidential elections in 1962. In the words of Murphy: "There is no suffering or actual inconvenience resulting from the OAS embargo. The effect of it is disturbing in the psychological and political sense and of course it is deeply resented."[29] Influenced by Trujillo's savoir-faire, Murphy recommended that the economic and diplomatic sanctions be lifted and that the Dominican portion of the Cuban windfall be reinstated. A US diplomat in Ciudad Trujillo, however, astutely pointed out: "As long as the US continues to be the principal market for the major share of DR exports, Trujillo will be able to pursue his present policies, and there will be no real inducement for him to look for other, if less green pastures."[30] Bundy, who also disagreed with Murphy's assessment of the situation, concluded: "There can be little doubt that the whole concept of the Alliance for Progress would be gravely shadowed in the eyes of Latin Americans if we were to move to anything like a policy of friendly guidance toward Trujillo."[31]   The Kennedy administration, therefore, ignored Murphy's recommendations and continued to seek alternatives to Trujillo.

On 3 May, the CIA, seeking authorization to supply the dissidents with more weapons, asked Kennedy's special advisor Adolph Berle what the administration's policy was regarding Trujillo's assassination. Berle answered: "I do not care what happens to Trujillo, and that is the general sentiment in the State Department. However, we want nothing to do with an assassination plan."[32] Still upset over the failed Bay of Pigs invasion, Kennedy decided that the United States should not support an attempt to assassinate Trujillo unless a successor government was clearly identified.[33] What Kennedy did not know was that on the very day that he prohibited the support of the dissidents, Lorenzo Berry (the owner of Wimpy's Supermarket in Ciudad Trujillo) and Thomas Stocker delivered three .30 caliber M-1 carbines, along with extra magazine clips and 500 rounds of ammunition, provided by the CIA, to Antonio de la Maza at the Embajador Hotel's polo grounds.[34]

Nevertheless, in his last month of life, Trujillo was confident that he had convinced Kennedy, via Murphy, that resuming diplomatic relations and lifting the economic sanctions would be the policy most beneficial to the United States. On 24 April, Dominican Consul in New York Luis Mercado informed Trujillo: "I have just received a phone call from Cassini telling me that Kennedy's father told him that the president was very impressed with the magnificent report prepared by Robert Murphy."[35] Trujillo believed that he was indispensable and that he had convinced the Kennedy administration of his indispensability. According to the dictator, "Now the Americans realize that my presence is required to ensure stability in the Dominican Republic."[36] Mercado and Cassini, however, were providing Trujillo with false information in an attempt to justify their high salaries.

Trujillo augmented the democratic facade begun in August of 1960 to convince the United States that his regime was liberalizing and worthy of receiving an increased sugar quota. Radio Caribe, Trujillo's internal mouthpiece, limited its verbal attacks to employees of the US consulate in Ciudad Trujillo, many of whom were working for the CIA.[37] In a further attempt to portray his regime in a favorable light, Trujillo publicly offered an interchange of prisoners: captives of the Cuban invasion of the Dominican Republic in 1959 for captives taken during the recent Bay of Pigs invasion.[38] On 6 May 1961, Balaguer offered guarantees of safety to the members of the opposition Movimiento Popular Dominicano (MPD) who chose to campaign in the proposed 1962 presidential elections.[39] The most interesting example of the liberalization facade came on 6 May, when four new members, all of them admirers of the Cuban revolution, appeared in the Dominican Congress: Gregorio García, Euclides Gutiérres Félix, Manolín Jiménez Rodríguez, and Luis Dhimes Pablo. The objective of this action, according to Johnny Abbes, the director of the Servicio de Inteligencia Militar (SIM), was to strengthen the anticlerical position of the government in Congress and to show the rest of the world that there was political freedom and congressional debate in the Dominican Republic.[40]

Despite Trujillo's machinations, Kennedy had no intention of lifting the economic and political sanctions against the Dominican Republic as long as Trujillo dominated the island nation. On 22 May, the United States formally protested the persecution of the Roman Catholic bishops in Ciudad Trujillo, especially Bishop Thomas Reilly, who was a US citizen.[41] In the words of the US Consul:

However one adds it up, on whichever set of alternatives he chooses, it would appear that the DR is going to be an increasing headache for the US, regardless of whether Trujillo stays or falls; and that the problems of the US in this troubled country are bound to increase rather than diminish over the immediately perceptible future.[42]

On 30 May, at approximately 10 P.M., at kilometer 9 on the highway leading to San Cristóbal, Trujillo was assassinated by a group of Dominicans who had been both accomplices in his tyranny and victims of it. Although some of the weapons used to destroy Trujillo were US-supplied, there was no evidence of direct US participation in the killing.[43] Of the thirteen conspirators in Trujillo's assassination, only Antonio de la Maza, Amado García Guerrero, Pedro Livio Cedeño, Huascar Tejeda Pimentel, Roberto Pastoriza, Salvador Estrella Sadhalá, and Antonio Imbert Barreras participated in the gunfight against Trujillo and his driver. Led by Antonio de la Maza, the brother of the slain Octavio de la Maza of the Galíndez-Murphy embroglio, many of the conspirators were tied together by compadrazgo, a formidable force in Latin America.[44] In the words of Bernard Diederich, "The opposition which succeeded in killing him might never have passed beyond the talking stage had not godfatherly ties held many of them together."[45]

Trujillo's death, however, did not immediately open up the floodgates of democracy in the Dominican Republic. Three decades of Trujilloism could not produce a viable new political system overnight. Within twenty-four hours of the dictator's assassination, Ramfis returned from Paris as chief of the joint chiefs of staff of the armed forces, a position created for him by his father. Although Joaquín Balaguer was kept on as president, Ramfis was in charge.[46]

JUNE–AUGUST 1961

In the aftermath of Trujillo's assassination, the main US policy objectives toward the Dominican Republic were to preserve order, eliminate the remaining vestiges of Trujillo's dictatorship, and prevent the coming to power of a communist regime. Kennedy, who wanted to export US-style democracy to the Dominican Republic, was concerned that an anti-US, pro-communist government might come to power in the fluid political situation following Trujillo's death. Thus, the idealistic, yet pragmatic, Kennedy asserted: "There are three possibilities in descending order of preference: a decent democratic regime, a continuation of the Trujillo regime, or a Castro regime. We ought to aim at the first but we really can't renounce the second until we are sure that we can avoid the third."[47] Nevertheless, on 7 June at a special meeting held in the White House to discuss possible courses of action in the Dominican Republic, Consul Dearborn reassured Kennedy that it would be possible to have a democratic government in the Dominican Republic without a communist takeover.[48]

Owing to the lack of an organized political opposition, the Kennedy administration first dealt only with Balaguer and Ramfis. US diplomats tried to convince Balaguer and Ramfis to move along the path toward democracy and pave the way for democratic elections. The possibility of lifting political and economic sanctions, especially the promise of removing the ban on full Dominican participation in the windfall quota, became an increasingly useful incentive for political change. At the same time, Kennedy decided to play the two major US trump cards in the Dominican equation, its cuota y flota threats. Kennedy immediately sent a convoy of three aircraft carriers, 280 fighter planes, 5,000 thousand Marines, and a submarine to waters off the coast of Ciudad Trujillo. The threat of sending in the US Marines and the potential suspension of the basic sugar quota deterred Dominican political digression.[49]

Aware of the economic and political impossibility of continued unfriendly relations with the United States, Balaguer and Ramfis began to liberalize Dominican politics in the hope of reducing US pressure. Balaguer insisted that his "primary mission consisted of convincing the Trujillo family of the necessity to initiate, for the benefit of everybody, the democratization process."[50] On 4 June, Balaguer declared that he would accept any formula suggested by the United States that would provide evidence to the rest of the world that the 1962 elections would be free. He even invited the OAS to send a special commission to visit the Dominican Republic to observe the liberalization progress.[51] Foreign Minister Herrera Báez explained that Balaguer "considered his government a transition between dictatorship and democracy, whose only purpose was to guarantee the celebration of free elections."[52]

Balaguer and Ramfis, therefore, sought to change the image of Trujilloism by instituting a series of reforms. They curbed police brutality, forced some of the most oppressive collaborators of the Trujillo regime into exile, allowed opposition political movements and parties to organize, permitted nongovernment-sponsored labor movements to form, and encouraged the Trujillo family to turn over some of its vast economic holdings to the state. After Balaguer proclaimed that the Dominican Republic's foreign policy was "closely aligned" to that of the United States, all anti-US rhetoric disappeared from the Dominican press and radio.[53] On 11 June, Johnny Abbes García, Trujillo's most anti-US henchman, and José Martí Otero, the anti-US director of Radio Caribe, were deported.[54]

On 13 June, in an effort to continue the liberalization process, Balaguer announced that he was inviting all Dominican exiles to return to the country.[55] After lifting restrictions on political activity, the Dominican political system experienced a rapid transformation. Within weeks, a variety of legal political organizations, including Viriato Fiallo's Unión Cívica Nacional (UCN), Juan Bosch's Partido Revolucionario Dominicano (PRD), Manuel Tavárez Justo's Agrupación Política 14 de Junio (AP1J4), and Máximo López Molina's Movimiento Popular Dominicano (MPD), were legalized and began campaigning.[56] In the words of historian Frank Moya Pons: "The death of Trujillo awakened the social and political energies of the nation and gave birth to an intense process of democratization. Groups that had been repressed or marginalized during the dictatorship gained strength."[57] These efforts, however, only served to heighten public opposition to the old regime, as well as to anger the remaining members of the Trujillo family.[58]

On 3 July, in yet another attempt to convince the Kennedy administration that he was liberalizing his regime, Balaguer accepted the resignation of his entire cabinet. The new cabinet, which included historian Emilio Rodríguez Demorizi as the new secretary of education, was more professional and less tainted by its association with the Trujillo era. Balaguer and his new cabinet promised to move the nation further along the path toward democracy and to restore diplomatic relations with the OAS nations as quickly as possible.[59] On the following day, Balaguer repeated his promise that free elections would take place in 1962, and that he would not be a candidate for the presidency.[60] On 20 July, Dominican Consul in Washington Oscar Ginebra reported to Balaguer that during his recent meeting with Lyndon B. Johnson, the US vice president told him that the Kennedy administration was pleased with the progress of the Balaguer government and that he believed that it was almost time to lift the economic sanctions and reinstate the Dominican portion of the windfall quota.[61]

Meanwhile, on 15 June, an OAS special commission led by Colombian Ambassador Augusto Arango completed a weeklong fact-finding trip to the Dominican Republic. Officially, the mission of the delegation was to determine if the Dominican Republic had ceased to be a threat to hemispheric peace and security. In reality, the delegation was to verify that a communist government would not fill the power vacuum.[62] Ironically, there was very little chance of a communist takeover in the Dominican Republic. Ambassador Martin explained that "there weren't many Communists" in the Dominican Republic, but that hardly mattered because paranoia over communism had gripped US policy makers.[63] Although a few Dominicans had been trained by the Cubans, they hardly constituted a threat to Dominican stability. In addition, by this time, Castro had already decided that the support of Dominican exile invasions would be counterproductive to his goals since they might provide a justification, as well as set a precedent, for similar attempts by Cuban exiles. Nevertheless, US policy makers who heard the story of Castro's success in the Cuba with a handful of men were intimidated by the couple dozen communists roaming the Dominican countryside.[64]

Although Arango claimed that Balaguer was moving the island nation along the path toward democracy, Rusk indicated that the committee should have stayed longer than six days to study local conditions. Rusk claimed that Balaguer had produced a spectacular facade of liberalization solely for the benefit of the OAS delegation. Although most members of the delegation preferred a rapid lifting of diplomatic sanctions, US representative DeLesseps Morrison preferred a longer period of "wait and see."[65] Consequently, the decision to lift economic and diplomatic sanctions was postponed. In the words of Rusk: "Balaguer has given indication of good intentions with respect to liberalizing Dominican politics, but he has not yet thoroughly proved those good intentions and the past record indicates the need for considerable skepticism."[66]

Nevertheless, by 17 July, the State Department was convinced that the anti-communist liberals were not strong enough to rule on their own. The only thing they had in common was their shared desire to overthrow Trujilloism. In the words of Ambassador Martin, the opposition was "divided, its leaders child-like and politically naive, patriotic, but of doubtful ability to govern."[67] Kennedy defended his belief in Balaguer's ability to move the nation along the path toward democracy as follows: "Balaguer is our only tool. The anti-Communist liberals aren't strong enough. We must use our influence to take Balaguer along the road to democracy."[68] According to the State Department, "The situation in the Dominican Republic is precarious. From the US point of view, it would be desirable to strengthen President Balaguer and moderates within the government and to encourage and support an anti-Castro, middle-of-the-road opposition."[69]

The State Department, however, pointed out that the continuation of Ramfis as chief of the armed forces had prejudiced many democratic elements against the Dominican president. To correct this problem, it advocated improving Balaguer's image in Latin America by disassociating him from the Trujillo family. The new policy, however, cautioned that any attempt to remove the Trujillo family from the island before a solid base for representative government was established would be an invitation to civil war. On the other hand, to reestablish diplomatic and economic relations while Ramfis was still in charge of the military could give other Latin American countries the impression that the United States supported dictatorships. In addition, it might convince Balaguer's government to move more slowly in its reforms, while giving the opposition forces the impression that the United States accepted the continued domination of the Trujillo family and thus stimulate the opposition to take more revolutionary measures.[70]

On 18 July, therefore, Kennedy met with US Consul John Calvin Hill, who had replaced Dearborn, in the White House to discuss the Dominican situation. Kennedy instructed Hill to inform Balaguer that he was pleased with the steps taken by Balaguer to establish representative democracy in the Dominican Republic. But Kennedy also wanted Balaguer to know that he was specifically interested in the "progress of anti-Communist laws in [the] Dominican Congress, measures taken [to] exclude [the] return [of] Communist and Castroist exiles, and other actions taken [to] prevent infiltration and agitation by Communist-Castroist elements."[71] In addition, Kennedy told Hill to allude to the possibility of reinstating the Dominican share of the Cuban windfall should Balaguer continue to facilitate the democratization process.[72] On 27 July, Hill reported that Balaguer had reassured him that he was doing everything in his power to institutionalize democracy. In the words of Consul Hill: "The next several weeks [are] likely to have high content of danger to our objectives but some chance [to] get through successfully. If unreconstructed Trujillistas do not move to restore their power in that period, [it] will probably be too late for them oppose tide of reforms and they know it."[73] Hill also reported that the Trujillo family, now led by an elusive Ramfis, refused to deposit sugar export earnings in the Central Bank. Because of this, Dominican importers were unable to obtain dollars in the Central Bank to pay for their purchases. This led Hill to believe that the entire Trujillo family planned to abandon the country.[74]

As the summer progressed, US and Dominican politicians realized that the OAS-imposed sanctions were having an enormous psychological and economic effect on the Dominican political economy. On 27 July, Charles McLaughlin, a former US Marine officer whose daughter was married to Héctor Trujillo, visited Assistant Secretary of State Robert F. Woodward and Robert Murphy in Washington to discuss recent events in the Dominican Republic. McLaughlin, who represented the interests of the Trujillo family, argued that the political and economic sanctions were causing unemployment and could very well benefit the communists. McLaughlin was informed that the sanctions would be lifted promptly, as soon as Balaguer "proved his democratic credentials."[75]

On 31 July, Consul Hill finally met Ramfis at his luxurious Boca Chica retreat. Hill observed that Ramfis "entered confidently into conversation, effectively conveying both opposition to Castro/Communism and determination to back President Balaguer's liberalization program."[76] According to Hill, the most interesting part of the evening's conversation came when Ramfis cautioned the United States to keep an eye on Manuel Tavárez Justo, a communist and the leader of the AP1J4 movement, because "I [Ramfis] don't intend to spend the rest of my life here in this job."[77] Ramfis also claimed that the economic sanctions were contributing psychologically more than materially to a situation wherein communists could be incited. He suggested, therefore, that the United States take the initiative in the OAS to push for lifting economic and diplomatic sanctions against the Dominican Republic.[78]

On 2 August, Kennedy held a meeting at the White House to discuss events in the Dominican Republic. It was decided that Hill would be instructed to inform Balaguer that the United States would investigate the technical and political problems involved in the partial lifting of the OAS sanctions, except those that applied to weapons and sugar.[79] The partial lifting of sanctions, however, required Venezuela's approval.[80] The Venezuelan government insisted that the sanctions remain until Balaguer had proven himself completely.[81] Regardless, for the first time the United States seriously contemplated the possibility of reducing the economic sanctions. In practical terms this was not very important, but in political terms it meant support for the Balaguer-Ramfis regime.

On 7 August, the OAS convened in Punta del Este, Uruguay. Within a few days, the Special Committee for Dominican Matters decided to send Ambassador

Arango's investigative team back to Ciudad Trujillo. Luis Mercado, the Dominican representative to the conference, sent a cable to Balaguer informing him that Morrison had assured him that if all went well, the economic sanctions would be lifted by September. Balaguer was thrilled. The only problem was that Mercado was telling a lie to ingratiate himself with Balaguer. That same night, Hill spent the evening convincing Ramfis that Mercado was lying. Ramfis immediately telephoned Mercado, ordering the man to return to the Dominican Republic.[82]

On 11 August, Ramfis announced to the *New York Times* that if diplomatic and economic relations were not restored with his country promptly, there would be a revolution in the Dominican Republic stimulated by the leftist opposition or within the military, and this would produce problems worse than those in Cuba. Ramfis concluded: "I believe that if relations are not resumed before the elections, there will not be any elections, because the current government cannot maintain itself in power without the help of the other American nations."[83]

The political situation in Ciudad Trujillo grew worse in August. The same elements that assassinated Trujillo increased their pressure on Ramfis to democratize the nation. A series of political clashes between the opposition political parties and the military threatened to negate Balaguer's efforts. The military was worried about its future and was reacting with violence against the opposition forces. In order to calm the military, on 25 August, Balaguer announced that any crimes committed by the military against the people during the Trujillo regime were the responsibility of Trujillo, and not the individual military members who carried out their instructions.[84]

Meanwhile, on 27 August, Secretary Rusk informed the president that any attempt to convince the OAS to lift the economic sanctions on petroleum and spare parts would be impossible because of recent acts of repression in Ciudad Trujillo against the opposition. Rusk cautioned that the Dominican Republic would earn an extra $28 million from windfall sugar sales to the United States as soon as diplomatic relations were restored. Since one of the biggest problems was the Trujillo family's ownership of the majority of the Dominican sugar industry, Rusk suggested that the Trujillo family give the sugar mills to a government foundation, because failure to do so would provide the Trujillo family with two-thirds of the extra $28 million, and this would cause an international scandal.[85]

Rusk explained that the Kennedy administration's four negotiating strengths were: (1) the promise to reestablish diplomatic relations; (2) the promise to reinstate the valuable windfall quota; (3) the threat of removing the basic Dominican sugar quota; and (4) the threat of the US military forces off the coast of Ciudad Trujillo.[86] Rusk suggested that it would be wiser to first induce the Trujillo family to flee the country, and then reconsider establishing diplomatic relations with the country. If the Trujillo family obtained the extra $28 million, it would be one less incentive to encourage democratization. According to Rusk: "Our capacity to influence events in the Dominican Republic is greatly strengthened by the promise of a valuable sugar quota."[87] It should also be noted, however, that Rusk took a very pragmatic approach to US foreign policy making. Rusk noted: "It will be noted that our bargaining assets, although important, do not afford us the ability to control the situation in the Dominican Republic."[88] The United States, therefore, continued to publicly and privately support Balaguer's government. Rusk explained:

Assuming [the] Trujillo family complies with transfer schedule [of the sugar properties] and OAS has acted favorably, USG reestablishes diplomatic relations. This action immediately makes GODR technically eligible receive part of Cuban windfall sugar quota at premium prices but [it is] unlikely any such benefits would be available for calendar 1961.[89]

AUGUST–DECEMBER 1961

Balaguer and the opposition forces anxiously awaited the arrival of the OAS delegation, but for different reasons. Viriato Fiallo, the leader of the UCN, believed that it was too soon to lift the economic and political sanctions imposed on the Dominican Republic at San José in August 1960. According to Fiallo, if the United States reinstated the benefits of the windfall quota while the Trujillo family still controlled the country, many Dominicans would think that the United States supported the Trujillo family, and this would cause considerable hostility toward the United States.[90] On the other hand, although his democratization process experienced difficulty in August, Balaguer believed that significant progress had been achieved and hoped that the special OAS delegation would recommend the immediate lifting of the diplomatic and economic sanctions.[91] Fearful that the OAS delegation would not recommend lifting the sanctions if it perceived excessive violence in the Dominican Republic, on 7 September, Balaguer named Marcos A. Jorge Moreno chief of police to replace José Caonabo Fernández, who was tainted by the police violence of August.[92] On 10 September, Balaguer ordered the police and army not to interfere in political rallies. Balaguer declared that any member of the police or intelligence service who used violence against political activists would be suspended from service and subjected to a trial.[93]

On 12 September, DeLesseps Morrison and the OAS delegation arrived in a US Air Force plane. The delegation was met at the international airport by 2,000 people carrying pro-Balaguer placards.[94] The opposition forces, however, had prepared their welcome for the delegation at the Duarte Bridge, on the outskirts of Ciudad Trujillo. The delegation was met by an angry mob with the corpse of Dr. Víctor Rafael Estrella Liz, a prominent dissident, wrapped in a flag with a banner that read: "OAS—This is the kind of brutality that we ask you to end."[95] After leaving the scene, the OAS delegation fled to the Hotel Embajador in speeding cars.

That night, Morrison had a secret meeting with Balaguer, who apologized to Morrison for the incident on the bridge. Balaguer announced that he was planning to invite the leaders of the three principal opposition groups to join his cabinet. When Morrison recommended that Balaguer deport communist activists,

Balaguer replied he would try, but that it would be difficult because it would destroy the image of free elections. Obviously, neither Morrison nor Balaguer was worried about democracy—Morrison was worried about communism and Balaguer was worried about a democratic facade.[96] On the following morning the entire OAS delegation met with Balaguer. Later that afternoon, the delegates met with Ramfis.[97] The delegates also met with opposition leaders Viriato Fiallo (UCN), Manuel Tavárez Justo (AP1J4), and Angel Miolán (PRD).

Although Morrison had come to the Dominican Republic with a desire to lift the economic and diplomatic sanctions, after his exploratory visit he concluded that lifting the sanctions and granting the benefits of the windfall quota while the Trujillo family was still in power would give the impression to the Dominican people that the United States supported the Trujillo family and encouraged the return of dictatorial rule. At the end of his two-week visit, Morrison met privately with Ramfis at Boca Chica. Morrison candidly explained to Ramfis: "I began my trip believing that this government could save itself. I thought that it could serve as an interim government until elections. I cannot say that now. I do not think that it will last much longer. The hatred against your family is just too great."[98] In response, Ramfis proposed: "If the OAS sanctions are lifted, I will resign as Chief of the Armed Forces and leave the country."[99] Morrison helped Ramfis write the following to the chairman of the OAS delegation: "Conscious of the need for the Dominican Republic to reintegrate itself into the family of American nations, I will irrevocably resign my position as Chief of the Armed Forces as soon as the sanctions against my country are lifted."[100]

On 17 September, Ramfis mentioned the possibility of a military coup if the Dominican government failed to progress rapidly with the democratization process. He claimed that the economic sanctions were hurting the Dominican economy by diverting funds from public works projects, and thus causing unemployment and poverty among the masses. Ramfis concluded by stating that his fate was tied to that of Balaguer, and if the Balaguer government should be overthrown, then he would resign his commission.[101] That afternoon, Balaguer announced that he was developing a coalition government made up of representatives from the major political parties. Balaguer concluded his message by saying that unless the economic sanctions were removed and the windfall quota reinstated, the economy would continue to deteriorate and the political violence that followed would cause a military coup.[102]

On 30 September, Balaguer flew from Ciudad Trujillo to New York City with the special OAS delegation. On 2 October, in an emotional speech before the General Assembly of the United Nations, Balaguer publicly criticized the Trujillo dictatorship. He conceded that the attempt on Betancourt's life deserved punishment and acknowledged that the diplomatic and economic sanctions were correctly applied against the Trujillo regime. Balaguer, however, insisted: "It is not fair that the punishment should continue after the fall of the culprit. The sentence punishing a personal act, the result of hatred between two political rivals, cannot be maintained against the whole people."[103] Trujillo's widow chided

Ramfis for allowing Balaguer to insult his father in the United Nations.[104] Nevertheless, on 8 October, Ramfis welcomed Balaguer home as a hero. In spite of his mother's nasty letters and telephone calls, Ramfis hugged Balaguer profusely at the airport. Balaguer and Ramfis were confident that the economic sanctions would be lifted promptly.[105]

Meanwhile, on 26 September, Kennedy's special investigator John Bartlow Martin sent the president a 115-page report on the Dominican Republic. Martin emphasized that sugar quota legislation and the US Navy, commonly referred to as the cuota y flota threat, were Kennedy's most powerful inducements to convince Balaguer and Ramfis to continue the democratization process. Regarding the potential of sugar quota legislation, Martin stated:

I would guess that the Republic's current economic difficulties were begun by the [Trujillo] family's plundering and that they continue because sanctions, particularly diplomatic, have dried up foreign investment, destroyed outside and local confidence, and stopped domestic credit and foreign exchange. Nothing short of a lifting of sanctions, foreign investment, and perhaps US government aid will get the economy moving again.[106]

Regarding the potential of the US military, Martin stated:

All negotiations with Balaguer and Ramfis should be negotiated with the US fleet just over the horizon. This will create a very dramatic atmosphere. It would please the opposition, who would believe that the fleet was there to protect them; and Ramfis, who understands force, would be more pliable if we confront him with the fleet.[107]

Martin recommended that Kennedy support Balaguer in his drive toward democratization, encourage the creation of a coalition government, send Héctor and Arismendi Trujillo into exile, convince Ramfis to give the sugar mills to a public foundation, disarm the terror apparatus within the government, and eventually send extensive economic and military aid to the nation.[108]

Kennedy read Martin's report one afternoon while listening to the World Series.[109] Martin's ideas became the basis of Kennedy's new policy toward the Dominican Republic—the so-called Kennedy Plan. The Kennedy administration outlined its strengths as follows: "We have considerable bargaining power since recognition, relinquishment of sanctions, trade with US, etc. are essential to the success of the government. We can, in my estimation, use this bargaining power much more effectively if we use it with a realization of the realities of the situation."[110] The Kennedy Plan, whose primary goal was the prevention of the establishment of a pro-communist state in the Dominican Republic, consisted of several major components, the most essential being the following: (1) the donation of the Trujillo sugar properties to a public foundation; (2) the formation of a coalition government under Balaguer; and (3) the departure of Héctor (Negro) and Arismendi (Petán) Trujillo from the island. After these requirements were completed, the United States planned to resume diplomatic relations.[111]

On 13 October, Assistant Secretary of State George McGhee met with Ramfis to discuss the Kennedy Plan. Ramfis initially balked at the idea of donating without compensation the Trujillo family's vast sugar estates to a public foundation. Ramfis suggested that the best way to keep the Trujillo family from benefiting from the windfall quota would be for Balaguer to assign all of the windfall quota to sugar enterprises not owned by the Trujillo family. He implied that the problem would eventually be solved when the Trujillo family sold its sugar properties to foreign businessmen.[112] After McGhee explained that the Kennedy administration disapproved of the sale of the Trujillo sugar properties to US citizens while the sanctions were still in effect, Ramfis agreed to the salient points of the Kennedy Plan.[113] On 24 October, various members of the Trujillo family, among them the notorious Arismendi and Héctor Trujillo, left the island in order to facilitate a solution to the crisis.[114]

On behalf of Trujillo's heirs, on 25 October, Ramfis donated the Azucarera Haina, the largest of the three Trujillo sugar properties on the island, to an autonomous foundation called La Entidad 24 de Octubre, Fundación Trujillo Martínez. Ramfis decreed:

All profits obtained by the foundation which I have decided to establish will be used exclusively for the benefit of the Dominican people and that under no circumstances shall they be employed on behalf of foreign investors. By transferring the titles to the Azucarera Haina, which is worth more than RD$ 100 million, I not only offer an important asset for the betterment of the Dominican people, but also a monument to the glorious work of my father for the happiness of the national Dominican family.[115]

On 3 November, Ramfis donated the rest of his family's sugar mills to the foundation.[116] This was a major step in fulfilling the Kennedy Plan's request for the disbursement of the Trujillo family's economic holdings in the Dominican Republic.

On 28 October, Ramfis gave *El Caribe* a copy of the letter that he had given to the chairman of the special OAS delegation. In the letter, Ramfis explained that the economic sanctions were destroying the country. He promised to resign his position as chief of the armed forces as soon as the economic and political sanctions were removed. Significantly, Ramfis left out his previously made verbal promise to leave the country.[117] In order to maintain his position and give himself time to export his wealth, Ramfis maintained a facade in the Dominican press that he was not planning to leave the country.

Believing that Balaguer's progress in democratization required OAS recognition, the Kennedy administration sought to convince Venezuela to support the partial lifting of sanctions. In the words of Dean Rusk: "Because of the danger of a military takeover or a Fidelista alternative, it is hoped that Venezuela might refrain from opposing, if it could not support, a partial removal of the economic sanctions."[118] On 7 November, Venezuela responded to Rusk's initiative. Both the United States and Venezuela agreed that the main objective in the Dominican Republic was the creation of a stable, democratic government friendly to the inter-American community. Venezuela therefore advocated the immediate lifting of all sanctions "provided all Trujillos—including Ramfis—leave the Dominican Republic."[119]

Although he was unable to get Venezuelan support for the partial lifting of economic sanctions with Ramfis remaining in Ciudad Trujillo, Rusk pushed ahead with his proposal to seek the partial lifting of economic sanctions. He explained: "There has occurred in the Dominican Republic sufficient change to justify lifting minor sanctions (affecting petroleum, trucks, and spare parts), but not sufficient change to justify lifting San José sanctions, which are vastly more important."[120] Therefore, on 13 November, the United States suggested that the sanctions on petroleum and spare parts be lifted as a sign of acknowledging the constructive efforts of the Dominican government. The proposal would only affect the sanctions imposed in January of 1961, not those adopted at San José in August of 1960.[121] This pleased nobody in Ciudad Trujillo.

On the evening of 14 November, when he received the official notice that the United States would merely support the partial lifting of sanctions, a disappointed Ramfis called his uncles in Jamaica and told them that they could return whenever they wanted. Colonel Santiago (Chango) Rodríguez Echavarría flew to retrieve them in a military plane.[122] Although the Dominican press announced that this was a great triumph for the nation, Ramfis personally felt as though he had been tricked. Ramfis, who was expecting a complete lifting of the sanctions, decided to abandon the country and leave it in the hands of his uncles. That evening, he sent Balaguer his letter of resignation as chief of the armed forces.[123] On the afternoon of 15 November, Arismendi and Héctor, the so-called "wicked uncles" because of their attempt to revive the authoritarian military regime, returned to the Dominican Republic. The Kennedy Plan, which depended on the stability of Ramfis and the exile of the uncles, was in jeopardy.

On 17 November, a disgusted Rusk formally withdrew his nation's petition for the partial removal of sanctions against the Dominican Republic because of the return of Arismendi and Héctor Trujillo. The return of the wicked uncles threatened the advances made by the Dominican government and people towards democracy.[124] Meanwhile, events were moving rapidly in Ciudad Trujillo. At six o'clock in the evening on 18 November, six of the eight surviving cohorts in Trujillo's assassination were taken to the Hacienda María and executed by Ramfis, who boarded the frigate *Mella* afterwards and sailed into exile.[125] At the same time, Kennedy, who feared a military coup by Héctor and Arismendi, put the US Second Fleet on alert.[126] The fleet, commonly referred to as Operation Seagull, arrived off the coast of Ciudad Trujillo the following morning. As the US fleet positioned itself off the Dominican coast, crowds lining the *malecón* (Avenida George Washington) shouted *viva los imperialistas* (long live the imperialists), an ironic but sincere reflection of their pleasure that US warships were preserving the democratization process.[127]

US military intervention, however, was not needed to thwart the coup proposed by the wicked uncles. On 19 November, Santiago-based Air Force General Pedro Rafael Ramón Rodríguez Echavarría ordered his planes to bomb the perimeters of all major military bases in the country. Rodríguez Echavarría stated that the Air Force was proud of the recent movement toward democracy and "supported the civilian government and would not tolerate any attempts to reestablish a tyrannical and reactionary regime in the country."[128] While all of this was happening, Balaguer and Hill were in the National Palace convincing Héctor and Arismendi Trujillo to abandon the country. The wicked uncles understood that the United States would never grant the benefits of the Cuban windfall to the Dominican Republic as long as it appeared that they had access to the Dominican treasury. That night Héctor and Arismendi Trujillo left the country forever.[129]

On 22 November, the newly appointed chief of the armed forces, General Rodríguez Echavarría, called for an immediate lifting of the economic and diplomatic sanctions. He claimed that communist agitators infested the countryside, and that unless the United States and the other OAS members lifted the sanctions, the Dominican government would find it difficult to maintain order. Kennedy, however, felt that it was still too soon to remove the economic sanctions. The State Department contended:

Given the heated political climate of the Dominican Republic, the removal of OAS sanctions would surely be widely interpreted, both in the Dominican Republic and in Latin America generally, as further, conclusive evidence that the United States is committed to an indefinite continuation of the present regime. Longer term US interests dictate that a friendly, anti-Castro, anti-Communist government succeed the present one. The attainment of the latter objective hinges upon the state of US relations with the opposition which are deteriorating, because of the latter's belief that the US is, in effect, supporting the present government. With growing dissatisfaction in the Dominican Republic over OAS and US policy, Castro-minded influence in the opposition is increasing.[130]

Regardless, the principal objectives of the Kennedy Plan had been salvaged: (1) Arismendi and Héctor Trujillo had permanently abandoned the country, and the Trujillo family no longer maintained economic and political control over the country; (2) the Trujillo family sugar mills had been donated to a foundation, so that when the windfall quota was reinstated it would not benefit the Trujillo family; and (3) communist groups in the country had been contained and the threat of a Castroist revolution had diminished greatly. It only remained to create a coalition government.

Once Ramfis left the country, however, the State Department saw that Balaguer's leadership position represented neither order nor democracy. Balaguer no longer had the military support of Ramfis, but he was tainted by his association with the Trujillo family. Arturo Morales Carrión, a Puerto Rican working for the State Department, reminded Rusk that a Consejo de Estado was the formula implemented in Venezuela after the overthrow of Pérez Jiménez in 1958, and that it would be a good transition government for the Dominicans to organize elections. Kennedy liked the idea and sent Morales Carrión to the Dominican Republic in December to convince Balaguer to establish a Consejo de Estado.[131]

Although willing to form a transitional government, Balaguer was initially unwilling to resign before his constitutional term expired in August 1962. On 15 December, Balaguer agreed to resign from the Consejo de Estado after the sanctions were lifted and the windfall quota reinstated.[132]   On 17 December, Balaguer announced the formation of a Consejo de Estado, over which he would preside until economic sanctions against the Dominican Republic were lifted. When Consul Hill offered Balaguer his congratulations, Balaguer smirked and remarked: "After all, it was President Kennedy's plan."[133]   The members of the new Consejo de Estado—old Trujillo supporters who had recently become anti-Trujillo—were selected by Balaguer, Rodríguez Echavarría, Fiallo, and Hill.[134]

The Consejo de Estado was heralded by Kennedy as the cornerstone of the Dominican democratization process. In the words of Kennedy:

It represents, in my judgement, an impressive demonstration of statesmanship and responsibility by all concerned. This accomplishment by the opposition and the Dominican government is all the more remarkable when it is recalled that only recently the Dominican Republic emerged from three decades of a harshly repressive regime which dedicated itself to stifling every democratic voice. This victory of the Dominican people and its leaders is a striking demonstration of the fact that dictatorship can suppress but cannot destroy the aspirations of a people to live in freedom, dignity, and peace. The Dominican people still face long and difficult efforts to transform their aspirations into an effective, soundly based democratic system. In this struggle they have our sympathetic and tangible support. I understand that the OAS is now considering the lifting of the sanctions imposed upon the Dominican Republic by collective action in August 1960 and January 1961. If the Council of the OAS takes such action—and our representatives are supporting that step—we will resume diplomatic relations with the Dominican Republic shortly. When this takes place, the Department of Agriculture will authorize the purchase under the Dominican allocation of non-quota sugar for the first six months of 1962.[135]

JANUARY–DECEMBER 1962

On 4 January 1962, the OAS voted unanimously to lift all diplomatic and economic sanctions against the Dominican Republic. On 6 January, the United States resumed full diplomatic relations with the Dominican Republic.[136] As a result, the Dominican Republic was entitled to a basic quota of 96,308 tons and a nonquota allocation of the former Cuban sugar quota of 862,081 tons. At US premium prices this would have earned $104 million with a net profit on this amount of $27.5 million.[137] As long as Cuba and the United States did not resume diplomatic relations, it seemed that the Dominican Republic would continue to receive a huge share of the windfall quota at preferential prices. The concern that the United States might resume diplomatic relations with Cuba after Castro left the political scene prompted a member of the Consejo de Estado to later exclaim: "We hoped that the United States and Cuba would never settle their differences. The end of the Cold War has justified our fears. Vast amounts of development assistance have been diverted from the Third World toward Russia and Eastern Europe."[138]

Thus, the Kennedy administration decided to "continue to take an active part in Dominican affairs and not be unduly concerned about intervention."[139] The ensuing US policy toward the Dominican Republic, therefore, consisted of the following four objectives: "1) The maintenance of the Council in effective power; 2) control of the threat from the far left and the far right; 3) resolution of the current Dominican economic and financial difficulties; 4) sound preparation of the Dominican people for participation in the electoral process."[140] In early January it seemed that the Kennedy administration's plan to make the Dominican Republic a showcase of democracy was making headway.

On 17 January, however, a new wave of left-wing political violence broke out in Santo Domingo that threatened the Kennedy plan. Rodríguez Echavarría, the chief of the armed forces, claimed that Balaguer's Consejo de Estado was responsible for the political turmoil and staged a military coup. Balaguer took refuge with his next-door neighbor, the papal nuncio, and council members Bonnelly, Read, and Pichardo were imprisoned. Rodríguez Echavarría immediately set up a new Consejo de Estado.[141]

The Kennedy administration, however, strongly disapproved of the coup. US officials let it be known that the United States would suspend diplomatic relations, discontinue the windfall quota, and terminate all economic assistance unless the first Consejo de Estado was immediately restored.[142] These threats convinced most elements of Dominican society to work toward an appropriate settlement. Within two days, Dominican Air Force officials sent Rodríguez Echavarría, as well as Balaguer, into exile and reinstated the previous Consejo de Estado. Bonnelly became the president of the reinstated council and Donald Reid Cabral was brought in to fill Bonnelly's vacant seat.[143] The newly reinstated Consejo de Estado energetically committed itself to Kennedy's reform agenda in return for a generous sugar quota. Fearful that leftists might overthrow the Consejo de Estado, the Kennedy administration provided a $25 million Agency for International Development (AID) loan for economic and social development projects. A few weeks later, on 8 March, the United States agreed to provide the Consejo de Estado with over $1 million in military aid to maintain internal security.[144]

There still existed the volatile question of the $22.6 million in special fees charged against Dominican sugar exports during the last quarter of 1960 and the first quarter of 1961. The collected fees had reverted to the US treasury, and no provision had been made for their eventual return. The US-owned South Porto Rico Sugar Company had filed suit against the United States government for its share of the fees, about $7 million, and the Dominican government inherited from the Trujillo regime a suit against the United States government for the return of about $14 million. The principal basis for the suits was the claim that the executive branch of the US government did not have authority to impose the fees.[145] Since the topic had become a major political issue in the Dominican Republic, the Consejo de Estado considered the resolution of this question important to its ability to continue its political and economic programs. According to Dominican Foreign Minister José Bonilla Atiles, the return of the $22.6 million was "more a political than a technical problem for his government, which was only interested in getting the money as soon as possible."[146] A much larger problem, however, loomed on the horizon. The US Sugar Act was about to expire on 30 June.

The Kennedy administration energetically sought an increased sugar quota for the Dominican Republic. Rusk explained: "Without a sizeable quota for the sale of sugar at premium US market prices, the Dominican government will be forced either to subsidize the sugar industry, close down sugar mills, or reduce wages."[147] Domestic lobbyists, however, were pushing for diminished foreign sugar quotas. Congressman Cooley, who had previously championed a large sugar quota for the Dominican Republic during the Trujillo era, now wanted to decrease the Dominican Republic's basic quota to 190,000 tons and limit its participation in the Cuban windfall to 160,000 tons annually. To make matters worse, Cooley wanted to abolish the premium price paid for windfall quotas.[148] The Kennedy administration opposed Cooley's bill. Rusk stated: "In the emotional Dominican scene, with a critical election period rapidly approaching, the sugar legislation issue has given an important propaganda advantage to the Castro/Communist elements. Even the moderate, pro-US political groups have been forced to take a nationalist anti-US stand."[149]

Dominican politicians were outraged by the proposed quota cutbacks. In the words of Consul Hill, "Even our best friends here feel betrayed. They feel the US Executive has, by its promises of help, put them out on a limb and now Congress has sawed the limb off."[150] President Bonnelly, who looked to the income from sugar exports as the means to establish the Dominican economy on a firm basis, finance needed economic and social reforms, and coopt the various pillars of the corporatist society, warned that "general suffering" would occur if new legislation adversely affected the Dominican sugar industry.[151] Secretary of Agriculture Héctor Aristy claimed that a reduction of the Dominican quota would be "the grossest monstrosity committed by Congress in recent times."[152] The president of the Santo Domingo Chamber of Commerce argued that Cooley's proposition threatened to weaken fragile democratic institutions and "would without doubt make the best and most effective contribution to the establishment of a new base for international communism."[153] A representative for the UCN stressed the theme that the Dominican Republic "was intended as a show-window [the literal translation of showcase in Spanish] of the Alliance for Progress and that the proposed legislation would represent a brick through that window."[154]

Nevertheless, on 30 June, the US Congress passed a new sugar bill that gave the Dominican Republic a basic quota of 190,000 tons, plus a windfall quota (not at premium prices) of 440,000 tons. Under the old legislation, the Dominican sugar industry would have earned a profit of $27.3 million on the 954,390 tons of sugar exported to the United States at premium prices. Under the Cooley bill, the Dominican Republic would earn a profit of $5.5 million on the 190,000 tons of sugar exported to the United States at premium prices, but would lose $20.4 million on the 768,389 tons sold at world market prices.[155] In order to preempt the position of the extremists, the Consejo de Estado immediately issued a statement suspending the $25 million AID loan for social and economic projects that was granted in January 1961. According to the Consejo de Estado,

> If the situation created by the sugar legislation is not reconsidered satisfactorily, the Council of State will study the need of a basic reorientation of the economic and social problems of the country, in both its domestic and foreign aspects, because the present attitude of the US government frustrates the purpose of the Alliance for Progress. The Council has taken the position that it cannot agree to loans as a substitute for a sugar quota on the grounds that it cannot commit a successor government to a large foreign debt.[156]

The highly charged situation in Santo Domingo was kindled by the still unresolved issue of the return of the $22.6 million in sugar taxes.

Ambassador Martin immediately contacted Washington. On 1 July, Kennedy proposed a solution to the Dominican sugar crisis. He decided that the new quota, plus the Cuban windfall, was worth $31 million less in profits than the Dominicans would have received in 1962 under the old legislation. Recognizing the special case of the Dominican Republic, Kennedy undertook to make up the difference. An Agency for International Development economic grant worth over $30 million was designed to assist the Dominican government in the diversification of its economy and to help cushion the impact of the new sugar quota legislation.[157] As a result, the Dominican Republic received more aid per capita in 1962 than any other Alliance for Progress country. US economic aid to the Dominican Republic amounted to over $22 for each Dominican—more than three times the average per capita amount for the rest of Latin America taken as a whole. Although this strengthened the Dominican political economy, it reinforced Dominican dependency on the United States.[158] On 9 July, a grateful President Bonnelly stated: "Only the understanding attitude of the US Executive has prevented what would have been an economic catastrophe of unforeseeable political and social consequences."[159]

The Kennedy administration and the Consejo de Estado spent the rest of the year planning for presidential elections in December. Kennedy continued to use sugar policy to push the Dominican Republic along the path toward representative democracy. A piece of legislation passed by the US Congress in July, the so-called Honeybee Bill, gave the Dominican Republic an extra basic quota of 130,000 tons annually. Kennedy explained the purpose of the legislation as follows: "It is my intention to use this authority to allocate 130,000 tons annually to the Dominican Republic, in recognition of that nation's economic dependence upon sugar and its problems of transition from the Trujillo regime."[160] To make the pot even sweeter, on 7 December, the Kennedy administration announced that the Dominican Republic would receive a special $23,750,000 grant distributed through the Alliance for Progress. The grant, which represented the sum withheld from Dominican sugar exports from 1960 to 1961 as a punitive measure against the Trujillo regime, was earmarked for economic and social development projects.[161]

On 20 December, Juan Bosch, poet and lifelong opponent of Trujillo, won the presidential elections. His election seemed to mark the success of US policy in the

Dominican Republic.[162]   In his congratulatory note to Bosch, an exuberant Kennedy stated:

The 20 December elections, which marked an important milestone in the return of the Dominican nation to the ranks of representative democracy, heartened free men everywhere as an example to the world of a people's determination to build a free society after long years of dictatorial rule. The government of the United States, acting in the spirit of friendship which has joined our peoples, looks forward to cooperating with you and your government under the Alliance for progress in the continuing and arduous work of reconstruction.[163]

From the dismantling of Trujilloism and the successful installation of the Consejo de Estado to the election and inauguration of a constitutional government in 1963, the United States used the sugar quota to pursue its goals in the Dominican Republic. US political and economic hegemony had been upheld and the Dominican Republic, which greatly benefited from expanded sugar exports at preferential prices and other forms of foreign aid, represented a showcase for pro-US democracy in Latin America.

NOTES

1. Henry Dearborn to the State Department, 24 February 1961; Decimal File 739.00/4-161, Box 1637; Dominican Republic, 1960–63; RG 59; NA.

2. Dean Rusk to the President, 15 February 1961; General Files 1/61– 6/61, Box 66; Country Series, National Security Files (CSNSF, hereafter); John F. Kennedy Library (JFK, hereafter); Boston, MA (MA, hereafter).

3. John Hugh Crimmins to Robert Woodward, 6 March 1962; Decimal File 839.235, Box 2459; Dominican Republic, 1960–63; RG 59; NA. Notwithstanding the tax on Dominican sugar, Trujillo still earned millions of dollars from sugar exports to the United States.

4. Charles L. Hodge to the State Department, 29 May 1961; Decimal File 839.00/5-2961, Box 2457; Dominican Republic, 1960–63; RG 59; NA.

5. John D. Martz, "Democracy and the Imposition of Values: Definitions and Diplomacy," in Latin America, the United States, and the Inter-American System, ed. John Martz and Lars Schoultz (Boulder, CO: Westview, 1980), p. 149.

6. Ibid. The economic and social reforms called for in Kennedy's new program included enfranchisement of the masses, constitutional government, industrialization, land reform, expansion of the education system, and health care reform.

7. Harold Molineu, US Policy Toward Latin America: From Regionalism to Globalism (Boulder, CO: Westview, 1986), p. 29. In the words of Molineu, "Although the rhetoric of the Alliance was one of cooperation and reform, the actions of the Kennedy administration showed that US priority was being given to its own security needs."

8. Dean Rusk, speech, 25 January 1962, to the Eighth Meeting of Ministers of Foreign Affairs of the OAS, Punta del Este, in Department of State Bulletin 46 (January–June 1962), p. 275.

9. Department of State Bulletin 44 (3 April 1961): 471–474.

10. Memorandum from the State Department to McGeorge Bundy, 5 May 1961; General Files 1/61–6/61, Box 66; CSNSF; JFK; MA.

11. Although the phrase "showcase for democracy" was never employed by Kennedy or the State Department, it was soon given wide currency in the mass media. I am grateful to Eric Roorda for bringing this to my attention.

12. *New York Times*, 23 February 1961.

13. Charles L. Hodge to the State Department, 23 February 1961; Economic Conditions Folder, Box 244; Dominican Republic, Narrative Reports, 1955–61; RG 166; NA.

14. John D. Barfield to the State Department, 30 January 1961; Decimal File 839.235, Box 2459; Dominican Republic, 1960–63; RG 59; NA.

15. Richard M. Bissel to McGeorge Bundy, 17 February 1961; General Files 1/61–6/61, Box 66; CSNSF; JFK; MA.

16. Thomas Mann to the Secretary of State, 17 March 1961; Decimal File 739.00/4-161, Box 1637; Dominican Republic, 1960–63; RG 59; NA.

17. Charles L. Hodge to the State Department, 23 February 1961; Economic Conditions Folder, Box 244; Dominican Republic, Narrative Reports, 1955–61; RG 166; NA.

18. *New York Times*, 3 July 1962.

19. *Washington Post*, 3 April 1961. Cooley had a point. Haitian dictator Francois Duvalier continued to receive his sugar quota.

20. *Washington Post*, 14 March 1961.

21. Henry Dearborn to the State Department, 23 March 1961; Decimal File 739.00/1-561, Box 1642; Dominican Republic, 1960–63; RG 59; NA. The Dominican government refused to allow any mention of the Kennedy administration's attempts to exclude the Dominican Republic from the Cuban windfall in the public media.

22. Porfirio Herrera Báez to Igor Cassini, 13 November 1960; File 10491; APG; PND; SD.

23. Igor Cassini to Porfirio Herrera Báez, 18 February 1961; File 87230; APG; PND; SD.

24. Dean Rusk to the President, 15 February 1961; General Files 1/61–6/61, Box 66; CSNSF; JFK; MA.

25. César A. Saillant, *Revalaciones a Sánchez Cabral* (Santo Domingo: El Caribe, 1962), pp. 13–14. Saillant was personal secretary for Ramfis until February 1962, when he and Ramfis fought over Saillant's long distance telephone calls.

26. Ibid.

27. Philip W. Bonsal to Augusto G. Arango, 12 May 1961; Sugar Folder, Box 246; Dominican Republic, Narrative Reports, 1955–61; RG 166; NA. The Dominican quota had increased annually for two reasons: greater US consumption needs and rewards to the Trujillo regime.

28. Ibid.

29. Robert Murphy to McGeorge Bundy, 16 April 1961; Murphy Files 5/61–7/61, Box 66; CSNSF; JFK; MA.

30. Charles L. Hodge to the State Department, 26 April 1961; Economic Conditions Folder, Box 244; Dominican Republic, Narrative Reports, 1955–61; RG 166; NA.

31. McGeorge Bundy to the President, 2 May 1961; Murphy Files 5/61–7/61, Box 66; CSNSF; JFK; MA. Trujillo obtained a distorted picture of US policy toward the Dominican Republic since Murphy persisted in trying to modify and soften the official US policy.

32. US Senate, Committee on Foreign Relations, *Alleged Assassination Plots Involving Foreign Leaders*, Report No. 94-465, 20 November 1975, pp. 203–209.

33. Lt. General Earle G. Wheeler to General Clifton, 5 May 1961; General Files 1/61–6/61, Box 66; CSNSF; JFK; MA. Kennedy demanded that contingency plans be developed to enforce a naval blockade of the Dominican Republic should Trujillo be removed from power without US support.

34. Bernard Diederich, *The Death of the Dictator* (Maplewood, NJ: Waterfront, 1990), p. 88. These were some the weapons that de la Maza's group used to assassinate Trujillo later in the month.

35. Luis Mercado to Trujillo, 24 April 1961; File 30101; APG; PND; SD.

36. César Saillant, "Mis Memorias Junto a Ramfis," unpublished manuscript, 1962, p. 87.

37. *El Caribe*, 5 April 1961.

38. *New York Times*, 23 April 1961. Castro refused the offer.

39. *El Caribe*, 25 May 1961.

40. Manuel de Jesús Javier García, *Mis Viente Años en el Palacio Nacional Junto a Trujillo y Otros Gobernantes Dominicanos* (Santo Domingo: Plus Ultra, 1962), p. 152.

41. *New York Times*, 23 May 1961. In January, Trujillo had accused Reilly of inspiring terrorism and of manufacturing bombs in his home. After Bishop Reilly's home in San Juan de la Maguana was destroyed by SIM agents he took refuge in a Catholic girls' school in Ciudad Trujillo. The Dominican press and radio were clamoring for the expulsion of Bishop Reilly and Bishop Francisco Panal of La Vega.

42. Charles L. Hodge to the Department of State, 29 May 1961; Decimal File 839.00/5-2961, Box 2457; Dominican Republic, 1960–63; RG 59; NA.

43. Stephen Rabe, "The Caribbean Triangle: Betancourt, Castro, and Trujillo and US Foreign Policy, 1958–1963" *Diplomatic History* 20 (winter, 1996): 73.

44. Diederich, *The Death of the Dictator*, pp. 82–121. Amiama Tió was *compadre* (the relationship between a father and a godfather) of Modesto Díaz and Román Fernández. Román Fernández was compadre of Juan Tómas Díaz, Modesto's brother. Livio Cedeño was compadre of Juan Tómas Díaz and Tejeda Pimentel. Antonio de la Maza was a childhood friend of Juan Tómas Díaz. Cáceres was Antonio de la Maza's cousin. Estrella Sadhalá was compadre of Antonio de la Maza. Imbert Barreras was Estrella's compadre. García Guerrero was Estrella's wife's cousin. Báez Díaz was Modesto and Juan Tómas Díaz's cousin. Pastoriza was Livio Cedeño's best friend.

45. Ibid., p. 30.

46. John Calvin Hill to the Department of State, 6 June 1961; Decimal File 739.00(w)/6-661, Box 1642; Dominican Republic, 1960–63; RG 59; NA. Within six days of Trujillo's assassination, eleven of the thirteen conspirators had been killed or captured. García Guerrero was killed on 2 June; Juan Tómas Díaz and Antonio de la Maza were killed on 4 June; Báez Díaz and Román Fernández were killed in October; Livio Cedeño, Tejeda Pimentel, Pastoriza, Modesto Díaz, Cáceres, and Estrella Sadhalá were killed by Ramfis on 18 November. Amiama Tió and Imbert Barreras were never captured.

47. Arthur M. Schlesinger, Jr., *A Thousand Days: John F. Kennedy in the White House* (New York: Houghton Mifflin, 1965), p. 769.

48. Richard Goodwin to McGeorge Bundy, 8 June 1961; General Files 1/61–6/61, Box 66; CSNSF; JFK; MA.

49. Dean Rusk to Henry Dearborn, 1 June 1961; Decimal File 739.00/6-161, Box 1637; Dominican Republic, 1960–63; RG 59; NA.

50. Joaquín Balaguer, *Memorias de un Cortesano de la "Era de Trujillo"* (Santo Domingo: Corripio, 1989), p. 151.

51. *El Caribe*, 4 June 1961.

52. *El Caribe*, 8 June 1961.

53. Carmine S. Bellino to P. Kenneth O'Donnell, 28 June 1961, *John F. Kennedy National Security Files: Latin America, 1961–1963*, Reel 4, pp. 442–43.

54. José G. Guerrero, "La Política Norteamericana y el Gobierno de Joaquín Balaguer (Junio–Diciembre 1961)," *Revista Dominicano de Antropologia e Historia* 12 (1982): 183–244. Abbes was one of those most responsible for the anti-US Radio Caribe attacks.

55. *El Caribe*, 13 June 1961.

56. Piero Gleijeses, *The Dominican Crisis: The 1965 Constitutional Revolt and American Intervention* (Baltimore, MD: The Johns Hopkins University Press, 1978), p. 39. The PRD, formed by Dominican exiles in Cuba in 1939, was a moderate, middle-of-the-road group. Juan Bosch, its leader, was comparable to Venezuela's Betancourt and other sanitized, liberal democrats in Latin America. A 7 June PRD rally in the capital attracted close to ten thousand people. The UCN was founded by members of the old elite on 17 July. They were ready to sacrifice democracy in order to maintain the status quo. The AP1J4, born on 30 July, was a Castroist party ready to sacrifice democracy for social justice. The MPD was a small communist party.

57. Frank Moya Pons, *Manual de la Historia Dominicana* (Santo Domingo: Academia Dominicana de la Historia, 1977), p. 527.

58. Dean Rusk to the President, 12 July 1961; Folder 6, Box 115A; CSNSF; JFK; MA.

59. *El Caribe*, 5 July 1961.

60. *El Caribe*, 7 July 1961.

61. Oscar Ginebra to Balaguer, 20 July 1961; File 30356; APG; PND; SD. Balaguer, who was very pleased to hear this information, did not realize that Johnson was relatively uninvolved in the formulation of foreign policy.

62. L. D. Battle to McGeorge Bundy, 16 June 1961; General Files 1/61– 6/61, Box 66; CSNSF; JFK; MA.

63. John Bartlow Martin, *Overtaken by Events* (Garden City, NY: Doubleday, 1966), p. 80.

64. Ibid.

65. *New York Times*, 16 June 1961.

66. Dean Rusk to the President, 12 July 1961; Folder 6, Box 115A; CSNSF; JFK; MA.

67. Martin, *Overtaken by Events*, p. 80.

68. Schlesinger, *A Thousand Days*, p. 770. Schlesinger was referring to a quote made by Kennedy at a meeting held in the White House on 25 August.

69. Department of State to the President, 17 July 1961; General Files 7/61–8/61, Box 66; CSNSF; JFK; MA.

70. Ibid.

71. Dean Rusk to John Calvin Hill, 21 July 1961; General Files 7/61–8/61, Box 66; CSNSF; JFK; MA.

72. Ibid.

73. John Calvin Hill to the Secretary of State, 27 July 1961; General Files 7/61–8/61, Box 66; CSNSF; JFK; MA.

74. John Calvin Hill to the Secretary of State, 28 July 1961; General Files 7/61–8/61, Box 66; CSNSF; JFK; MA. On 27 August, Trujillo's widow, Doña María, went into exile. Historian Bernardo Vega argues that one of the reasons that Ramfis returned to the island after his father's death was to collect as many dollars as he possibly could. Bernardo Vega, interview with author, December 1992.

75. Dean Rusk to the President, 27 July 1961; Murphy File 5/61–7/61, Box 66; CSNSF; JFK; MA.

76. John Calvin Hill to the Secretary of State, 1 August 1961; General Files 7/61– 8/61, Box 66; CSNSF; JFK; MA.

77. Ibid.

78. Ibid.

79. Dean Rusk to John Calvin Hill, 2 August 1961; General Files 7/61–8/61, Box 66; CSNSF; JFK; MA.

80. Dean Rusk to Ambassador Moscoso, 28 August 1961, *John F. Kennedy National Security Files: Latin America, 1961–1963*, Reel 10, pp. 576–77. US Ambassador to Venezuela Moscoso was instructed to contact the Venezuelan foreign minister to ascertain the Venezuelan reaction to a US push for partial lifting of sanctions—petroleum, trucks, and spare parts—to support Balaguer's program of gradual democratization. It would "enable Balaguer to better withstand pressures from the military, and thus afford continuing opportunity for effective development of moderate political opposition."

81. Ambassador Moscoso to the Secretary of State, 29 August 1961, *John F. Kennedy National Security Files: Latin America, 1961–1963*, Reel 10, p. 582. According to Moscoso, "Finance Minister informed me that Venezuela will be unable to support GUS proposal lift suspension trade GODR. Foreign Minister responded that democracy in hemisphere undergoing heavy strains these days and no action should be taken which would indicate compromise with high principles."

82. John Calvin Hill to the State Department, 12 August 1961; Cable Folder 8/61–9/61, Box 66; CSNSF; JFK; MA.

83. *New York Times*, 18 August 1961.

84. Saillant, "Mis Memorias Junto a Ramfis," pp. 344–49.

85. Dean Rusk to the President, 27 August 1961; General Files 8/61–5/62, Box 66; CSNSF; JFK; MA.

86. Dean Rusk to US Consulate in Ciudad Trujillo, 31 August 1961; Economic Conditions Folder, Box 244; Dominican Republic, Narrative Reports, 1955–61; RG 166; NA.

87. Dean Rusk to the President, 27 August 1961; General Files 8/61–5/62, Box 66; CSNSF; JFK; MA.

88. Ibid.

89. Dean Rusk to John Calvin Hill, 1 September 1961; Cables Folder 8/61–9/61, Box 66; CSNSF; JFK; MA.

90. John Bartlow Martin to the President, 25 September 1961; Folder 9, Box 115A; CSNSF; JFK; MA.

91. *El Caribe*, 1 September 1961. On 31 August, the AP1J4 offices in Ciudad Trujillo were attacked and looted by the military.

92. *El Caribe*, 7 September 1961.

93. *El Caribe*, 11 September 1961.

94. DeLesseps Morrison, *Latin American Mission* (New York: Simon & Schuster, 1965), p. 5. Morrison points out, however, that this was a counterfeit welcome. As the US delegate left the airplane, he saw the line of busses that had brought the cheering crowd parked on a side street.

95. Balaguer, *Memorias de un Cortesano de la Era de Trujillo*, p. 161. Earlier in the day, 4,000 people had gathered to await the arrival of the OAS delegation. At 10:00 A.M., José Alfonso León Estévez tried to cross the bridge in a red Mercedez Benz owned by Luis José León Estévez, the husband of Trujillo's daughter Angelita. The crowd recognized the car as belonging to a member of the Trujillo family and started to throw rocks at it. The chauffeur opened fire on the crowd, killing the famous doctor and four others.

96. Morrison, *Latin American Mission*, pp. 8–10.

97. Ramfis Trujillo to Augusto Arango, 14 September 1961; Folder 6, Box 115A; Country Series, President's Office Files (CSPOF, hereafter); JFK; MA.

98. Morrison, *Latin American Mission*, pp. 9–11.

99. Ibid.

100. Ibid.

101. *El Caribe*, 17 September 1961.

102. *El Caribe*, 18 September 1961.

103. *New York Times*, 3 October 1961.

104. Saillant, "Mis Memorias Junto a Ramfis," p. 406. Doña María was living comfortably in Paris.

105. Balaguer, *Memorias de un Cortesano de la Era de Trujillo*, p. 164.

106. John Bartlow Martin to the President, 25 September 1961; Folder 9, Box 115A; CSPOF; JFK; MA.

107. Ibid.

108. Ibid.

109. Schlesinger, *A Thousand Days*, p. 642.

110. Richard N. Goodwin to the President, 3 October 1961; Murphy File 8/61–5/62, Box 66; CSNSF; JFK; MA.

111. Ibid.

112. John Calvin Hill to the State Department, 14 October 1961; Decimal File 739.13/2-1960, Box 1643; Dominican Republic, 1960–1963; RG 59; NA. Ramfis had been secretly negotiating to sell the Trujillo sugar holdings for $40 million to a US consortium.

113. John Calvin Hill to the State Department, 13 October 1961; Decimal File 739.13/2-1960, Box 1643; Dominican Republic, 1960–1963; RG 59; NA. All attempts by Ramfis to sell the family sugar properties met with failure because investors were aware that titles to many of the properties were open to dispute and that guarantees by the present regime might be meaningless under a successive government.

114. John Calvin Hill to the State Department, 26 October 1961; Decimal File 739.00/10-1561, Box 2459; Dominican Republic, 1960–63; RG 59; NA.

115. Charles L. Hodge to the State Department, 25 October 1961; Decimal File 839.00/10-2561, Box 2457; Dominican Republic, 1960-63; RG 59; NA. The corporation was named in honor of the dead dictator's birthday, 24 October.

116. *El Caribe*, 3 November 1961.

117. *El Caribe*, 29 October 1961. In the letter, Ramfis explained his father's philosophy of "from here to the grave." Trujillo had argued that the only way that he would leave the Dominican Republic would be on a stretcher. In the case of Ramfis it would be "from here to Paris." Ramfis had no intention of being as melodramatic.

118. Dean Rusk to Ambassador Teodoro Moscoso, 1 November 1961, *John F. Kennedy National Security Files: Latin America, 1961–1963*, Reel 10, pp. 616–17.

119. Ambassador Teodoro Moscoso to Dean Rusk, 8 November 1961, *John F. Kennedy National Security Files: Latin America, 1961–1963*, Reel 10, p. 621–22.

120. Dean Rusk to Ambassador Teodoro Moscoso, 9 November 1961, *John F. Kennedy National Security Files: Latin America, 1961–1963*, Reel 10, pp. 624–25.

121. *El Caribe*, 14 November 1961.

122. Saillant, "Mis Memorias Junto a Ramfis," p. 507.

123. Ramfis Trujillo to Joaquín Balaguer, 14 November 1961; File 44303; APG; PND; SD.

124. John Calvin Hill to Dean Rusk, 30 November 1961; Economic Conditions Folder, Box 244; Dominican Republic, Narrative Reports, 1955–61; RG 166; NA.

125. Diederich, *The Death of the Dictator*, pp. 236–38. Two of the conspirators in the Trujillo assassination plot, Luis Amiama Tió and Antonio Imbert Barreras, were still in hiding.

126. *New York Herald Tribune*, 18 January 1962.

127. Gineida Castillo, interview with author, December 1992.

128. *El Caribe*, 20 November 1961.

129. *New York Times*, 30 November 1961.

130. L. D. Battle to McGeorge Bundy, 22 November 1961; General Files 9/61–12/61, Box 66; CSNSF; JFK; MA.

131. *El Caribe*, 15 April 1989.

132. Dean Rusk to John Calvin Hill, 18 December 1961; General Files 9/61–12/61, Box 66; CSNSF; JFK; MA.

133. John Calvin Hill to the State Department, 19 December 1961; General Files 9/61–12/61, Box 66; CSNSF; JFK; MA.

134. *El Caribe*, 6 January 1962. The members of the Consejo de Estado were: Dr. Joaquín Balaguer; Lic. Rafael F. Bonnelly, a former minister during the Trujillo Era and associated with the UCN; Dr. Nicolás Pichardo, a cardiologist who was Trujillo's minister of health and associated with the UCN; Eduardo Read Barreras, a lawyer, ex-president of the Supreme Court, former minister of labor during the Trujillo Era, and associated with the UCN; Monseñor Eliseo Pérez Sánchez; and Antonio Imbert Barreras and Luis Amiama Tió, the two surviving members of the conspiracy group that killed Trujillo.

135. *New York Times*, 21 December 1961.

136. N. L. Parks to the State Department, 6 January 1962; Decimal File 739.00/1-262, Box 1642; Dominican Republic, 1960–1963; RG 59; NA.

137. William H. Brubeck to McGeorge Bundy, 23 June 1962; General Files 4/62–12/62, Box 66; CSNSF; JFK; MA.

138. *El Caribe*, 11 December 1992. The quote is attributed to Donald Reid Cabral.

139. L. D. Battle to McGeorge Bundy, 30 April 1962; General Files 4/62–12/62, Box 66; CSNSF; JFK; MA.

140. Ibid.

141. *El Caribe*, 18 January 1962. The new Consejo de Estado was composed of Humberto Bogaert (president), Armando Oscar Pacheco, Enrique Valdez Vidaurre, Wilfredo Medina Natalio, Neit Nivar Seijas, and two leftovers from the old council, Imbert and Amiama.

142. *Washington Post*, 18 January 1962.

143. *El Caribe*, 20 January 1961. The son of a Scottish bank teller who had married into one of the most prominent Dominican families, Donald Reid Cabral was a well-known used car salesman in Santo Domingo.

144. CIA Report to the President, 19 March 1962, General Files 1/62–3/62, Box 66; CSNSF; JFK; MA.

145. L. D. Battle to McGeorge Bundy, 29 March 1962; General Files 1/62– 3/62, Box 66; CSNSF; JFK; MA.

146. Edwin Martin to the President, 4 April 1962; General Files 4/62–12/62, Box 66; CSNSF; JFK; MA.

147. Dean Rusk to the President, 2 July 1962; General Files 4/62–12/62, Box 66; CSNSF; JFK; MA.

148. William H. Brubeck to Myer Feldman, 23 June 1962, General Files 4/62–12/62, Box 66; CSNSF; JFK; MA.

149. Dean Rusk to the President, 2 July 1962; General Files 4/62–12/62, Box 66; CSNSF; JFK; MA.

150. John Calvin Hill to the State Department, 20 June 1962; Decimal File 839.235, Box 2959; Dominican Republic, 1960–63; RG 59; NA.

151. John Bartlow Martin to the State Department, 18 May 1962; Decimal File 739.00(w)/5-1862, Box 1642; Dominican Republic, 1960–63; RG 59; NA.

152. Ibid.

153. Marino Auffant Pimentel to President Kennedy, 22 June 1962," *John F. Kennedy National Security Files: Latin America, 1961–1963*, Reel 9, Frame 871.

154. John Bartlow Martin to the State Department, 18 May 1962; Decimal File 739.00(w)/5-1862, Box 1642; Dominican Republic, 1960–63; RG 59; NA.

155. William H. Brubeck to Myer Feldman, 23 June 1962, General Files 4/62–12/62, Box 66; CSNSF; JFK; MA.   Sugar legislation did not come up for renewal until 31 December 1964.

156. John Bartlow Martin to the State Department, 6 July 1962; Decimal File 739.00(w)/7-662, Box 1642; Dominican Republic, 1960–63; RG 59; NA.

157. John Calvin Hill to the State Department, 3 July 1962; Decimal File 839.235, Box 2459; Dominican Republic, 1960–63; RG 59; NA.

158. Abraham F. Lowenthal, "Limits of American Power: The Lesson of the Dominican Republic," *Harper's Magazine* 228 (June 1964): 87.

159. John Bartlow Martin to the State Department, 13 July 1962; Decimal File 739.00/7-622, Box 1642; Dominican Republic, 1960–63; RG 59; NA.   On 10 July, the Dominicans decided to proceed with their AID-funded projects.

160. Dean Rusk to John Bartlow Martin, 13 July 1962; Decimal File 839.235, Box 2459; Dominican Republic, 1960–63; RG 59; NA.

161. John Bartlow Martin to the State Department, 26 December 1962; Decimal File 739.00/7-622, Box 1642; Dominican Republic, 1960–63; RG 59; NA.

162. John Bartlow Martin to the State Department, 21 December 1962; Decimal File 739.00/12-1562, Box 1641; Dominican Republic, 1960–63; RG 59; NA.   Although Bosch was inaugurated on 27 February 1963, his democratic experiment was ended by a military coup on 25 September 1963.

163. John F. Kennedy to Juan Bosch, 31 December 1962; Folder 4/62–12/62, Box 66; CSNSF; JFK; MA.

Conclusion

Sugar was the primary ingredient in diplomatic relations between the Dominican Republic and the United States throughout the twentieth century, and particularly during the watershed period from 1958 to 1962. Dominican and US policy makers repeatedly focused on sugar legislation to pursue the national interests of their respective nations. The contrasting definitions of national interest that Dominican and US leaders applied in their dealings with each other consistently revolved around sugar.

Since the nineteenth century, a colorful array of Dominican elites have consistently manipulated their country's national resources to preserve a hierarchical social order and line their own pockets. Primarily concerned with elite self-preservation, during the last quarter of the nineteenth century they encouraged the modernization of the sugar industry and the expansion of sugar exports for their own self-serving reasons. During the first three decades of the twentieth century, these elites facilitated US domination of the sugar industry in return for lucrative jobs and substantial revenues from sugar exports.

When General Trujillo came to power in 1930, he saw in the sugar industry a powerful tool to increase his power and prestige at home as well as abroad. Whereas lucrative revenues from an expanding sugar industry provided the dictator with the necessary funds to run his authoritarian state, the prestige of doing business with the US reinforced Trujillo's control over the island nation. During the Trujillo era, therefore, the sugar industry represented an essential pillar of the dictator's authoritarian corporatist power structure. During his lengthy rule, income from sugar taxes accounted for the majority of Dominican foreign currency revenues.

US policy makers, for their part, were motivated by a combination of national security, economic, and ideological concerns. Throughout the twentieth century, the United States promoted a policy of keeping the hemisphere free from the influence of hostile powers, especially the Nazis during the 1930s and the Soviets after World War II. The United States repeatedly attempted to impose its political and economic hegemony over its smaller neighbors to the south. At times, when the US felt that its security and economic interests in the hemisphere were not at jeopardy, it also sought to transplant its cherished institutions, especially democracy, to the Dominican Republic. In return for lip service to US ethnocentric civilizing efforts, acquiescence to US hegemonic assumptions, and support for US policies on the floor of international forums, Dominicans were rewarded with economic aid, military aid, and increased sugar quotas. Convinced that the Trujillo regime was not a threat to political and economic hegemony, the United States did not protest the dictator's acquisition of the Dominican sugar industry, which was primarily US-owned, during the 1950s. The US sugar corporations were adequately compensated, and the United States continued to be the island nation's largest trading partner.

A period of relatively friendly reciprocal manipulation, therefore, existed between the United States and the Dominican Republic until 1957. These friendly relations, however, were disrupted during the remaining years of Trujillo's lengthy rule. By 1958, the United States was concerned that Trujillo's harsh authoritarian style was setting the stage for a communist revolution in the Dominican Republic. Disturbed by the possible loss of US hegemony in the region, which was enhanced by Fidel Castro's victory in neighboring Cuba, the Eisenhower administration began to cool its relations with the Trujillo regime. Eisenhower was not merely distancing himself from an authoritarian dictator, he was attempting to defend US hegemony in the region by portraying the US on the side of democratic forces.

The Eisenhower administration initiated economic sanctions against Trujillo's authoritarian regime in an effort to convince the aging dictator to resign and begin the democratization of the Dominican political economy. In 1960, the removal of the Cuban sugar quota and its redistribution to other foreign nations—the so-called Cuban windfall—provided the United States with an enticing new economic opportunity to manipulate Dominican policy. Eisenhower's attempt to deny the Dominicans their share of the Cuban windfall, however, was blocked by a US Congress packed with Trujillo supporters in key positions. Trujillo's years of bribery and blackmail had apparently paid off. Unable to thwart Trujillo's access to the Cuban windfall, Eisenhower placed a punitive tax of $.02 per pound on the Dominican Republic's windfall quota sugar exports to the United States.

Notwithstanding the punitive tax on the windfall quota, Trujillo continued to export sugar to the United States and earn valuable foreign currency revenues. Trujillo still earned the preferential price on his basic quota, which was untouched by Eisenhower, and the world price (which was about two cents less than the US price) for his windfall quota. Although the Eisenhower administration wanted Trujillo to leave the Dominican political arena, it was not yet willing (or able) to play hardball with the dictator. Although Eisenhower wanted to prohibit Trujillo from receiving his share of the windfall quota, he never tried to deny the aging dictator his basic quota.

Emphasizing the threat of international communism, Trujillo continued to claim that the US sugar quota provided the economic resources that would help forestall communist infiltration. He warned US policy makers that failure to continue sugar purchases from the Dominican Republic would cause severe economic hardship and facilitate the coming to power of an anti-US, pro-Castro government on the island. For those US politicians not convinced by Trujillo's compelling, albeit overdramatic, anticommunist rhetoric, the dictator increased his bribery attempts to win supporters in the US Congress. Many US politicians, therefore, were reluctant to cancel the dictator's participation in the sugar quota. Not surprisingly, the termination of Trujillo family bribes in 1961 coincided with Representative Cooley's withdraw of support for a generous Dominican sugar quota.

The Kennedy administration, however, successfully expanded Eisenhower's sanctions, especially as they pertained to Dominican participation in the preferential US sugar market, in an attempt to liberalize the Dominican political system and stave off the possibility of a Castro-like communist takeover of the Dominican Republic. Although Kennedy obtained permission from a Democratic-controlled Congress to cancel Trujillo's participation in the Cuban windfall, he was unable to disrupt the Dominican Republic's basic quota of 130,000 tons. Thus, like his predecessor, he was unable to use economic sanctions to their fullest extent because of congressional obstacles. Although the US presidents had tremendous power and important bargaining assets, they were never able to completely control events in the Dominican Republic or the US Congress.

After Trujillo's assassination on 30 May 1961, the Kennedy administration used threats and promises revolving around the sugar quota to push the dictator's successors along a path toward democracy. The United States played an instrumental role in the transition from authoritarian dictatorship to democracy in the Dominican Republic. Since sugar remained the basis of the Dominican political economy, the principal vehicle of persuasion used by the United States to push the Dominican Republic along the path toward democracy was the promise of an increased sugar quota and the reinstatement of the windfall quota.

From June to December 1961, Dominican President Joaquín Balaguer, who was promised a generous preferential sugar quota, guided his nation along the road to democracy. The US offer to reinstate the Cuban windfall and expand the sugar quota became an increasingly useful incentive to Dominican political change. On the other hand, Dominican threats that the failure to obtain a generous preferential sugar quota inhibited the Dominican government's efforts to thwart possible communist menaces that might arise at home invariably conditioned US initiatives and responses.

After Trujillo's assassination, Dominican policy makers—haunted by the fear of not being able to sell their massive sugar harvest at a profit to coopt the various pillars of their corporatist society—eagerly acknowledged US hegemony and initiated democratization in return for a preferential US sugar quota. Although the US was not able to implant its particular variety of democracy in the

Dominican Republic, it was able to promote a more benign form of authoritarianism with a thin veneer of democracy. Dominican policy makers exaggerated the communist threat to scare the United States into giving more military and economic aid, especially an expanded sugar quota. The path to democracy, however, increased Dominican dependency on the United States. After 1962, more than 80 percent of Dominican sugar exports went to the United States.

The steps taken by the Eisenhower administration to replace the Trujillo regime with a government composed of moderate leaders, and the policies of the Kennedy administration to establish democracy in the Dominican Republic, illustrate the power of sugar quota legislation in US-Dominican relations. Kennedy was not merely interested in preventing a Castroist revolution in the Dominican Republic: he believed that the Dominican Republic could become a showcase of democracy and development. An effort to preempt a second Cuba and push the Dominicans along the path of democracy, the US decision to strip the Trujillo regime of its windfall quota was a statement against authoritarianism and a realistic political move to gain support in Latin America. The democratic election of Juan Bosch on 20 December 1962 and the subsequent allotment of a generous sugar quota indicated the apparent restoration of friendly reciprocal manipulation between the Dominican Republic and the United States.

In the period from 1958 to 1962, the United States used threats and promises revolving around sugar to uphold traditional US policies. Cold War anti-communism was the underlying factor for these actions. The Eisenhower and Kennedy administrations were merely the latest in a long line of US governments that used sugar policy to maintain US hegemony, expand trade and investment, and exclude hostile foreign influences. Trujillo, his predecessors, and his successors—although obviously playing from a weaker hand—consistently tried to manipulate US policy makers into granting them lucrative economic deals. Dominican elites frequently acknowledged US hegemonic assumptions in return for economic favors. These yearnings for self-preservation were the underlying factor for their behavior. For this reason, sugar policy has been a decisive factor at key moments in US-Dominican relations, especially between 1958 and 1962.

Bibliography

ARCHIVAL SOURCES

Archivo del Palacio Nacional Dominicano (PND), Santo Domingo
    Oficios de la Secretaría de Estado de Relaciones Exteriores (SRE)
    Archivo Particular del Generalísimo (APG)
Dwight D. Eisenhower Library (DDE), Abilene, Kansas
    Eisenhower, Dwight D.,
        Papers as President of the United States, 1953–61
        White House Central Files (WHCF), 1953–61
    Herter, Christian, Papers, 1959–61
    Oral History Program
Franklin D. Roosevelt Library (FDR), Hyde Park, New York
    Berle, Adolph, Papers
Herbert Hoover Library, West Branch, Iowa
    Pawley, William, Oral History
John F. Kennedy Library (JFK), Boston, Massachusetts
    Kennedy, John F.,
        Country Series, National Security Files (CSNSF)
        Country Series, President's Office Files (CSPOF)
    Oral History Program
Seeley G. Mudd Library, Princeton University, Princeton, NJ
    Martin, John Bartlow, Papers
Universidad Nacional Pedro Henríques Ureña (UNPHU), Santo Domingo
    Balaguer, Joaquín, Book Collection, 1948–78
US National Archives (NA), Washington, DC
    RG 59—Records of the Department of State
    RG 80—Records of the Army
    RG 84—Records of the Foreign Posts of the State Department
    RG 139—Records of the Dominican Customs Receivership
    RG 166—Records of the Foreign Agricultural Service

PUBLISHED DOCUMENTS

Declassified Documents Reference System. Washington, DC: Carrollton, 1977–81; Woodbridge, CT: Research Publications International, 1982–.

Foreign Relations of the United States (FRUS). Washington, DC: Government Printing Office, 1941–.

Herring, George C., ed. *John F. Kennedy National Security Files: Latin America, 1961–63.* Bethesda, MD: University Publications of America, 1987.

Minutes of Meetings of the US National Security Council. Washington, DC: Government Printing Office, 1986–.

Oficina Nacional de Estadística de la República Dominicana. *La Industria Azucarera en Marcha.* Ciudad Trujillo: Oficina Nacional de Estadística de la República Dominicana, 1955.

Oficina Nacional de Estadística de la República Dominicana. Estadística Industrial de la República Dominicana. Ciudad Trujillo: Oficina Nacional de Estadística de la República Dominicana, 1958.

Oficina Nacional de Estadística de la República Dominicana. *Comercio Exterior de la República Dominicana.* Ciudad Trujillo: Oficina Nacional de Estadística de la República Dominicana, 1960.

Oficina Nacional del Presidente de la República Dominicana. *Discursos, Mensajes y Proclamas.* Ciudad Trujillo: Oficina Nacional del Presidente de la República Dominicana, 1948–57.

Organization of American States. *Declaration of Santiago.* Washington, DC: Organization of American States, 1959.

Organization of American States. Marketing Problems of Sugar at the Hemisphere and World Levels. Washington, DC: Organization of American States, 1964

President Dwight D. Eisenhower's Office Files, 1953–61. Bethesda, MD: University Publications of America, 1986.

Rosenman, Samuel, ed. *The Public Papers and Addresses of Franklin D. Roosevelt,* vol. 9 (New York: Random House, 1941).

US Agency for International Development. *From Debt to Development.* Washington, DC: US Agency for International Development, 1985.

US Cuban Sugar Council. *Sugar: Facts and Figures, 1952.* Washington, DC: US Cuban Sugar Council, 1953.

US Department of Agriculture. *The Dominican Republic: Agriculture and Trade.* Washington, DC: Department of Agriculture, 1963.

—. *A History of Sugar Marketing.* Washington, DC: Department of Agriculture, 1978.

US Department of Commerce. *Economic Developments in the Dominican Republic, 1962.* Washington, DC: Department of Commerce, 1963.

US Tariff Commission. *Report to the President of the United States on Sugar.* Washington, DC: US Tariff Commission, 1934.

CONGRESSIONAL HEARINGS, HOUSE OF REPRESENTATIVES

Committee on Agriculture. *Amendment and Extension of the Sugar Act of 1948.* 86th Congress, 2nd Session, 1960.

—. *Amendments to the Sugar Act of 1948.* 84th Congress, 1st Session, 1955.

—. *Amendments to the Sugar Act of 1948.* 88th Congress, 1st Session, 1963.

—. *Extension of the Sugar Act of 1948.* 82nd Congress, 1st Session, 1951.
—. *Extension of the Sugar Act of 1948.* 87th Congress, 1st Session, 1961.
—. *History and Operations of the US Sugar Program.* 87th Congress, 2nd Session, 1962.
—. *Inclusion of Sugar Beets and Cane Sugar as Basic Commodities.* 73rd Congress, 2nd Session, 1934.
—. *Revision and Extension of the Sugar Act of 1948.* 84th Congress, 1st Session, 1955.
—. *Study of the Dominican Republic Agriculture and Sugar Industry*, 84th Congress, 1st Session, 1955.
—. *The Sugar Act of 1948.* 80th Congress, 1st Session, 1947.
Committee on Appropriations. *Mutual Security Appropriations for 1957.* 84th Congress, 2nd Session, 1956.
—. *Mutual Security Appropriations for 1958.* 85th Congress, 1st Session, 1957.
—. *Mutual Security Appropriations for 1959.* 85th Congress, 2nd Session, 1958.
—. *Mutual Security Appropriations for 1960.* 86th Congress, 1st Session, 1959.
—. *Mutual Security Appropriations for 1961.* 86th Congress, 2nd Session, 1960.
Committee on Foreign Affairs. *Report on US Relations with Latin America.* 86th Congress, 1st Session, 1959.

CONGRESSIONAL HEARINGS, SENATE

Committee on Finance. *Inclusion of Sugar Beets and Sugar Cane as Basic Agricultural Commodities.* 73rd Congress, 2nd Session, 1934.
Committee on Foreign Relations. *Activities of Nondiplomatic Representatives of Foreign Principals in the United States.* 88th Congress, 1st Session, 1963.
—. *Alleged Assassination Plots Involving Foreign Leaders.* 4th Congress, 1st Session, 1975.
—. *Report of a Study Mission by George D. Aiken to the Caribbean in December 1957.* 85th Congress, 2nd. Session, 1958.

NEWSPAPERS AND PERIODICALS

Ahora (Santo Domingo)
Annals of the Organization of American States
Boletín Mensual (Banco Central de la República Dominicana)
El Caribe (Santo Domingo)
Christian Science Monitor
Congressional Record
Department of State Bulletin
Journal of Commerce
Listín Diario (Santo Domingo)
Miami Herald
La Nación
New York Herald Tribune
New York Times
La Noticia (Santo Domingo)
Statutes at Large
Sugar Report (US Department of Agriculture)
Washington Post

BOOKS

Albert, Bill, and Adrian Graves, eds. *Crisis and Change in the International Sugar Economy, 1860–1914*. Edinburgh: ISC Press, 1984.

—. *The World Sugar Economy in War and Depression*. London: Rutledge, 1988.

Alemán, José Luis. *Veintisiete Ensayos sobre Economía y Sociedad Dominicana*. Santiago: Universidad Católica Madre y Maestra, 1982.

Alexander, Charles. *Holding the Line: The Eisenhower Era, 1952–61*. Bloomington: Indiana University Press, 1975.

Alvarez, Julia. *In the Time of the Butterflies*. New York: Penguin, 1994.

Ambrose, Stephen E. *Eisenhower, Volume II: The President*. New York: Simon & Schuster, 1983.

Ascuasiati, Carlos. *Diez Años de Economía Dominicana*. Santo Domingo: Taller, 1980.

Atkins, G. Pope. *Arms and Politics in the Dominican Republic*. Boulder, CO: Westview, 1981.

Atkins, G. Pope, and Larman C. Wilson. *The United States and the Trujillo Regime*. New Brunswick, NJ: Rutgers University Press, 1972.

—. *The Dominican Republic and the United States: From Imperialism to Transnationalism*. Athens: University of Georgia Press, 1998.

Báez Evertsz, Franc. *Azúcar y Dependencia en la República Dominicana*. Santo Domingo: Universidad Autónoma de Santo Domingo, 1978.

—. *La Formación del Sistema Agroexportador en el Caribe: República Dominicana y Cuba, 1515-1898*. Santo Domingo: Universidad Autónoma de Santo Domingo, 1986.

Balaguer, Joaquín. *Entre la Sangre del 30 de Mayo y la del 24 de Abril*. Madrid: Pareja, 1983.

—. *La Isla al Revés: Haití y el Destino Dominicano*. Santo Domingo: Corripio, 1984.

—. *Memorias de un Cortesano de la "Era de Trujillo."* Santo Domingo: Corripio, 1989.

—. *Mensajes Presidenciales*. Barcelona: Pareja, 1979.

—. *La Palabra Encadenada*. Santo Domingo: Corripio, 1984.

—. *El Pensamiento Vivo de Trujillo*. Ciudad Trujillo: Impresora Dominicana, 1955.

Baldwin, Robert E. *Nontariff Distortions on International Trade*. Washington, DC: Brookings Institute, 1970.

Bass, William. *Reciprocidad*. Santo Domingo: La Cuna de América, 1902.

Baud, Michiel. *Peasants and Tobacco in the Dominican Republic, 1870–1930*. Nashville: University of Tennessee Press, 1995.

Bell, Ian. *The Dominican Republic*. Boulder, CO: Westview Press, 1981.

Benítez, José A. *Las Antillas: Colonización, Azúcar e Imperialismo*. La Habana: Casa de las Américas, 1977.

de Besault, Lawrence. *President Trujillo: His Work and the Dominican Republic*. New York: Washington Publishing, 1936.

Bernhardt, Joshua. *The Sugar Industry and the Federal Government*. Washington, DC: Sugar Statistics Service, 1948.

Betances, Emelio. *State and Society in the Dominican Republic*. Boulder, CO: Westview, 1995.

Black, Jan Knippers. *The Dominican Republic: Politics and Development in an Unsoveriegn State*. Boston: Allen & Unwin, 1986.

Blasier, Cole. *The Hovering Giant: US Responses to Revolutionary Change in Latin America, 1910–85*. Pittsburgh: University of Pittsburgh Press, 1976.

Bosch, Juan. *Crisis de la Democracia de América en la República Dominicana*. Mexico City: Centro de Estudios y Documentación Sociales, 1964.

—. De Cristobal Colon a Fidel Castro: El Caribe, Frontera Imperial. Santo Domingo: Corripio, 1993.

—. *Trujillo: Causas de una Tiranía sin Ejemplo*. Santo Domingo: Impresora Arte y Cine, 1962.

—. *The Unfinished Experiment: Democracy in the Dominican Republic*. London: Pall Mall Press, 1968.

Bovard, James. *The Farm Fiasco*. San Francisco: Institute for Contemporary Studies, 1991.

Brea Franco, Julio. *Introdución al Proceso Electorial Dominicano*. Santo Domingo: Taller, 1984.

Calder, Bruce. *The Impact of Intervention: The Dominican Republic during the US Occupation of 1916–1924*. Austin: University of Texas Press, 1984.

Cardoso, Fernando, and Enzo Faletto. *Dependency and Development in Latin America*. Berkeley: University of California Press, 1979.

Cassá, Roberto. *Capitalismo y Dictadura*. Santo Domingo: Universidad Autónoma de Santo Domingo, 1982.

—. *Historia Social y Economía de la República Dominicana*. Santo Domingo: Alfa y Omega, 1977.

—. *Los Doce Años: Contrarevolución y Desarollismo*. Santo Domingo: Alfa y Omega, 1986.

Castro García, Teófilo. *Intervención Yanqui 1916–1924*. Santo Domingo, Taller, 1978.

Cepero Bonilla, Raúl. *Politica Azucarera*. Mexico City: Editora Nacional, 1958.

Chomsky, Noam, and Edward S. Herman. *The Washington Connection and Third World Fascism: The Political Economy of Human Rights*. Boston: South End Press, 1979.

Cohen, Benjamin. *In Whose Interest?* New Haven, CT: Yale University Press, 1986.

Coleman, Kenneth. "The Political Mythology of the Monroe Doctrine: Reflections on the Social Psychology of Hegemony." In *Latin America, the United States, and the Inter-American System*. Ed. John Martz and Lars Schoultz. Boulder, CO: Westview, 1980.

Connell-Smith, Gordon. *The United States and Latin America*. New York: John Wiley, 1974.

Corten, Andrés. *Azúcar y Política en la República Dominicana*. Santo Domingo: Taller, 1973.

Crassweller, Robert D. *Trujillo: The Life and Times of a Caribbean Dictator*. New York: Macmillan, 1966.

Curry, E. R. *Hoover's Dominican Diplomacy and the Origins of the Good Neighbor Policy*. New York: Garland Publishing, 1979.

Dalton, John E. *Sugar: A Case Study of Government Control*. New York: Macmillan, 1937.

Deere, Carmen, ed. *In the Shadows of the Sun: Caribbean Development Alternatives and US Policy*. Boulder, CO: Westview Press, 1990.

del Castillo, José. *Entre el Autoritarianismo y la Democracia: El Dilema del Sistema Político Dominicano*. Santo Domingo: Instituto Technológico de Santo Domingo, 1982.

—. "La Formación de la Industria Azucarera Moderna en la República Dominicana." In *Tobacco, Azúcar y Mineria*. Ed. Antonio Lluberes. Santo Domingo: Banco de Desarrollo Interamericano, 1984.

—. *La Gulf & Western en la República Dominicana*. Santo Domingo: Taller, 1974.

—. *La Inmigración de Braceros Azucareros en la República Dominicana, 1900–30*. Santo Domingo: Universidad Autónoma de Santo Domingo, 1968.

de la Rosa, Antonio. *Las Finanzas de Santo Domingo y el Control Americano*. Santo Domingo: Nacional, 1969.

Díaz Grullón, Virgilio. *Antinostalgia de una Era*. Santo Domingo: Fundación Cultural Dominicana, 1989.

Diederich, Bernard. *The Death of the Dictator*. Maplewood, NJ: Waterfront, 1990.

Dreirer, John C. *The Organization of American States and the Hemisphere Crisis*. New York: Harper & Row, 1962.

Eisenhower, Dwight D. *Mandate for Change, 1953–56*. Garden City, NY: Doubleday, 1963.

—. *Waging Peace, 1956–61*. Garden City, NY: Doubleday, 1965.

Eisenhower, Milton. *The Wine Is Bitter*. Garden City, NY: Doubleday, 1963.

Espaillat, Arturo. *Trujillo: El Ultimo de los Césares*. Santo Domingo: Editorial Nacional, 1963.

Espinal, Rosario. *Autoritarianismo y Democracia en la Política Dominicana*. San José: Centro de Asesoría y Promoción Electoral, 1987.

Ferguson, James. *Beyond the Lighthouse*. London: Latin American Bureau, 1992.

Fernández, Leonel. *Los Estados Unidos en el Caribe: De la Guerra Fría al Plan Reagan*. Santo Domingo: Alpha y Omega, 1984.

Gaddis, John Lewis. *Strategies of Containment: A Critical Appraisal of Postwar American National Security Policy*. New York: Oxford University Press, 1982.

Galíndez Suarez, Jesús. *La Era de Trujillo*. Tucson: University of Arizona Press, 1973.

Gallegos, Gerardo. *Trujillo: Cara y Cruz de una Dictadura*. Madrid: Ediciones Iberoamericanas, 1968.

García, José Gabriel. *Compendio de la Historia de Santo Domingo*. Santo Domingo: Universidad Autónoma de Santo Domingo, 1878.

Gardner, Lloyd C. *Economic Aspects of New Deal Diplomacy*. Madison: University of Wisconsin Press, 1964.

Gil, Federico. *Latin American-United States Relations*. New York: Harcourt Brace Jovanovich, 1971.

Gimbernard, Bienvenido. *Trujillo*. Santo Domingo: Editora Cultural Dominicana, 1976.

Gleijeses, Piero. *The Dominican Crisis: The 1965 Constitutional Revolt and American Intervention*. Baltimore: The Johns Hopkins University Press, 1978.

Goff, Fred, and Michael Locker. "The Violence of Domination: US Power and the Dominican Republic." In *Latin American Radicalism*. Ed. Irving Horowitz. New York: Random House, 1969.

Goldwert, Marvin. *The Constabulary in the Dominican Republic and Nicaragua: Progeny and Legacy of United States Intervention*. Gainesville: University of Florida Press, 1962.

Green, David. *The Containment of Latin America: A History of the Myths and Realities of the Good Neighbor Policy*. Chicago: Quadrangle Books, 1971.

Grissa, Abdessatar. *Structure of the International Sugar Market and Its Impact on Developing Countries*. Paris: Development Centre of the Organization for Economic Co-Operation and Development, 1976.

Grow, Michael. *The Good Neighbor Policy and Authoritarianism in Paraguay*. Lawrence: Regents Press of Kansas, 1978.

Grupo de Países Latinoamericanos y del Caribe Exportadores de Azúcar. *Report on United States Sugar Policy and its Effects Towards the Economy of GEPLACEA's Member Countries*. Mexico City: GEPLACEA, 1984.

Gutierrez, Carlos María. *The Dominican Republic: Rebellion and Repression*. New York: Monthly Review Press, 1972.

Hagelberg, G. B. *The Caribbean Sugar Industries: Constraints and Opportunities*. New Haven, CT: Antilles Research Program, 1970.

Harding, Bertita. *The Land that Columbus Loved*. New York: Gorden, 1979.

Harrison, Lawrence. *Underdevelopment Is a State of Mind: The Latin American Case*. Lanham, MD: Madison Books, 1985.

Hartlyn, Jonathan. *The Struggle for Democratic Politics in the Dominican Republic*. Chapel Hill: University of North Carolina Press, 1998.

Healy, David. *Drive to Hegemony: The United States in the Caribbean, 1898-1917*. Madison: University of Wisconsin Press, 1988.

Heine, Jorge, and Leslie Manigat. *The Caribbean and World Politics: Cross Currents and Cleavages*. New York: Holmes & Meier, 1988.

Hetson, Thomas J. *Sweet Subsidy: The Economic and Diplomatic Effects of the US Sugar Acts, 1934–1974*. New York: Garland, 1987.

Hillman, Richard S. and Thomas J. D'Agostino. *Distant Neighbors in the Caribbean: The Dominican Republic and Jamaica in Comparative Perspective*. New York: Praeger, 1992.

Hoetink, Harry. *The Dominican People: Notes for a Historical Sociology*. Baltimore: The Johns Hopkins University Press, 1982.

—. "The Dominican Republic, c. 1870–1930." In *The Cambridge History of Latin America*, vol. 5. Ed. Leslie Bethell. London: Cambridge University Press, 1984.

Hybel, Alex Roberto. *How Leaders Reason: US Intervention in the Caribbean Basin*. Oxford: Basil Blackwell, 1990.

International Sugar Council. *The Sugar Club Annual (1960)*. London: International Sugar Council, 1961.

—. *The World Sugar Economy: Structure and Politics*. London: International Sugar Council, 1963.

Javier García, Manuel de Jesús. *Mis Viente Años en el Palacio Nacional Junto a Trujillo y otros Gobernantes Dominicanos*. Santo Domingo: Taller, 1985.

Johnson, D. Gale. *The Sugar Problem: Large Costs and Small Benefits*. Washington, DC: American Enterprise Institute for Public Policy Research, 1974.

Johnson, Harry G. *Economic Policies Toward Less Developed Countries*. Washington, DC: Brookings Institute, 1968.

Kaufman, Burton I. *Trade and Aid: Eisenhower's Foreign Economic Policy, 1953–61*. Baltimore: The Johns Hopkins University Press, 1982.

Kindleberger, Charles P. "The 1929 World Depression in Latin America from the Outside." In *Latin America in the 1930s: The Role of the Periphery in World Crisis*. Ed. Rosemary Thorpe. New York: St. Martin's Press, 1985.

Knight, Franklin. *The Caribbean: The Genesis of a Fragmented Nationalism*. New York: Oxford University Press, 1978.

Knight, Melvin. *The Americans in Santo Domingo*. New York: Vanguard Press, 1928.

Kryzanek, Michael J. *US-Latin American Relations*. New York: Praeger, 1985.

Kryzanek, Michael J., and Howard J. Wiarda. *The Politics of External Influence in the Dominican Republic*. Stanford: Hoover Institute Press, 1988.

LaFeber, Walter. *The American Age: United States Foreign Policy Home and Abroad since 1750.* New York: W. W. Norton & Company, 1989.

LaTorre, Eduardo. *Política Dominicana Contemporanea.* Santo Domingo: Instituto Technológico de Santo Domingo, 1975.

—. *La República Dominicana y las Relaciones Internacionales.* Santo Domingo: Instituto Technológico de Santo Domingo, 1973.

—. *Sobre Azúcar.* Santo Domingo: Instituto Technológico de Santo Domingo, 1988.

Lemoine, Maurice. *Bitter Sugar: Slaves Today in the Caribbean.* Chicago: Brenner Press, 1985.

Lozano, Wilfredo. *La Dominación Imperialista en la República Dominicana, 1900–1930.* Santo Domingo: Universidad Autónoma de Santo Domingo, 1976.

—. *El Reformismo Dependiente.* Santo Domingo: Taller, 1985.

Lucero Vásquez, Jaime. *Anonimos Contra el Jefe.* Santo Domingo: Taller, 1987.

Lugo, Amérigo. *Historia de Santo Domingo.* Santo Domingo: Editorial Librería Dominicana, 1952.

Lynsky, Myer. *Sugar Economics, Statistics, and Documents.* New York: United States Cane Sugar Refiners' Association, 1940.

Madariaga, Salvador. *Latin America between the Eagle and the Boar.* New York: Praeger, 1962.

Madruga, José Manuel. *Azúcar y Haitianos en la República Dominicana.* Santo Domingo: Amigo del Hogar, 1986.

Martin, John Bartlow. *It Seems Like Only Yesterday.* New York: Morrow & Company, 1986.

—. *Overtaken by Events.* Garden City, NY: Doubleday, 1966.

—. *US Policy in the Caribbean.* Boulder, CO: Westview, 1978.

Martz, John D. "Democracy and the Imposition of Values: Definitions and Diplomacy." In *Latin America, the United States, and the Inter-American System.* Ed. John Martz and Lars Schoultz. Boulder, CO: Westview, 1980.

Mecham, Lloyd J. *The United States and Interamerican Security, 1889–1960.* Austin: University of Texas Press, 1961.

Mejía, Luis. *De Lilís a Trujillo.* Caracas: Editorial Elite, 1944.

Mintz, Ilse. *US Import Quotas: Costs and Consequences.* Washington, DC: American Enterprise Institute for Public Policy Research, 1973.

Mintz, Sidney Wilfred. *Sweetness and Power: The Place of Sugar in Modern History.* Brattleboro, VT: Elizabeth Sifton Books, 1985.

Molineu, Harold. *US Policy Toward Latin America: From Regionalism to Globalism.* Boulder, CO: Westview Press, 1986.

Morrison, DeLesseps. *Latin American Mission.* New York: Simon & Schuster, 1965.

Moya Pons, Frank. *El Batey: Estudio Socioeconómico de los Bateyes del Consejo Estatal de Azúcar.* Santo Domingo: Fondo para el Avance de las Ciencias Sociales, 1986.

—. "The Dominican Republic since 1930." In *The Cambridge History of Latin America*, vol. 7. Ed. Leslie Bethell. London: Cambridge University Press, 1984.

—. *Manual de la Historia Dominicana.* Santo Domingo: Academia Dominicana de la Historia, 1977.

—. *El Pasado Dominicano.* Santo Domingo: Fundación J. A. Caro Alvarez, 1986.

Palmer, Bruce. *Intervention in the Dominican Caribbean.* Lexington: University Press of Kentucky, 1989.

Paulino, Aliro. *Balaguer: El Hombre del Destino.* Santo Domingo: Mundo Diplomático Internacional, 1986.

Pearce, Jenny. *Under the Eagle.* London: South End Press, 1982.

Peguero, Valentina. *Vision General de la Historia Dominicana.* Santo Domingo: Corripio, 1978.

Peña Rivera, Víctor A. *Trujillo: Historia Oculta de un Dictador.* Madrid: Ultra, 1977.

Perkins, Whitney T. *Constraint of Empire: The United States and Caribbean Interventions.* Westport, CT: Greenwood Press, 1981.

Petras, James. "United States Wealth and Power in Latin America." In *Trends and Tragedies in American Foreign Policy.* Ed. Michael Parenti. Boston: Little & Brown, 1971.

Pike, Fredrick B. *The United States and the Andean Republics: Peru, Bolivia, and Ecuador.* Cambridge, MA: Harvard University Press, 1977.

Plant, Roger. *Sugar and Modern Slavery.* London: Zed Books, 1987.

Rabe, Stephen. *Eisenhower and Latin America: The Foreign Policy of Anticommunism.* Chapel Hill: University of North Carolina Press, 1988.

Rodríguez, Alberto. *El Azúcar como Hacedor de Historia y de Comunidades.* Santo Domingo: Universidad Autónoma de Santo Domingo, 1985.

Roorda, Eric Paul. *The Dictator Next Door: The Good Neighbor Policy and the Trujillo Regime in the Dominican Republic, 1930–1945.* Durham, NC: Duke University Press, 1998.

Rosario, Esteban. *Los Dueños de la República Dominicana.* Santo Domingo: Iodized, 1992.

Saillant, César. *Revelaciones a Sánchez Cabral.* Santo Domingo: El Caribe, 1962.

Sánchez, Juan J. *La Caña en Santo Domingo.* Santo Domingo: Hermanos García, 1893.

Sang, Mu-kien Adriana. *Una Utopia Inconclusa: Espaillat y el Liberalismo Dominicano del Siglo XIX.* Santo Domingo: Instituto Technológico de Santo Domingo, 1997.

Schlesinger, Arthur M. Jr. *A Thousand Days: John F. Kennedy in the White House.* Boston: Houghton Mifflin, 1965.

Schoultz, Lars. *National Security and United States Policy Toward Latin America.* Princeton: Princeton University Press, 1987.

Schwarz, Jordan A. *Liberal: Adolf A. Berle and the Vision of an American Era.* New York: Free Press, 1987.

Scott, C. D. *Technology, Employment and Income Distribution in the Sugar Industry of the Dominican Republic.* Geneva: International Labour Office, 1978.

Slater, Jerome. *Intervention and Negotiation: The United States and the Dominican Revolution.* New York: Harper & Row, 1970.

Smith, Gaddis. *The Last Years of the Monroe Doctrine 1945–93.* New York: Hill & Wang, 1994.

Steward, Dick. *Trade and Hemisphere: The Good Neighbor Policy and Reciprocal Trade.* Columbia: University of Missouri Press, 1975.

Strausz-Hupé, Robert. *Democracy and American Policy: Reflections on the Legacy of Tocqueville.* New Brunswick, NJ: Transaction Books, 1994.

Swerling, Boris C. *International Control of Sugar, 1918–41.* Stanford, CA: Stanford University Press, 1949.

Thomas, Hugh. "Cuba, c 1750–1860." In *Cuba: A Short History.* Ed. Leslie Bethell. Cambridge, MA: Cambridge University Press, 1993.

Timoshenko, Vladimir, and Boris C. Swerling. *The World's Sugar: Progress and Policy*. Stanford, CA: Stanford University Press, 1957.

Turner, Jack T. *The Marketing of Sugar*. Homewood, IL: Irwin, 1955.

Vargas-Lundius, Rosemary. *Peasants in Distress: Poverty and Unemployment in the Dominican Republic*. Boulder, CO: Westview, 1991.

Vedovato, Claudio. *Politics, Foreign Trade and Economic Development: A Study of the Dominican Republic*. London: Croom Helm, 1986.

Vega, Bernardo. *Control y Represión en la Dictadura de Trujillo*. Santo Domingo: Fundación Cultural Dominicana, 1986.

—. *En la Decada Perdida*. Santo Domingo: Fundación Cultural Dominicana, 1991.

—. *Eisenhower y Trujillo*. Santo Domingo: Fundación Cultural Dominicana, 1991.

—. *Los Estados Unidos y Trujillo—Año 1945*. Santo Domingo: Fundación Cultural Dominicana, 1982.

—. *Los Estados Unidos y Trujillo—Año 1946*. Santo Domingo: Fundación Cultural Dominicana, 1982.

—. *Los Estados Unidos y Trujillo—Año 1947*. Santo Domingo: Fundación Cultural Dominicana, 1984.

—. *Estudio de las Implicaciones de la Incorporación de la República Dominicana a la Comunidad del Caribe*. Santo Domingo: Fondo para el Avance de las Ciencias Sociales, 1978.

—. *Kennedy y los Trujillo*. Santo Domingo: Fundación Cultural Dominicana, 1991.

—. *Nazismo, Fascismo y Falangismo en la República Dominicana*. Santo Domingo: Fundación Cultural Dominicana, 1985.

—. *La Problemática Economía Dominicana*. Santiago: Universidad Católica Madre y Maestra, 1973.

—. *Trujillo y el Control Financiero Norteamericano*. Santo Domingo: Fundación Cultural Dominicano, 1990.

—. *Trujillo y Haiti*, vol. 1. Santo Domingo: Fundación Cultural Dominicana, 1988.

—. *Trujillo y Haiti*, vol. 2. Santo Domingo: Fundación Cultural Dominicana, 1995.

—. *Los Trujillo se Escriben*. Santo Domingo: Fundación Cultural Dominicana, 1987.

—. *La Vida Cotidiana Dominicana a través del Archivo Particular del Generalísimo*. Santo Domingo: Fundación Cultural Dominicano, 1986.

Vicini, José. *La Isla del Azúcar*. Ciudad Trujillo: Editora Dominicana, 1957.

Watts, David. *The West Indies: Patterns of Development, Culture and Environmental Change since 1492*. Cambridge, MA: Cambridge University Press, 1987.

Welles, Sumner. *Naboth's Vineyard: The Dominican Republic, 1844–1924*. New York: Payson & Clarke, 1928.

Wiarda, Howard J. *Dictatorship and Development: The Methods of Control in Trujillo's Dominican Republic*. Gainesville: University of Florida Press, 1968.

—. *The Dominican Republic: A Nation in Transition*. New York: Praeger, 1969.

—. *Finding Our Way: Toward Maturity in US-Latin American Relations*. Washington, DC: American Enterprise Institute for Public Policy Research, 1987.

—. *Política y Gobierno en la República Dominicana*. Santiago: Universidad Católica Madre y Maestra, 1968.

Wiarda, Howard J., and Michael J. Kryzanek. *The Dominican Republic: A Caribbean Crucible*. Boulder, CO: Westview, 1982.

Wiarda, Howard J., and Janine T. Perfit. *Trade, Aid and US Economic Policy in Latin America*. Washington, DC: American Enterprise Institute for Public Policy Research, 1983.

Wilgus, A. Curtis. *The Caribbean: Its Hemispheric Role*. Gainesville: University of Florida Press, 1967.

Wilson, Earl B. *Sugar and its Wartime Controls*. New York: Statistical Press, 1948.

Woodson, Drexel G. *The Caribbean Presence*. Washington, DC: Woodrow Wilson International Center for Scholars, 1982.

Wright, Philip. *Sugar in Relation to the Tariff*. New York: McGraw-Hill, 1924.

ARTICLES

Abel, Christopher. "Crisis and Change in the International Sugar Economy." *Hispanic American Historical Review* 66 (August 1986): 603–4.

Ascuasianti, Carlos. "Diez Años de Economía Dominicana." *Revista de Ciencias Económicas y Sociales* 1 (March–June 1972): 5–18.

Bates, Thomas H. "The Long-Run Efficiency of the United States Sugar Policy." *American Journal of Agricultural Economics* (October 1968): 521–35.

Block, Alan A. "Violence, Corruption and Clientelism: The Assassination of Jesús de Galíndez, 1956." *Social Justice* 16 (1989): 64–88.

Boggs, Hale. "Views of a United States Congressman." *The Sugar Club Annual* 3 (1963): 33–43.

Bosch, Juan. "Why I was Overthrown." *The New Leader* 46 (14 October 1963): 3–4.

Bryan, Patrick. "The Transition to Plantation Agriculture in the Dominican Republic, 1870–1884." *Journal of Caribbean History* 10 (1978): 82–105.

Cater, Douglas, and Walter Pincus. "Our Sugar Diplomacy." *The Reporter* 24 (13 April 1961): 24–28.

Ceara Hatton, Miguel. "El Ciclo de la Política Económica." *Revista de Ciencia y Cultura* 1 (January–April 1989): 23–38.

Christopher, Ian. "US Fails Sugar Ally." *Contemporary Review* 256 (February 1990): 68–9.

Coughlin, Cletus C. "A Non-Tariff Barrier in Practice: The US Sugar Import Quota." *Review* 71 (January–February 1989): 41–2.

Echenique, Federico. "La Industria Azucarera Dominicana en Perspectiva." *Azúcar y Diversificación* 4 (May 1975): 27–31.

Espinal Jacobo, Flavio Darío. "El Concepto de la Democracia en la Sociedad Contemporánea." *Revista de Ciencia y Cultura* 1 (January–April 1989): 15–22.

Guerrero, José G. "La Política Norteamericana y el Gobierno de Joaquín Balaguer (Junio–Diciembre 1961)." *Revista Dominicana de Antropología e Historia* 12 (1982): 183–244.

Kunz, Diane B. "When Money Counts and Doesn't: Economic Power and Diplomatic Objectives." *Diplomatic History* 18, no. 4 (fall 1994): 451–62.

Kryzanek, Michael J. "The Dominican Republic: Politics and Development in an Unsoveriegn State." *The Hispanic American Historical Review* 67 (August 1987): 533–52.

LaTorre, Eduardo. "El Futuro del Mercado Azucarero." *Azúcar y Diversificación* 3 (August 1974): 6–10, 77.

—. "Hacia una Política Azucarera Dominicana en la Década de los 80." *Ciencia y Sociedad* 5 (July 1980): 253–68.

LeGrand, Catherine C. "Informal Resistance on a Dominican Sugar Plantation during the Trujillo Dictatorship." *Hispanic American Historical Review* 75, no. 4 (1995): 555–96.

Lowenthal, Abraham F. "Foreign Aid as a Political Instrument: The Case of the Dominican Republic." *Public Policy* 14 (1965): 141–60.

—. "Limits of American Power: The Lesson of the Dominican Republic." *Harper's Magazine* 228 (June 1964): 87–95.

Lozano, Wilfredo. "Azúcar, Fuerza de Trabajo y Desarrollo en la República Dominicana." *Ciencia y Sociedad* 5 (July–December 1980): 3–19.

Martínez Fernández, Luis. "Caudillos, Annexationism, and the Rivalry between Empires in the Dominican Republic, 1844–1874." *Diplomatic History* 17 (fall 1993): 571–97.

Moya Pons, Frank. "Import-Substitution Industrialization Policies in the Dominican Republic." *Hispanic American Historical Review* 70 (November 1990): 539-577.

Rabe, Stephen. "The Caribbean Triangle: Betancourt, Castro, and Trujillo and US Foreign Policy, 1958–1963." *Diplomatic History* 20 (winter 1996): 55–78.

Reed, Karaim. "What Do Cory Aquino, Cocaine Addicts, and American Consumers Have in Common?" *The Washington Monthly* (November 1987): 18–20.

Rippy, James Fred. "The Initiation of the Customs Receivership in the Dominican Republic." *Hispanic American Historical Review* 17 (November 1937): 419–57.

—. "Sugar in Inter-American Relations." *Inter-American Economic Affairs* 9, (spring 1956): 50–64.

Roorda, Eric Paul. "Genocide Next Door: The Good Neighbor Policy, the Trujillo Regime, and the Haitian Massacre of 1937." *Diplomatic History* 20 (summer 1996): 1–19.

Schreiber, Anna. "Economic Coercion as an Instrument of Foreign Policy: US Economic Measures Against Cuba and the Dominican Republic." *World Politics* (1973): 387–419.

Stern, Steve J. "Feudalism, Capitalism, and the World System in the Perspective of Latin America and the Caribbean." *The American Historical Review* 93 (October 1988): 829–97.

Swerling, Boris. "A Sugar Policy for the United States." *The American Economic Review* 43 (June 1952): 347–57.

Tejada, Adriano Miguel. "Política Exterior de los Estados Unidos Hacia el Caribe: Cuatro Casos de Intervención en la República Dominicana." *Eme Eme* 9 (July 1980): 3–37.

Trujillo Molina, Rafael L. "Los Principios de no Intervención y la Solidaridad Panamericana." *Revista de las Fuerzas Armadas* 10 (January 1959): 53–54.

Vidal, Máximo Luis. "La Industria Azucarera y su Mercado." *Azúcar y Diversificación* 1 (September 1973): 26–33.

Walters, Ingo. "Nontariff Barriers and the Export Performance of Developing Economies." *American Economic Review* (May 1971): 191–205.

Whitney, Thomas P. "The US and the Dominicans: What Will be Done with the Trujillo Properties?" *New Republic* 146 (12 February 1962): 13–14.

Wright, Theodore P. "The United States and Latin American Dictatorship: The Case of the Dominican Republic" *Journal of International Affairs* 14 (1965): 152–57.

OCCASIONAL PAPERS, DISSERTATIONS, UNPUBLISHED WORKS

Espinal, Rosario. "Classes, Power, and Political Change in the Dominican Republic." Ph.D. diss. Washington University, 1985.

Hagelberg, G. B. "Sugar in the Caribbean: Turning Sunshine into Money." Working paper, Woodrow Wilson International Center for Scholars, 1985.

Kraus, Theresa. "Prelude to the Storm: The United States Navy and the Dominican Republic, 1959–1964." Paper presented at the Colloquium on Contemporary History at the Naval History Center in Washington, DC, 9 January 1990.

Moya Pons, Rafael Francisco. "Industrial Incentives in the Dominican Republic, 1880-1983." Ph.D. diss. Columbia University, 1987.

Saillant, César. "Mis Memorias Junto a Ramfis." Unpublished manuscript, 1962.

Segundo Volmar, Gustavo. "The Impact of the Foreign Sector on the Domestic Economic Activity of the Dominican Republic from 1950 to 1967." Ph.D. diss. Columbia University, 1971.

Wiarda, Howard J. "The Aftermath of the Trujillo Dictatorship: The Emergence of a Pluralistic Political System in the Dominican Republic." Ph.D. diss. University of Florida, 1965.

Index

About the Author

MICHAEL R. HALL teaches Latin American and Diplomatic History at Armstrong Atlantic State University in Savannah, Georgia. He served in the Peace Corps in the Dominican Republic from 1984 to 1987.

ISBN 0-313-31127-7

90000>

EAN

9 780313 311277

HARDCOVER BAR CODE